# BRIGHT MORNING

# BRIGHT MORNING

## IMAGES OF A
## LANCASHIRE BOYHOOD

## DON HAWORTH

*With line drawings by*
Roy Newton

Methuen

First published in Great Britain 1990
by Methuen London
Michelin House, 81 Fulham Road, London SW3 6RB

Copyright © 1990 Don Haworth

The author has asserted his moral rights
Illustrations copyright © 1990 Roy Newton

A CIP Catalogue record for this book is available
from the British Library

ISBN 0 413 64440 5

Phototypeset by Input Typesetting Ltd, London
Printed in Great Britain
by St Edmundsbury Press, Bury St Edmunds

To Elaine and Robbie

# CONTENTS

# 1 · SUMMER OF THE STRIKE

In summer the colliery slag heaps burned internally through spontaneous combustion. The smell was welcome like the unpleasant smell of marigolds because it was the scent of hot days. In 1932 when I was eight the breeze carried the summer smell and also a sound I had not heard before, a distant prolonged moaning as though of some animal in pain but containing within it the voices of women. Thousands of people were in the streets booing. Douggie Cubbons said they were called strikers; he knew where to go to see them. A Catholic woman who lived opposite overheard him. We mustn't dream of going, she said; they were wicked creatures. When the breeze strengthened we were fearful for a moment that they might be coming our way.

Extra mounted police arrived from Manchester to contain the wickedness. My grandfather Sephton made it his business to put them under observation. He was a dapper little man of sixty-four with a silver quiff and moustache. Nobody regarded him as unemployed for the good reason that since he had lost his job as an insurance agent three years previously he had turned his back on work and wholeheartedly embraced retirement. Living with us or with cousins, they got by on my grandmother's old-age pension of ten shillings a week, and indeed he always seemed rich. On our afternoon saunters round Burnley town centre he bought each edition of the *Northern Daily Telegraph* as it reached the streets and we stopped for a snack at the market stalls: tripe in summer, black puddings with mustard in the cold of winter.

We went and inspected the strike from a vantage point up

on the canal bank. A crowd of workers was hemmed in
tight and inert between high mill walls. There came a surge
from amongst them and a clattering counter-move by the
police horses. Frightened voices echoed. There were eyes
everywhere, in the crowd, under the peaks of helmets, in
the upraised heads of horses, all frightened.

Later in a side street we came across two of the Manchester
mounted policemen hustling a man who was trying to sell
the *Daily Worker*. My grandfather intervened.

'Who do you think you are?' one of the policemen
demanded.

'I'm a citizen of this town,' my grandfather said, echoing
Paul and raising his finger like Mr Gladstone at the dispatch
box, 'and that is more than either of you officers can claim.'

. The policemen, who no doubt had enough to bear without
rhetoric, gave us all a warning look and rode on. My grandfather invited the newspaper-seller to continue his lawful
trade.

The incident, recounted many times by my grandfather
with the underlying libertarian principles made explicit, is
my clearest memory of the cotton strike. It took me a long
time to sort everything out. I had begun by supposing that
strikers were persons who struck others, emitting the booing
noise we heard on the wind. Wicked people seemed an apt
description. I thought of them as a separate category of
humankind, who had no identity except being wicked, and
who had fallen upon the town from some foreign place like
the police from Manchester. It was a shock to learn that they
were residents, familiar people who clattered through the
streets morning and evening, lived nearby and queued at the
chip shop. Booing I then took to be the sound people naturally emitted when striking, just as they roared at football
matches, sang in chapel and whistled in the lavatory. But
no, it turned out that it had a purpose. It was directed at
'blacklegs' who, it again took me some time to understand,
were not an imported foreign category of people. With a
name like that they were obviously wrong 'uns, the Blackburn Rovers of the business, but that too proved to be a
misapprehension. My grandfather, who took the side of the
strikers against the police, took the side of the blacklegs

against the strikers, on those very principles, as he explained, by which he had defended the sale of the *Daily Worker*.

It further transpired, to add to the ideological complexity, that he had never read the *Daily Worker* and did not intend to. I gathered it was one of those journals, like the *Manchester Guardian* and the *Methodist Recorder*, which were esteemed but never bought because they were hard to read, carried no football news and came without the gifts of dictionaries, Dickens and free insurance which it was regarded as the duty of a newspaper to provide.

The booing on the breeze became fainter. With familiarity it lost its menace. It sounded like wailing, and that is how across the years I remember it, a lament for the industry, once Britain's greatest, which had created and sustained our world and now was dying. The decline of cotton was a story that was to be repeated in the next fifty years through most of our industries. A huge complacency, grown in the bounding success of the nineteenth century, persisted blind and deaf long after other countries had left us behind.

Perhaps it was inevitable. Nothing comparable to mechanised industry had happened before in the experience of humankind. It conferred what must have seemed a magical power, the ability actually to create wealth and on a scale vastly exceeding the hoards scraped together by the enthroned brigands and pirates who up to then ruled the earth. It was an El Dorado that, far from running to exhaustion, had yielded up bounty in growing abundance.

Cotton was the first industry of the industrial revolution. In the nineteenth century the damp rural landscape of Lancashire was transformed as though in an animated cartoon. Towns sprang up, mill chimneys rose, coal mines were sunk, canals dug, railways laid. Workers flocked in from the countryside and from Ireland. A procession of horses, dwarfed by their loads of raw cotton, plodded up the valleys from the docks at Liverpool and Salford and returned laden with cloth for the markets of the world. Cotton was by far Britain's greatest export. By 1913 it brought in a quarter of all overseas earnings and employed directly or indirectly a million people. Nobody imagined it could ever end.

Least questioning were the mill-owners. They collared the lion's share of the new wealth and took its possession to be a sign of God's approval. They built chapels, a sort of nod to a partner, commissioned mansions and laid out parks. Downturns in the trade cycle they learned to accept as the bad seasons of capitalism and met with resolution, prayer and reductions in wages. Righteousness hung round like them like the whiff of cigar smoke. They ruled the work force with severity and their families with the bank book. They did not borrow money and they did not enter joint-stock companies. They ran their mills independently and thanked nobody for advice. When changes in equipment and organisation should have been made towards the end of the century none was made. In boom years they could not find the time for change; in recession they could not find the money. The general tendency was so powerfully onwards and upwards that nobody worried. Some came to believe that they and their industry possessed a unique and unrepeatable talent, voiced in the following quotation from a mill-owner addressing himself to the prospect of foreign competition:

In the first place we've got the only climate in the world where cotton piece goods in any quantity can ever be produced. In the second place no foreign johnnies can ever be bred that can spin and weave like Lancashire lassies and lads. In the third place there's more spindles in Oldham than in the rest of the world put together. And last of all, if they had the climate and the men and the spindles, which they never can have, foreigners could never find the brains Lancashire cotton men have for the job. We've been making all the world's cotton cloth that matters for more years than I can tell and we always shall.

I do not know whether the quotation is authentic, but it has a convincing ring of bumptiousness and complacency. A class of entrepreneurs in less than a century had become conservative with success while enjoying the illusion created by their political Liberalism of marching at the head of progress.

As late as 1919 scores of new mills started building and hundreds were bought and sold at rising prices. A few years later it became evident that countries of the Far East had learned to roll their own and that British cotton would never again compete with foreign prices. The strike of 1932 was against reorganisation to meet the productivity of Japanese two-shift working. A compromise ended the strike but won no markets back from Japan. Between the wars eight hundred mills closed down.

The cotton slump impoverished all of us. 'Trade's bad,' people said.

My grandfather Haworth put it down to parsimony. 'Money's not circulating,' he said. Throughout his best years he had promptly and generously returned to circulation most of his earnings. He had enjoyed a particularly good thrash at the time of Queen Victoria's Diamond Jubilee, and he looked forward to a revival of prosperity at King George V's jubilee, which now in 1932 was only three years away. Mills would work late to produce millions of yards of Union Jacks; shops and the market stalls would stay open till midnight; the pubs would be loud with roistering, the streets full of rolling drunks. It would be 1913 again. And from the cascade of spending, torrents of lifeblood would flow through England's slow arteries and revive the extremities of the vast and languishing empire.

The jubilee when it arrived fell some way short of the vision.

One Sunday morning my father got out his knives for cutting leather and sharpened them on an oil stone. He was to work half the next week at the last because there were no longer enough shoe repairs coming to the Co-op's central factory to keep busy all the stitching and finishing machines. People had gone back to clogs. Boots and shoes they kept for weekends, and many repaired them themselves with stick-on rubber soles and screwed-on circular heels from Woolworth's.

Soon there was no work at all for my father on the machines. He was demoted full-time to the bench, and that too became less than a week's work. They were put on piecework, paid by the job. They sat around until the van brought in shoes collected from Co-op grocery branches, then hammered into the work in furious competition to get the extra pairs that did not divide evenly between them. Their earnings sank to just above the level of the dole. Thus ended the executive career on which my father had hopefully embarked when he sold his one-man business to become a Co-op branch manager only three years previously.

I do not remember any lamentation. My parents were no doubt better able to bear their disappointment because it was part of a general misfortune and at least he was not on the dole. That really would have been cause for despondency.

In fact, rather than sit around half the day waiting for work, my father and his mates would have been better off to have made a full week's work for a few of them by going on the dole in turn, but when the management proposed this they refused. They had been brought up to work for their living; they wanted no dole nor any form of charity. They thought of themselves primarily not as citizens, trade unionists or children of God but as workers. A man was known by his trade to friends, neighbours and every official record. When he lost his job he lost his identity.

The employment exchange was in a big wooden hut at the top of Hammerton Street. The long-term unemployed, pale men in dark rags, hung around for hours after they had signed on. There was nothing to go home for. In good weather they filtered through the streets and parks as the day wore on. On Mondays most of them finished up on the cattle market, where cheapjacks and quacks set up their pitches and shouted themselves hoarse at a lethargic crowd with no money to spend. A broad-chested woman offered rolls of oilcloth which were bounced down from the back of a lorry.

'Roll it out, Sam,' she would command. 'Show 'em the quality.'

Noses in the crowd tweaked at the sharp smell that rose as the bright-coloured rolls were spread on the cobbles. I never saw anybody buy.

A fat bald man selling tonic did little better. It was an

orange-coloured liquid in which bits like dried peel floated about. He charged the crowd with looking run-down and dispirited. He shamed them by accusing them of sexual over-indulgence in the indolence of their days. Then, changing tack, he hoisted a brimming fish-bowl full of his tonic into the air and proclaimed: 'I am going to do what no doctor in Burnley would do today. I am going to drink my own medicine.' He drained the vessel. Curious people with nothing pressing to do hung on to see how many bowlsful he could down without relieving himself. He never left the stand.

On rainy days many took refuge in the library reading room, which steamed up from their wet clothes, and in Woolworths and Calvary Hall, an abandoned factory up on the canal embankment where the Reverend Mr Watson, an evangelist from South Wales, promised paradise when the world came to an end in 1939 if only they would hang on patiently.

Most of the long-term unemployed looked ill. Some of them had fallen out of work in the first place because of poor physique or injury, possibly a war wound. After a time they were subjected to a means test and given a lower rate of benefit. The means test was only another of the daily humiliations they suffered, but it has a special place in the horrors of folk history because it was suffered in the home. The officials of the Public Assistance Committee included to my knowledge tactful and considerate people but their task was an invidious one – to snoop into every little source of household income, children's earnings, the pensions of aged parents, the value of eggs from a hen pen, to nose out any savings and to spot in the rubbish of the home any possession worth assessing – all with a view to calculating how little might be needed to keep the family alive. Angry scenes were infrequent. The long-term unemployed were too dispirited.

There was only one group in town below them, too small to be called a class, people mainly of low intelligence whose lives had gone to pieces through bad luck or drink or both. The men were ragged and unshaven, stank of beer and swore in every sentence. They barracked bitterly, without humour, at football and cricket matches. They were loners. Some muttered, some slavered, quite a few were lame. They lived in streets where families fought and children went without pants. It was they who came to mind when the Communists sang:

> Arise, ye prisoners of starvation.
> Arise, ye wretched of the earth.

Some hope. These were 'the poor'. The fear of being thought one of them or even in the same category as the long-term unemployed alarmed workers whose jobs had just gone. When they went for the dole they put on their best clothes and stood apart. They avoided crudely-stated arguments and swearing. I noticed the deliberately casual manner of those who, like ourselves at one time, could not afford the football match and went in free for the last ten minutes when the big gates were opened to admit newspaper boys. They sauntered up as though they just happened to be passing. They did not cluster about the gate nor rush through when it was opened. Some saved a cigarette to light on reaching the terraces. Others watched the play with detachment as though it was not the kind of thing they would choose to spend a whole afternoon on.

Feelings of humiliation passed. Because of a lifetime's conditioning in the work ethic, people at first felt their own unemployment as a personal failure, but they were not despised by those still in a job – it could happen to anybody and, because the dole was not much less than a wage, they continued to join in the same activities.

Once the stigma wore off, unemployment became more tolerable to those who had reason to believe it would not be permanent and it was even welcome in short stretches to some women workers who discovered they had always had too much to do, coming home to the housework after a day at the looms. 'Are you laiking?' they would mime to each other across the street in the lip language they used in the mills. They beamed and nodded in congratulation rather than by way of condolence. Being 'played off' from time to time became a sort of holiday.

Men found the free time harder to cope with. There was

nothing to do in the home. Few had indoor hobbies, almost none did housework, even if the woman was out at work all day. Where women stayed at home everybody was turned out, children, grandfathers, the cat and the dog and the unemployed husband. The purpose of having a home was to keep it like a museum. They 'couldn't get on' with people under their feet.

The younger unemployed in time established a quite agreeable social life about the streets. Most of them had a trade. Small businesses took on boys from school and sacked them on completion of their apprenticeship at twenty-one when they became entitled to a tradesman's wage. It was better than nothing. Skilled jobs for which they had qualified would come vacant, a few each month, as older workers retired.

In the meantime they made the best of it. On fine days hundreds stood at street corners talking and joking. They could afford the odd game of billiards or sixpence on a horse, and the pictures a couple of afternoons a week. They played a boys' game of skimming cigarette cards on the pavement and a game of their own on the recreation ground in which they belted a small wooden top with a stick. Few took on an allotment or kept a hen pen and few travelled far looking for work. Their response to bad times was patience.

William Horsfall deplored their lack of initiative. Industrial workers had become so conditioned to regular and regulated work, he said, that they had lost all personal drive. When the job stopped, they stopped and waited for somebody to tell them what to do.

Mr Horsfall, the father of a friend of later years, became something of a legend for his defiance of the depression and his own bad luck. He had been reared at Hebden Bridge, just over the frontier in Yorkshire, by his widowed mother, a bright illiterate little woman who, he said, banged him on one side of the head with her Bible and on the other with the bankbook. She taught her four children not to drink or smoke and to make a habit of adding to their savings every pay day. William grew up to be a leading light at the chapel and a power-loom overlooker at the mill. He was good at the job and the looms seldom broke down. He rigged up a hammock in the warehouse and read most of the day, and thus became a man of such learning and authority that nobody dared to rebuke him, not even the woman operatives.

Bad luck ended his career. One eye was already blind from a botched childhood operation; now the other was struck by a sliver of hot metal and his sight too badly impaired to continue in the job. He refused to sign on for the dole. He chopped firewood and sent his children out to sell it, then when he had learned to get around with the aid of a stick he found jobs on moorland farms which did not need good vision – dry-stone walling, manure-spreading, haymaking in summer.

Up there he got the idea of setting up as a pedlar. It was worth no tradesman's while to drive his horse and cart or his motor van to these isolated farms. William Horsfall did the rounds on foot, at first loading his pack with small articles he could buy from his savings – bootlaces, braces, socks, studs, knitting and sewing things – then as the business prospered working up to clothing, curtains and bed-clothes. He was a big man, little bowed by the weight of the pack, and to avoid stumbling he developed the habit of raising his knees high as he walked, like a horse in good fettle. His ascent at daybreak of the steep road that rises above the tops of the mill chimneys to Hardcastle Craggs was a sight that passed into folklore. His tales and aphorisms were published in the local paper. He became a parish councillor and a magistrate. He was an abstemious but affable man, much richer than when he worked at the mill, with time for everybody and tolerant of all human foibles except going on the dole.

That he did not understand. He could see no reason why the unemployed should not follow his example and shoulder the pack. He seems to have visualised an economy in which the countryside would be alive with the erstwhile industrial work force crossing moors and valleys humping varieties of supplies to the doors of farm kitchens. Nobody rose to the challenge of giving him any competition.

Mr Horsfall's venture was dependent not only on making initially a prodigious effort for small profit but on the discovery of a market which, though widely dispersed and often snowbound, had the essential virtue of being outside an industrial town. Inside, there was no money for any service people could manage without. I have read that coal-pickers who worked over the slagheaps sold their nuggets of coal by the sack- or barrow-load. I don't know to whom. Nobody could afford anything different or extra. It was well nigh impossible to earn pin money. My grandmother knitted pullovers for a local shop at a rate that hardly covered the wear of her needles. My father, after a day at work of alternating idleness and frantic effort, repaired boots and shoes in the kitchen after his tea. He did have the idea of taking in repairs, but by the time he had done ours and the grandparents' and our cousins the Kerrys' and those of friends in need, there was no time for paying customers. Nor, as far as I know, did anybody come inquiring; however much under the rate he charged it would still be more than Woolworth's sticker soles and revolving heels.

The only service I remember being offered by amateurs was for interior decoration. Quite a few of the poorer houses around Fulledge chapel had a notice in the window: 'Nine shillings papers your room.' The crude crayon gave an ominous clue to the kind of Laurel and Hardy effort to be expected – foot in the paste bucket, plank through the window, walls that after a week would peel like bananas.

Few people had nine shillings for a job they might some day do themselves for the cost of the paste and paper. Wallpaper lasted for donkeys' years. In living-rooms the designs were heavy fronds and peeping birds in black and purple, in bedrooms pink. The years had dimmed and darkened the original pattern. It was a delight to find at the back of some cupboard or behind a picture a patch of paper strong in colour and clear in pattern as the whole room must one day have been to eyes long dead.

Offers to paper people's rooms violated the notion of 'each man to his own trade' and also a deep conformity which disapproved of an unestablished enterprise conducted from the home. My father from time to time warmed to the idea

of going into retail greengrocery by converting the parlour
into a shop. 'You can't do that,' my mother would say.
When he asked why, she only repeated with a little laugh,
'Well, you can't.' It was not done, the neighbours would be
embarrassed to live next door to us, people at chapel would
say, 'They've opened a greengrocer's shop in their front
room.'

Workmen felt guilty about doing the jobs of another trade,
even about their own homes. Interiors were sombre for the
lack of decoration, whole streets were without a decently
painted door or window. Landlords, who owned ninety per
cent of the houses, were responsible for outside paintwork,
but most of them were only richer than the tenants by a
terraced house or two left under somebody's will, unsaleable
and let at low rent. They undertook repairs only when floors
collapsed or water poured through the roof in sufficient
volume to swill the tenants out of bed. There was no money
to pay a painter. But I never heard of anybody making the
obvious deal, for the landlord to buy the paint and the tenant,
with nothing to do all day but visit the labour exchange, to
apply it to doors and window frames. That would have
seemed less like a sensible arrangement than a conspiracy
against the established order of things. The town became
full of rotten woodwork, slimy in the wet, grey and cracked
in hot weather.

My father came to wallpapering through an emergency. He
was, as I later understood, one of the millions who bore
disappointment without complaint but with inner frus-
tration. He sometimes relieved it by punching us. A few
days before we were due to hold a children's party in the
unfurnished parlour he thumped me into the wall with sufficient force to burst the rotten paper. Dried plaster trickled
down like sand and formed a rising heap on the floor. My
mother was aghast. Across the width of the wall the plaster
shrugged behind the paper and cascaded out through the
widening gap. We were covered with dust. The window
became opaque. Whatever, my mother asked, was she to
say to people?

All right, my father said, containing himself, he would stick the wallpaper back.

Sticking it back wouldn't do, she said. Everybody would notice the hollow.

All right, my father said, glowering as though assailed by picadors, all right. When he charged it was in my direction. 'You always have to muck things up, don't you, lad?' My mother held him back before he burst another wall.

She came home next day with plaster and enough rolls of wallpaper to do the whole room. He worked till midnight, meticulously and in fury at any mistake he made. Neither my brother Eric nor I dared venture into the room. We could hear the scrape of the ladder and the slap of paste and at intervals outbursts of rage. When my mother went in with cups of tea he responded gently enough, but one time the paper had torn and he growled about wasting his time sticking rubbish on the wall. Like everything she bought, it was the cheapest, and it must have been like working with tissue paper. She said it was the best we could afford, which only added to his exasperation.

It was a dangerous night when he got to the last corner. Between the vertical lines of the pattern and the asymmetry of the room where the walls had subsided no compromise could be reached that satisfied his boiling perfectionism. We took refuge with the Benns family and suffered a recital on the organ from Arthur Benns until it was time to creep back into the house and upstairs to bed.

Auntie Nellie Battersby, arriving with cakes for the party, was the first outsider to view the finished work. The walls were still blotched by the drying paste and the air acrid from a fire burning in a long-empty grate. She was a simple soul. 'It couldn't be better if it had been done by a proper man,' she said.

My father enjoyed the joke but when she had gone it palled by repetition. 'All right,' he warned me, 'just don't let it happen again, lad.'

'You see what it's cost,' my mother said, 'and Dad having to work every night.'

'Just watch your step,' he glowered by way of closing the

incident and, including in his threat my brother Eric who had not been banged into a wall or done anything wrong at all, 'You too. I'm talking to both of you'.

# 2 · FATHER CHRISTMAS UNMASKED

In one of his films Groucho Marx, taking passage in an ocean liner, is shown into a tiny cabin which then fills up with luggage, visitors and stewards in a writhing pile wedged between the floor and the roof. 'Say, who installed me in this telephone kiosk?' Groucho demands.

Home must have felt like that at times to the adults. In the periods when my grandparents were with us, six of us shared the small living-room. My brother and I played on the table. We painted and fought out sieges with our fort and soldiers and we played cards with the grandparents. My grandfather handled a pack like a Mississippi steamboat gambler, having perfected the art on many an afternoon spent in the Liberal club to the neglect and ultimate demise of his insurance agency. He would lean a little in his chair, pretending to be stretching or merely looking around, and try to catch a glimpse of our cards and we would respond by making a small similar movement to see the reflection of his cards in his spectacles. My grandmother, a keen card-player and a woman of simple honesty, never knew what we were all smirking about.

We also played active games that involved circulating around the living-room. At one time we did a lot of march-ing, blowing tin whistles that tasted of bitter metal and beating a drum in time to the tune my grandfather played on a comb or to the words of the recruiting songs he sang.

> Soldier, soldier will you come,
> Fifty guineas on the drum.

The drum shall rattle and the band shall play.
Pray, good soldier, fire away.

We dived into the cover of the table and raked the room with machine-gun fire.

It must have been nerve-wracking for my mother, almost permanently in the scullery, and worse for my grandmother who got the full blast of it sitting by the fire mending clothes or preparing vegetables. They looked out for clearing skies; neither we nor my grandfather stayed in if we could go out.

He took no part in the housework. After breakfast he read the paper until ten o'clock, when he joined in singing the hymns of the BBC morning service audible from the new wireless next door. For this act of worship he stood on the rug, toasting his backside at the fire and shielding the heat from everybody else. He always wore a suit in the house and often his bowler hat. He kept a few pins concealed in the lapel of his jacket and developed the strange habit of tapping them into the table top with the back of his spoon after dinner.

Once a week in winter he made soup. He bought marrow bones from the butcher's on Monday and spent the week boiling them ready for the addition of the vegetables on Thursday. Everybody was kept in touch with his progress and when the soup was ready he handed out samples to all callers, friends and tradesmen alike. He found no praise too extravagant.

Occasionally he mended clocks and watches on the table, but he had no real hankering for his old trade. He liked to paint. He bought the cheapest paint and left tacky surfaces all over the house. When he painted the bath my brother stuck in it so firmly that it took the whole family, gripping his limbs and with boot soles braced against the walls, to prise him out.

My grandfather cut hair, anybody's. People who had left a visit to the barber's too long arrived at the door like tousled sheep. He performed with style and pride. He would prowl round, snip a few hairs, blow them clear with a great breath and flourish the snapping scissors in the air. He did not tolerate centre partings. Everybody got a quiff. It caused some anguish when we asked for short back and sides in order to look like footballers.

He rested from his labours after the midday dinner when he would wrap a blanket round his head and shoulders and nod off for half an hour. Sometimes he woke up lively and, still seated, took us on in a boxing match which he terminated by slapping hard enough to put us off for the next twenty-four hours.

In the evenings he often went out to political or church meetings and there was a sense of incompleteness, of time being rather suspended, until he returned. My father usually retired into the kitchen and repaired boots for family and friends. His work was received by most of us with perfunctory thanks, but my grandfather performed a ceremony of gratitude. He turned his boots in his hands, rapped the polished soles with his knuckles and held them high for contemplation. He bent and laced them up and marched round the table, looking down and lifting his feet high. They always shone like a guardsman's boots but now he gave them an extra clean, sitting over the hearth, his quiff falling forward, using many brushes and polishing rags until they shone silver on surfaces that caught the gaslight. Then he went out, and if there was no meeting on which he could inflict his company he went to auntie Abbie's and sat in the armchair by the fire, his newly repaired, size five boots thrust out on the rug in front of him.

The best winter evenings were when we all stayed in. Eric and I played blow-football or ping-pong on the table with the leaves extended and the adults sat round the fire. The celluloid ball added an element of drama. It could shatter the gas mantle and plunge us for the night into the gloom of a blue flame. There were no spares of anything; to replace the mantle we should have had to knock on the side window of a closed corner shop, which you were not supposed to do except for medicine. Likewise there was no spare ball if the one we had went into the fire or was trodden on.

Celluloid was thought both vulnerable and dangerous. There were cautionary stories of children who had been burned trying to grab their ping-pong ball off the fire. My grandfather recalled a companion of his youth who had gone up in flames with his celluloid cuffs and collar. My mother knew of a house burned down by a blaze that started among some of those pink celluloid dolls whose trunk and limbs were held together by elastic. My grandmother remembered some celluloid ducks my cousin Margaret had got for Christmas which had cracked and sunk at bath time. When our ball eventually expired under foot or in flame there was some sense that a potentially lethal danger had passed without mishap. It was months before we got another.

As Christmas approached the headmaster at morning assembly read a suitable lesson from the Bible, then harangued us for funds. Mr Smith was a tubby man with glinting gold-rimmed spectacles, and he managed to sound both aggrieved and threatening as he twiddled his fingers in front of him as though to tickle up contributions. The money, I thought he said, was for 'the Conqueror' and I took it that the hint of menace was because of what might happen to us in default of tribute.

'Conjuror, you clown,' a boy said. 'It's a bloke Smithie pays to perform tricks at the Christmas concert.'

An older boy said his dad said the conjuror himself was the trick. He didn't exist. When he had finished browbeating the school and raking in contributions Smithie would pocket the lot and decamp.

The boys pulled Christmas to bits. They said there was no big star over the manger, else where had it gone to now, and the wise men and the shepherds were just blokes who happened to be passing on their way home from the pub. Father Christmas, they said, didn't exist. My precocious cousin Stanley had come to the same conclusion at the age of five. It was hardly to be supposed, he thought, that one Father Christmas could visit thousands of children in the course of one night, particularly as he had to go through the ritual of climbing down the chimney of each house. Stanley was fiercely instructed to keep his apostasy to himself for the sake of his two younger sisters, who left supper for Santa Claus and were confirmed in their simple faith by seeing the supper gone and a load of toys left in the morning. My cousin confided his findings to me when I was seven and in danger, as he thought, of carrying a primitive and erroneous belief into adult years. Sybil Yates, who lived near him, said she had particular reason to know that Father Christmas was really your own father disguised by false whiskers.

My parents tried to preserve the myth for the sake of my brother, who was not yet beset by doubt. They took us into Woolworth's, where Father Christmas was handing out pink and blue boxes and a Mother Christmas was taking the money. She was no part of the tradition. Moreover, they had undone their top button to let the sweat evaporate. My parents said they were not the real Father Christmas.

He, they pointed out, was standing at the door of the Co-operative shoe shop. He certainly looked the part. He tolled a handbell, Ho-ho-hoed, patted heads, and lavishly promised dolls, bikes and footballs. He had a jolly face and a twinkling eye and a word for everyone who passed. He spoke to my father: 'How do, Archie.'

'How do, Hiram,' my father replied.

Hiram? We saw peering through his cotton-wool eye-brows Hiram Tempest, the man who worked next to my father on the bench in the Co-op shoe repair factory.

The real and undoubtable Father Christmas, my parents said with the enthusiasm of a final effort, was installed across the road in the toy department. We found him squatting in a grotto, hearing requests from a queue of children. Wooden reindeer waited on snow of white crêpe. Frost sparkled on sacks loaded high on the sleigh. Carols played and in an orb of sky a large star twinkled among a galaxy.

Father Christmas had a merry laugh and bright dark eyes. He really did seem authentic. Yet in his voice and his manner of joking there was something familiar. He raised his face to greet us. Under the hood and behind the whiskers we recognised Councillor Jack Yates, Sybil's father, failed com-edian and funeral director of the Co-op, doing his Christmas turn.

The best four meals of the year we consumed in the space of Christmas Day and Boxing Day. My brother Eric started to gorge the chocolates and sweets among his presents as he unpacked his pillow-case. He found a spinning top full of small octagonal biscuits and he downed them too. He was usually sick for the first time before Christmas Day dawned.

It was a morning of smells, the wood shavings and shredded paper in which presents were packed, the tingling dark smell of the Christmas tree, the chicken cooking in the oven and the acrid smell of the parlour fire. Christmas was the only time we ate chicken and one of the few days on which the fire in the unfurnished parlour was lit. We spread our toys on the floor. The year Father Christmas was unmasked I had a mechanical model motor car fitted with a battery which lit the headlights. Eric had a horse and cart with barrels and boxes all made out of wood, which now would cost so much that it would be displayed as an ornament rather than used as a toy.

Our cousins the Kerrys arrived in a gale of uncle Ben's jollity. These were his two hearty days of the year. Cabinet-makers on piecework were as thin as laths and the colour of wood. Often he was so tired that he slept wherever he sat. Sometimes he would put on a comic awakening, blinking and twiddling his fingers as though surprised to have been overtaken by sleep. Now he made looping movements to catch everybody in the vice of his handshake, chortling the while and repeating 'Happy Easter'. He ate prodigious amounts. He attacked Christmas tea five hours after the end of Christmas dinner as though he had not eaten for a month, and he went on reaching out for mince pies and Christmas cake in a comic circuitous way ('Just one more to keep the wind off') long after everybody else had finished.

My grandfather tried to smoke a cigar, which always made him groggy. My grandmother read out riddles for us to guess from Foulsham's Fun Book. 'When is a door not a door? When it's a-jar.' We played rowdy games. We made shadow pictures on a white cloth draped over the edge of the table. We drank ginger wine my grandmother made, which seared the throat but was accounted superior to alcoholic drink on moral and aesthetic grounds.

After supper, which for uncle Ben was another great meal, this time of snacks, the Kerrys departed. The room was strewn with cushions and paper and the table laden with uneaten food. We sat by the dying fire. My brother, who had been freeloading all day, gave a couple of groans, at which we took cover, and heaved his Christmas food into the fire.

'You always have to go the whole hog, lad,' my father ground out through his teeth, revolted by the sizzling coal.

'Don't go for him. It's Christmas,' my mother said.

'That's no excuse. Just watch your step tomorrow, lad. Don't try this on at somebody else's house.'

The next day was the return fixture at the Kerrys'. My brother complied with his order. At night he walked back home solemnly quiet, then, as we had been out and there was no fire, he let fly into the cold grate.

My mother's friends from Norfolk, the Benns family, came to join in our Christmas and had us back at New Year. Arthur Benns worked in the same cabinet-making factory as uncle Ben but, having only one child, Arnold, to pester him at home, was more lively in his use of leisure. He was a spiritual man. He went alone on long walks over the moors. At home he listened to gramophone records, oblivious to any domestic uproar, and played his organ which drowned out all dissension. At Christmastime he played carols with such zest that the floorboards vibrated under our feet. He then set off indoor fireworks sent by Arnold's grandmother from Great Yarmouth.

'Snake in the grass,' Arthur Benns announced selecting one.

'Pass no remarks, little man,' Mrs Benns warned Arnold.

The snake fizzled and left a trail. 'It's doing its business,' Arnold announced.

Mrs Benns dragged him to the kitchen, closed the door and pummelled him. Arthur suspended the display so his son should miss no enjoyment of the Yuletide gift. When he was brought back bruised but unrepentant, Arthur set off an indoor rocket, guaranteed safe, which set fire to the Christmas tree and the decorations.

After that we had another organ voluntary and, as the time approached to go home, Eric under menacing glances waned into silent pallor, which marked the penultimate stage of the passing of Christmas.

Snow seldom fell before Christmas but always in January, first up on the moors where it remained in the northern gullies until April, then on the town itself. It blanketed the noise of the mills so that in the middle of the recreation ground there was near silence and one could imagine oneself trudging to the South Pole.

We made slides in the snow but better ones on days of keen frost. Boys polished the ice on the pavement and in the schoolyard with their sliding clog irons, then burnished it with lashing caps. Women crossing at their peril would mime to each other, 'It's like a bottle.' Some adults teetered with mincing steps. Others, coming upon a slide unexpectedly, went down with their limbs flailing like swastikas. Whole pavements where children slid on their way to school were more or less impassable. Teachers got across by developing a wary, crouching walk. They punched children who accidentally slid into them.

When Good Friday arrived everybody went out to the country, most on foot, pushing children's trolleys and loaded

with paper carrier-bags. Some villages had become by tradition the goals of Easter pilgrimage and maintained Victorian attractions, rides in a high-sided cart or a monkey in a
cage. Thousands of people milled round, and some tried to
play football or cricket through the throng. It was chaotic
and the weather was usually cold or wet, but it marked the
end of winter and soon the air would be warm again and
filled with the smell of hedgerow flowers and of new grass
on the moors.

Summers seemed long. The cinder recreation ground
turned to dust and we came in at night with feet as black as
coal miners'. We went to the woods and gathered bluebells
and lost all sense of time until the sun set and search parties
came out for us. 'Heat waves' arrived, cheered on by the
daily papers. At school, where the windows remained closed
against the soot and cinders of the breeze, we sweated in
flannel shirts and trousers. There were days of sudden, frightening darkness. In atmospheric inversions smoke from the
mill chimneys cascaded back on to the town, so darkening
the school windows that the lights had to be switched on.
Evangelists had warned of the impending end of the world;
we feared it had now arrived. Even some of the teachers
were alarmed. They had all the desks made tidy as though
they thought we might shortly leave the room and be evacu-
ated to a place where there was still light.

All the year round on fine mornings we formed up in the
school yard at the sound of the bell and marched in to the
click of a wooden instrument the teacher held. Files of girls
came in the opposite direction from their separate yard. We
met in the central hall and marked time, clogs beating on
the wood-block floor, until the headmaster ascended the
platform and halted us.

'Good morning, children,' he greeted us.

'Good morning, sir,' three hundred voices replied.

We sang a hymn and he reminded us of any standing
orders that were in danger of being ignored. Teachers,
ranged round the walls, stepped quietly into the ranks and
punished any misbehaviour with a thump in the ribs. The
headmaster said a prayer: 'Teach us, good Lord, to serve

Thee as Thou deservest; to give and not to count the cost, to fight and not to heed the wounds, to toil and not to seek for rest, to labour and not to ask for any reward, save that of knowing that we do Thy will.'

We sang another hymn and filed out to a marching tune on the piano. In the classroom we stood by our desks until the teacher came in and commanded us to sit.

Those who arrived late were locked out of school until the end of assembly, when the caretaker admitted them to make their excuses to the headmaster at his desk in the hall. He imposed no punishment but he scorned almost all excuses. Everybody dreaded the interview.

Teachers taught from bell to bell, side-tracked by very few administrative duties. They marked the attendance register morning and afternoon, and on Monday mornings they collected the money for the Yorkshire Penny Bank and for milk, which was supplied on the headmaster's initiative long before the education authority's scheme began. The rest of the time they taught. We learned to read and write and do arithmetic and we also did handwork, singing, nature study, games in the yard, religious instruction, geography and history.

These last subjects, something of a bore in most classes, were made interesting by Miss Dale, a slight young woman with owlish spectacles, who had such a gift for story-telling that we were sorry to be brought back to the prosaic present by the sound of the bell. We learned nothing about the development of industry or anything that bore directly on our life because that was not the fashion then, but we were left with a notion of the achievement of determined men and of the glory and grandeur of past empires. Our own, the British Commonwealth of Nations, as it had become known, was presented as an enormous benevolent society in which white men in pith helmets coached the 'natives' towards Christianity and democracy. Our bearded King George was father to us all, the Royal Navy ruled the seas and oceans, and the dominions of the white Commonwealth stood ready to come to the aid of each other against any aggressor.

Miss Dale conveyed all this, but she also struck a note of

doubt and misgiving which must have troubled any histori-
cally-minded person by 1933. India, the jewel in the crown,
the keystone in the arch, was in turbulence which had been
stirred up and promoted by the very educational process of
which we were taught to be proud. 'Buy British from the
Empire at home and overseas,' the posters urged us, but the
parts of the Commonwealth continued to do their main trade
not with each other but with outsiders. As for defence, three
imperial conferences held since the war had revealed a lack of
will to work out anything remotely approaching a common
policy, and indeed a chronic lack of means. The total strength
of the Royal Canadian Air Force in 1934 was one aeroplane
on a year's loan from the RAF. The empire for which we
wagged our flags on Empire Day had become a strategic and
economic liability, an expensive job-creation scheme for the
colonising classes.

Suddenly in the winter of 1933 the empire was in crisis, not
through any historical forces but because of the turmoil
caused in Australia by an English bodyline bowler, Harold
Larwood. He bowled so fast that the ball could not be seen
on newsreel film, and he bowled at batsmen's heads. Only
two fielders were set on the off side. The rest were to leg,
most of them clustered obliquely behind the batsman, waiting for the snick he might make in attempting to dodge the
ball. Most of the Australians were knocked senseless, but
apparently they took it in a sporting manner. Harold always
ran the length of the pitch to console the felled batsman and,
as he told it in later years, a graceful dialogue ensued.

'I'm sorry, Jim,' Harold would say.

'It's all right, Harold,' the batsman would reply, stroking
a broken rib or a lump the size of an egg on his head. 'It's
not your fault.'

But the Australian press and Cricket Board thought it was
Harold's fault and also the fault of Bill Bowes, the bowler
who brained people from the other end, and also of the
captain, Douglas Jardine, whose determination to win the
Ashes seemed overdone in days when games were played
for pleasure. The Australian government went further. They

condemned the MCC for condoning bodyline and made their feelings known at the Court of St James.

Cables passed, diplomats met, the King and the Prime Minister and the Prime Minister of Australia were brought into consultation. The poor old empire had never been so rattled since the Boer War and it was not to be so rattled again until Roosevelt set about it.

The crisis passed with the end of the tour and was not to be repeated. Jardine won the Ashes but lost the captaincy. Harold Larwood never again visited Australia until, with fond memories of the place, he emigrated there in old age. But long before then he had lost his speed and was reduced to bowling at the wickets and addressing Sunday school classes. He was held up to us as a model for youth.

One day I came in too tired to eat my tea and the next scarlet fever was diagnosed. It was then a virulent disease but I had it only in a milder form and was allowed to remain at home instead of being sent to the fever hospital.

After the malaise of the first week it was a pleasant break from school. The parlour was made into a bedroom for me to spare my mother the stairs. Each morning she lit the fire and cleaned the room and made me ready for the doctor, who prescribed delicate and expensive food. I had a boys' magazine most days and my mother played draughts and ludo with me in the afternoons. My father, whose manner with us had become increasingly gruff, reverted to the gentleness of earlier years. I read in annuals about camping and making expeditions by canoe. He said I was to have a tent and a canoe when I was well again. I was never really ill but I enjoyed all the benefits due to a patient with a killer disease.

My brother Eric did even better. He was exiled beyond the reach of germs to grandfather and grandmother Haworth's house at Bacup, where he enjoyed the indulgences that old people bestow on young children. It was a cosy dark house, nestling with its neighbours into a steep bank and warmed by a fire in an iron grate which was fuelled with a bucketful of coal at a time.

The house that backed on to it was so small that in later

years when it was added to my grandfather's house it was
made into a kitchen and a single bedroom. But then it housed
a family of thirteen, whose small children regularly created
an agreeable diversion by falling over the parapet of the
bridge into the brown river that ran between high walls.
Bigger boys went vertically down to the rescue like flies in
clogs. A woman stood at her door shouting: 'They shouldn't
be pulled out. They should be given a good hiding.'

For Eric it was the best and longest holiday of his early
life. He did not go to school. There were kittens to play
with on the rug, our patient grandmother to talk to all day,
and in the evening uncle Walter who did exciting things like
experimenting with radio sets on the table. Above all, Eric
was free of parental admonitions and exhortations. The
grandparents were delighted to have a child about the place
again.

They were not quite equipped for it. They had not
replaced the child's bath brush when uncle Walter grew too
big for the zinc bath by the fire and my grandfather, a genial
man of broad solutions, took the scrubbing brush to Eric
and soaped and rasped him as though he was preparing a
pig for market. Eric came back home the whitish pink of
a porker in good fettle. But they became lifelong friends.
Grandfather Haworth took him everywhere and at all hours.
Sometimes it was approaching midnight when he went to
bed. On the night they saw King Kong my brother, left to
sleep in the darkness of the attic bedroom, imagined the
monster scaling the wall outside and watched the square of
the skylight waiting in dread for the huge eye to appear.

He shouted. Grandmother came up and lighted the candle,
Grandfather asked what the noise was about.

'He's not here in Bacup, he's in New York,' he said. 'He's
dead, he was shot off his skyscraper.'

My brother calmed down.

'Any road,' grandfather Haworth said, 'it's nobbut a great
ape.'

Eric was there six weeks, which was the duration of the
infection of scarlet fever, and at the age of six it gave him a
buoyancy that lasted for years. His robust and open nature,
which was a trial to our mother, met its like in grandfather

Haworth. Their obvious admiration of him helped my mother to see his virtues and to enjoy in him qualities different from her own.

He came back with some economic advice for her. He had gone errands for grandmother Haworth to the local grocer's, where daily transactions were entered into a credit book which he took to be a substitute for money.

'You want to get one,' he told my mother. 'You can have whatever you want and it costs nothing.'

# 3 · FRESH AIR AND FUN

On the second weekend in July everything in Burnley stopped and half the population left town. Holiday weeks had been allocated to the cotton towns years ago by the cotton employers meeting in Manchester, and the wakes week, as it was called elsewhere, belonged to a place as inalienably as the town hall. In Burnley it had been known as Fair Week from long before cotton came. Through the years the hiring and trading fair had been transformed into a travelling fun fair. Its tractors and trailers came puffing and rumbling over the cobbles of the cattle market the evening before the holiday began to give a whirl to those who would stay at home. Nearly all who went away went to Blackpool.

Blackpool was a complete change from the soot and decay of East Lancashire, a clean town freshly painted with tall windows and polished brass door knobs. It was sunnier than inland and vibrant with the hum of streamlined trams and the ring of the hooves of landau horses and the call of pitched voices from the booths along the promenade. The wind carried the scent of distant oceans and the nearer whiff of fried fish. On arrival old men breathed in deeply, hands on hips, eyes rolling, nostrils dilating like horses', an inhalation which would prolong life for years.

The better off went on Saturday, most of them in the early afternoon after work. The rest of us economised on a weekend's lodging and got the maximum stay out of four nights by arriving before breakfast on Monday and returning on Friday night. We set off for the station before dawn, humping our suitcases and spades and cricket bats, and joined a thickening procession of grey figures under the lamplight, hunched over their loads and silent with sleepiness and exertion.

Trains came in cold from the sidings, old six-wheeled engines, wheezing steam, with a number on a card on the front of the boiler. I do not know what it was for, perhaps only to proclaim that it was indeed an excursion train. There was no question of needing to have a correspondingly numbered ticket to be allowed on; unconditioned as yet by bureaucracy and air travel, nobody would have understood that kind of regulation.

They got aboard in an orderly way, everybody giving a hand to hoist suitcases into the racks and sitting with squeezed-in shoulders to make room for all. Once under way, experienced travellers plunged down with falling hair and reddening faces to try to turn up or down the heating regulator somewhere under the seat that either produced no heat or steamed everybody in the compartment like an invalid's fish. Children were subdued, first with sweets, then with exhortations to watch through the windows for the first appearance of Blackpool tower, and finally with a straightforward pasting.

We were safe. My father never assaulted us in public. He was a shy, private man and he confined his violence to the seclusion of the home. On holiday he turned over a new leaf, no growling or pummelling, all smiles, willing to run all day in games with us on the sands. The brief break from the monotony of work and the constraints of being hard up restored the happiness of past years. He became young again. He enjoyed splashing money around. Whatever we wanted he paid for. My poor mother spent the week aghast.

On arrival we poured out of the station under the soaring mesh of the tower girders and across the promenade. Most of the established holidaymakers were still in bed. Only the early birds were astir. Some were smoking pipes that went like bonfires in the breeze. A few brave souls wallowed at the edge of the ocean.

We descended to the unbroken sands, where the stalls and the donkeys would not arrive for two hours yet, and walked

along the firm side of the tidemark past the jetsam of boots
and bottles and rotted spars. We could have taken the tram
but convention required us not to arrive at the boarding
house before breakfast had been cleared. We lodged near the
Pleasure Beach at the south end of Blackpool, which was
thought to be posher and less rowdy than the central promenade, so we had a mile or more to walk. It was a memorable
walk on a good day. An occasional early tram passed above
on the promenade, seagulls soared and swooped, and the sea
broke and sparkled in the sunlight slanting between the high
façades of the promenade buildings.

The boarding house was palatial with polished wood and
shining glass and deep carpets pleasantly ingrained with sand.
It smelled of rich brown gravy. The landlady escorted us up
the well of the stairs, up and round, taking Eric and me to
an attic at the very top, from which in bed at night we could
watch the moving lights of the Pleasure Beach.

Boarding houses catered for those who could do better
than a day excursion but could not afford an hotel. But
within this class there were many strata and some of the
middle-aged ladies, themselves a little better off now their
children had left home, were at pains to establish a social
hierarchy among the week's guests. Those who paid the
extra tariff for a window table and a first-floor front bedroom
were indisputably rich; the fact could not be made more
clear if they had arrived on an elephant with a retinue of
servants. But the rest of us who sat in the darker part of the
dining-room and ascended to the higher floors had to be
sorted out. Clothes, manners and accents would be scrutin-
ished and sly questions put to tease out our status.

We had already stigmatised ourselves by arriving on a
Monday, nor could we conceal that we were staying on a
cheaper plan by which instead of having food provided by
the landlady we bought our own and she cooked it. At the
first meal the inquisitors rose a little in their corsets to peer
at what was brought to each table.

Under scrutiny people's accents became posher, men who
swore or blew their nose loudly were quietly and fiercely
admonished, children who shouted had their arms wrenched.
Everybody rose up the industrial scale. There were no wor-

kers there, certainly no unemployed. The house was filled
with foremen, proprietors of businesses, and gentlemen with
a position in a shop. We were warned not to speak of my
father's tumble from Co-op branch manager to repair-
factory benchman. He remained a branch manager for the
holiday period long after all the Co-op shoe branches had
been closed down.

One year some people, finding themselves by an accidental
give-away sliding down the status league, restored their position by threatening to turn their son or daughter loose on
the piano. It was a good tactic. Ability to play the piano was
a sure mark of social standing and there was little danger the
threat would be put to the test as the piano lid was kept
permanently closed under its load of framed doggerel and
bottles of pop.

Mrs Salt, a personable middle-aged woman, forestalled any
quizzing by brazenly promoting herself from nurse to
matron in a single day. She shocked everybody. She was
there alone, she had a lame leg, she smoked and she addressed
people in a loud voice across the dining-room. One day
when we were in the sea she paddled out to throw the beach
ball with us, then plunged in fully clothed, swam round the
pier, and went dripping across the promenade and up the
stairs of Mrs Lockwood's boarding house.

The guests were impressed. Only a real matron could
exhibit such eccentricity. My mother, ever gullible, consulted her about my upset stomach; was it just something I
had eaten? No, the matron replied, my stomach was my
weak spot; I would suffer from it all my life and it would
finish me off.

That was grave enough to have the ring of truth about it.
Word of the diagnosis spread and Matron Salt was consulted
about everybody's maladies. She shot to the top of the social
league, level in status with the family who occupied the
window table. Her stories of being romantically accosted
by men on the promenade were credulously received. She
claimed that she had cornered Lobby Lud and would have
caught him but for her lameness.

This man was an employee of the *Daily News* who had

himself chased round seaside resorts. The paper published a timetable of points he would pass and angled photographs in which his features were largely concealed by his hat brim. Carrying a *Daily News*, you had to sail up to him and say, 'You are Mr Lobby Lud. I claim the *Daily News* prize.' It was £50.

When he was in town hundreds of people came by excursion train and thousands passed the day accusing each other of being him. He was known to dart between booths and down alleys to shake off pursuers. Nobody in Blackpool could quicken his pace without having a shoal of hunters dart after him. My mother made my father accost a few males, after which he pitched his *Daily News* into a wastepaper basket and said something under his breath that would have relegated us to the very bottom of the boarding-house social league.

When Lobby Lud was caught, seldom until the late afternoon, a newspaper van drove around with a notice to say the chase was ended, and next day the paper carried an article by Mr Lud about his many near escapes in which hundreds of challengers were able to identify themselves. Often he evaded capture. One tactic he used repeatedly, knowing his hunters thought of him as a loner, was to tag on uninvited at the back of groups or to stroll along chatting to a companion or to help in pushing a wheelchair. His most persistent pursuers he taunted and rewarded by slipping an IOU for ten shillings into their pocket or shopping bag.

Matron Salt did not come quite as close as that, but she claimed to have had him under hot pursuit. He had dodged round promenade shelters and plunged down the steps to the sands in desperate efforts to shake her off, turning as he rounded corners to wink at her. But she so hung on that in the end he forsook taunting and tactics of evasion and galloped for it at a speed she could not equal on her gammy leg. Even to tell the story made her breathless. We felt her near success did honour to the boarding house and reflected some glory on ourselves as fellow guests.

My brother and I were among the first on the sands every morning. We went down at dawn through the silent house.

Old Mr Lockwood, the landlady's father, slid off the couch where he slept by the open door of the kitchen and without speaking unlocked the front door. The promenade was empty, a few early risers and the odd tram, but the soft-drink stalls were already open. Eric and I drank in the manner of cowboys. We drank sarsaparilla because it was dark-coloured like whisky looked on the cinema screen. 'Set 'em up,' we would say to the man, ringing a coin on the counter. We tossed the drinks back, wiped the back of our hands across our mouths and banged the glasses down for refills.

My brother owned a cowboy hat with a cardboard brim and was deeply into the lore of the West; the sarsaparilla brought it out in holiday weeks. 'This town ain't big enough for both of us,' he would say in the general direction of some startled old man on the sands. 'Beat it, you coyote. Hit the trail. I'll give you till sundown.'

When the donkeys were brought down he sounded the bugle calls of the US Cavalry. He trotted, reins high, between the deckchairs performing duologues. 'I'm a-coming to git yuh, Ringo – Well, come down a-shooting.' He specialised in an interrupted wedding. 'Has anyone any objections?' he intoned in the voice of a clergyman. A door was kicked open. 'Yeah, me. Plenty. Stick 'em up.' People in the deckchairs hardly glanced up. The world in those days was saner but there were a great number of idiots abroad. In the boarding house Eric demanded his chow and placed two imaginary six-shooters on the table if he was rebuked. He had to be restrained from standing with his thumbs down his belt, opening doors with his boot sole and eating with his fork in his right hand.

His act was well received. One year, sent for a sliced loaf, he galloped back with a thunder of hooves, dropping from under his arm a trail of slices. Only a single crust remained, lodged at the end of the wrapper. That confirmed him as a character. At night when he figured he'd hit the hay everybody responded.

People were very tolerant. The status-establishers were few in number. Live and let live was the usual practice. The old particularly were tolerant. It could have been no sort of rest for them to be in a noisy town packed with children, but to most old people in Lancashire a holiday could only mean Blackpool. They lived in crowded houses where they were given jobs to do or chucked out while a daughter did the housework. On the crowded beach they could sleep in deckchairs all day long, feet bare, a knotted handkerchief on their head or a newspaper over their face, with the sound of the trams and the sea and children's shrill voices mingling with dreams. Disturbances were momentary, the scuffle of a children's game that shook the chair, the opening bombardment from the promenade of the Salvation Army band, the buffet of bodies compressed on the narrow strip of beach when the tide came in. They stirred and went back to sleep, head lolling, mouth agape. They had lived and worked and played always in crowds and would have found no rest in solitude.

Some weeks the sun fried everybody. Either there was no sun-tan cream then or nobody used it. People went bright red; those who had worn sun specs looked like koala bears or black minstrels with two white circles round their eyes. Guests in the boarding house failed to recognise each other at first sight. At night, as the lights of the Pleasure Beach rose and fell in the attic window, we could not sleep for the burning of our livid arms and faces.

One year I suffered what was thought to be sunstroke, though I had been wearing a cap from the moment of arrival to conceal a rough haircut done by my father. It was not his job. It was my grandfather's, but he had gone elsewhere and taken his scissors. It was Sunday, the barber's shop was closed, so my mother set my father on, unskilled and armed only with the kitchen scissors. It was a painful bad-tempered session that left me looking like a half-sheared sheep. I wore my school cap in the train. On arrival at Blackpool I was marched straight to a promenade stall and bought a Foreign Legion cap with a flap at the back that concealed all my hair. It might have been good enough for the Sahara but it did not ward off the Blackpool sun. I was sick in the night, and the next day I stayed in bed, sleeping and waking, disappointed to have lost a day of the holiday and saddened to have imprisoned my mother who stayed in a chair by the window silhouetted against the blue sky. I was all right next day, which fortified her wish to believe that it had indeed been a sharp attack of sunstroke and not a recurrence of my fatal stomach complaint which Mrs Salt had diagnosed the previous year.

The matron was not there to comment but she was back next year when my father developed an itching that kept him awake all night. He swore it was caused by a yellow shirt, of which my mother had bought one for each of us. We sailed out of the boarding house in the morning like a flight of canaries. People looked round. My father felt conspicuous. He noticed the 'Foreign made' label in the shirt and decided some oriental impurity had brought on his affliction. Mrs Lockwood, anxious to dispel any suspicion that he might have been attacked by fleas in her boarding house, said a similarly tormented client had been found to be suffering from 'prickly heat'. Mrs Salt came upon the scene. It wasn't the shirt and it wasn't prickly heat, she said. It was an infrequent condition, unknown to lesser medical practitioners, caused by having been bitten by a fish rare in these northern seas. It would recur each year and eventually prove fatal.

Thus in three years she had finished off half our family. 'Sorry to see you bite the dust, pardners,' my brother said.

Once his cowboy act was accepted, Eric took the liberty of singing to the house. He had the knack of picking up rapidly the inane songs of pier comedians and he was sufficiently unselfconscious to render them.

> Two can't sit on a three-piece suite
> O dear, No, No, No.

The year we wore the canary shirts he had the whole boarding house tweeting to a new song.

> Let's all sing like the birdies sing
> Tweet, tweet, tweet, tweet.

Then at the Tower circus he discovered a new genre of songs, of which he would increase his repertoire in future years in his many months in hospital. After the monkeys had cycled round and the lions had clambered on to their drums, pierrots wheeled on a big double-sided screen on which the words of a lyric were struck by a bouncing dot of light in time with the music. He had never heard a song like it before nor seen singers with the stance and expression of the pierrots. He was fascinated. The song was sung by the pierrots and the audience over and over again. Eric learned it. Everybody who went to the circus learned it. People in the boarding house and about the town joined in whenever he sang. Ascending the steps from the sands he would circle his hands like a soulful minstrel and sing:

Have you ever been lonely, have you ever been blue?

People coming down would sportingly reply:

Have you ever loved someone just as I love you?

Approaching the boarding house, he would plead with sadly shaking head:

Can't you see I'm sorry for each mistake I've made?

And from the darkness behind the open door half a dozen people sitting waiting at the tables would join in the line:

Can't you see I've changed, dear? Can't you see I've paid?

It became like a production number, moving fluently from set to set about the town, a technique still years away in those days when singers on the screen simply faced the camera and sang.

Until the industrial revolution Blackpool was a fishing village on the fertile coast of the Fylde where, until the Tower rose, the flat horizon was broken only by windmills, a few of which remained in my childhood. It had nothing but a few miles of sand, but that made its fortune. The tide comes in close to and sometimes right up to the promenade wall, leaving the sand firm and smooth and good to play on. The beach shelves gently and is safe. A railway line was built last century and in the 'thirties the country road there was replaced by a three-lane highway.

The town was different from any in Lancashire, clean, fresh, American-looking. It was a bustling place. At rigidly observed hours the side streets filled with tides of people, tens of thousands, moving between lodgings and the promenade, out towards the sea at 9.30 after breakfast, back inland at 12.30, out again at 2, back at 5. Many who came to recuperate must have been killed off by the exertion.

The lodging house itself was a base, not a place of rest. Everybody had to leave the dining-room as soon as a meal was finished so the table could be set for the next, and there was nowhere else to sit except the form outside the window. People hadn't come to sit indoors; you could do that at home. On wet days boarders were turned out just the same. The old dozed in shelters along the promenade and in the parks. The rest of us trooped through the stinking zoo and the green aquarium, passing the time by making fish faces at the fish. We hung about the Pleasure Beach without going on any of the exposed rides. We played under the piers. We rode up and down the promenade in covered trams, looking out on the sodden beach and the undivided sea and sky. It seemed that the sun and bright colours would never return.

Those days were few. The prevailing memory is of bright days with a breeze coming off the sea. Blackpool was believed to be therapeutic. There is an apocryphal story about a man who died when he returned home. The woman from next door, seeing him laid out under the dining-room window, was moved to say: 'It's a pity, because he does look so well.'

'Look well?' his widow said, 'He ought to look well. He's just back from a week at Blackpool.'

My grandfather claimed to have enjoyed a remarkable recovery there, not directly from the breezes but from a huge helping of potato pie in a shop behind the promenade. He had suffered from an upset stomach and had been advised by the doctor, in line with the practice of those days, to cut all sorts of items out of his diet. At the sight of the huge sloppy pie steaming in the window, he rebelled against his finicking privations, went inside and downed a plateful. He had no more stomach trouble for the rest of his life. Blackpool got the credit for the cure; the pie, he admitted, might have occurred anywhere in Lancashire but it was the invigoration of Blackpool that had raised his morale to the point of defying doctor's orders.

The only sedentary people in the resort, apart from the aged, were those exhibited in the booths on the promenade and the Pleasure Beach. One poor chap sat with an expressionless face on a seat which collapsed and dropped him into a pool whenever a bull's eye was scored by wooden balls thrown at a target above his head. A young lady in a bathing costume, Frosty Godiva, reclined all day in a block of ice. And we discovered a pale youth who turned out to be the works of a machine. It was an octagonal kiosk with slots to take your money and windows in which prizes of jewellery were displayed on black velvet. On our way to the sarsaparilla in the early morning we stuck a penny in, hoping to win necklaces, rings and watches, but all that ever came down the chute was rubbish, tie-pins, pencils that would not write, collar studs. One hot day we spotted an open small door in the lower part of the kiosk and a youth squatting in the darkness. We put a penny in and whipped round in time to see him post some rubbish down the chute. We asked him to oblige us with a watch. He said, 'Bugger off.'

The most famous ever of the human exhibits on the promenade was the Reverend Harold Davidson, the unfrocked Rector of Skiffkey, who sat in a barrel between a performing flea circus and a cousin of Mahatma Ghandi who reclined on a bed of nails. The rector, five feet two inches and then around sixty, had been brought to this pass through neglecting his parish in Norfolk to rescue girls in London. He was so occupied in pursuing waitresses and in disputing with café managers who threw him out that the only full week he spent in his parish for several years was during the General Strike of 1926 when the trains stopped. Five years later he failed to get back in time to take the Armistice service. The squire complained to the Bishop of Norwich and the Reverend Davidson's twenty-five years as a country parson finished at a Consistory Court which deprived him of 'all ecclesiastic dues and rights and emoluments'.

The people were on his side. One Sunday before sentence was pronounced he ascended the pulpit wearing war medals to a standing ovation from the crowded church. He took as his text: 'I came not to call the saved but sinners to repentance.' After the service he lit a big cigar and signed autographs for those outside who had been unable to find seats. Thus began a series of publicity stunts which in a short time was bringing him in £2,000 a year, a huge income. By 1933 he had reached the big time in his barrel on Blackpool's Golden Mile.

But it wasn't the kind of thing stolid visitors from the mill towns approved of, and Blackpool corporation tried to get him jailed on a technicality. Ghandi's cousin in the next booth had mentioned what a boon fasting had been to the Mahatma's cause and Mr Davidson incorporated it into his own act. He pulled in the crowds by advertising that he was starving to death. Blackpool corporation had him arrested for unlawful intent to commit suicide. He was acquitted and awarded damages of £350 against the town for false imprisonment. He rolled away his barrel and shook the sand off his boots, departing for Skegness, 'a delightful place to be in,' he proclaimed, 'after the blatant vulgarity of Blackpool.'

It was his final place. He performed there with two lions, Freddie and his mate Toto. Standing outside their cage, he gave his audiences a short sermon in which he applied the symbolism of Daniel in the lions' den to his own brave struggle against the injustice of the Church. Then he changed his ebony walking-stick for a short stock whip and went in through the steel gates.

A crowd of about a hundred, who had paid threepence each, heard his last words. As he stepped into the cage he trod on Toto, and Freddie punched him to the ground. The crowd ran in panic. A sixteen-year-old girl lion-tamer beat Freddie back with a stick, and a more cautious helper waggled an iron rod through the bars.

But it was all up with the reverend. His dramatic end put Skegness on the map and left the publicity department at Blackpool silent with envy.

Blackpool was a self-contained world. When you were there nowhere else existed except in brief moments. My father would be seized by strangers, men who had served with him in the trenches and who now identified themselves by recalling the names of places in Flanders. We remembered the photographs of companies of soldiers which he kept at the back of a drawer with his cap badge and medals, and we caught a glimpse of a different world in which he was a different man, unknown to us. But it was a passing glimpse and the strong reality of Blackpool, the throngs and the noise, the seagulls and the sea smell, blanketed out thoughts of other places and the wider world.

That world in 1932 was speeding up. Jim Mollison flew solo to the Cape in 4 days 17½ hours, a Great Western express raced from Swindon to Paddington at 81.6 m.p.h., a Dutchman crossed the Channel on a hydrocycle and the Belgian Professor Piccard attempted to reach the stratosphere by balloon. The world was also becoming more dangerous as the demented dictators of the decade prepared their horrors. Hitler was on the point of taking power. Mussolini paraded his growing army and air force. Stalin sought the strength for war by desperate industrialisation and brutal collectivisation of the land.

I doubt whether anybody during their week at Blackpool cared very much. There may have been something in the newspapers, but they were used largely for sleeping under in a deckchair or as qualification for hunting Lobby Lud. Blackpool banished all other worlds. The journey home, away from the Tower and windmills back into the sooty mill towns, was a long moment of awakening from a bright dream.

# 4 · IN PURSUIT OF TRADE

Shop men dressed the part. Grocers wore ankle-length tass-elled aprons, butchers aprons of blue and white stripes, the fishmonger a straw boater, the greengrocer a floppy trilby hat. The chemist appeared in a wing collar at his counter in front of his framed certificates and between two big carboys of coloured liquid. Shops were full but took money slowly. Lacking refrigerators and cash, their customers bought in small quantities. Few items were packaged. Most purchases were to weigh out and to present in bags fashioned on the counter by deft fingers. Each customer was to be flattered by conversation. It took a long time.

The longest wait was at the Co-op grocer's on Saturday mornings. The shop had a marvellous smell – of the butter they slapped, of the bacon they cut on the machine that sang to the turn of the handle, of potatoes that rumbled down a chute, of nutmeg and ginger and all the spices in the bank of drawers behind the counter, of sawdust and flypaper, and of the carbolic smell of mill-workers scrubbed for the weekend and wearing new woollen shawls. One could wait for an hour. The grocers, besides selling grocery and writing out dividend tickets, took in boot and shoe repairs, collected money and issued receipts for payments for coal, and did some system of multiple entry for contributions to Mutu-ality, the Co-op's scheme for selling clothing and furniture on credit. There was a convention by which somebody in a hurry could shove through saying, 'Can I come before you? I'm pushing.' There was also a convention by which children in the shop were ignored for younger women, with whom

the shopmen could brighten the morning by exchanging
gallantries, and pushed aside with a basket in the ear by
ruthless crones.

Banter was a normal form of conversation in the Co-op
but not in privately-owned shops, where customers were
treated with deference, addressed by name and honorific and
not subject to the broad jokes that were part of a Co-op
grocer's stock in trade. Anybody was free to chastise children
and some shopkeepers, rankled by years of truckling to adult
customers, made a practice of it. The chemist, a mild man
with thinning hair and an unctuous manner, shot out like an
angry tiger when we rapped with a coin on the counter to
summon him from the back. He had it in for us. He had
sold some nostrum to my plump and precocious cousin
Stanley Kerry and instructed him to convey it to the mouth
by means of a spoon or some other suitable vehicle. My
cousin questioned the word. The chemist said it was correct.
Stanley looked it up in the dictionary and, a keen and inno-
cent student, returned to the chemist with his findings;
'vehicle' was correct but pedantic. After that neither of us
was persona grata in the shop.

The O'Briens were a tough pair. Their corner shop, like
most, was a converted house in which the front room had
been fitted with a big window and a small counter, lined
with shelves and strung across the ceiling with cords to carry
towels, table cloths and garments. The outside was bright
with tin advertisements for Fry's Five Boys' chocolate, Col-
man's mustard, and Bovril's bull. Inside there was hardly
room for customers to squeeze in, and for the O'Briens little
space to live, their room at the back being crammed with
boxes stacked up the walls and pushed under the dining-
table.

A corner shop would not make a living in itself. Somebody had to go out to work as well. Mrs O'Brien ran the
shop and Mr O'Brien had a job. At home he was kept in
the back except when summoned. He was a little man with
suspicious eyes and seldom seen out of his overalls. After a
day's work he may not have been up to the contortions
necessary to change in a bedroom full of cardboard boxes.

She summoned him not by name but simply by raising her voice.

'Are you smoking?' she shrilled at me, and there he was, swaying in the shadow of the doorway to the living-room, sizing me up through his specs and chewing his dinner. He must have fed well. I cannot remember an appearance when he was not chewing. 'Smoking, eh?'

I held up a stem of burning band, a hollow string of cotton which we scrounged from the mills and which would glow and smoulder. 'Burning band,' I said.

'Art thou smoking it? he asked, shifting his dinner to the other side of his cud.

'No,' I said, 'burning it.'

'Well, don't burn it here. Them ping-pong balls are inflammable. The whole premises could go up in a roar. And don't burn it anywhere else either. Same applies.'

He swayed a little while the message sank in, turned and disappeared into the darkness.

'Now, Mr O'Brien's told you,' Mrs O'Brien said. 'Mind you think on.'

She was impatient with children when the shop was full and it was difficult not to dither, we were so spoiled for choice. There were hundreds of bottles full of strong-tasting sweets – mint imperials, gob-stoppers, aniseed balls, fruit gums, clear mints, lemon drops, pear drops, lime and sarsaparilla tablets. Then there were trays of toffee which had to be broken with a little hammer and which became so sticky on hot days it could adhere permanently to a pocket lining. There were things parents did not like you to buy – chewing-gum, braided spanish spooled round a coloured sweet and sticks of liquorice which left soft splinters of wood in your teeth. My mother tried to warn us about chewing-gum by quoting a boy's epitaph:

> Chewing-gum, chewing-gum, made of wax
> Brought me to my grave at last.

The wonky rhyme made it seem authentic, but we discovered that chewing-gum was not made of wax but of rubber from the forests of South America. That, she thought, could only be worse. Accidentally swallowed, it would swell in your stomach like the bladder of a football.

One week we resisted sweets and spent our pennies on water pistols, for which there was a craze. They consisted of a rubber bulb and a thin lead barrel an inch long through which water was drawn in and squirted out. They fired only a couple of feet and soon ceased to work altogether. We took them back.

'You've been filling 'em wi' mucky water out o' t' gutter,' Mrs O'Brien shrilled.

Mr O'Brien appeared chewing in the doorway.

'They've bunged 'em up wi' muck,' she said.

He shifted his dinner. 'Don't bung 'em up wi' muck.'

He advanced and took them off us. We heard him threading through the boxes in the back and the splash of the tap.

He returned, held up a pistol and fired a loop of water on to some bundles of firewood. 'What's up wi' that?'

'Nowt,' we agreed.

He handed the pistols back. 'Scatter,' he said. 'Don't bung 'em up and don't bring 'em back.'

We did go back. With use the neck of the bulb stretched and the barrel kept falling out. We spread the pieces on Mrs O'Brien's counter.

'He's mended them once,' she complained, loud enough to summon him.

He contemplated the dirty oozing heap of broken pistols, chewed long enough to decide repair was impossible and impassively pushed the pieces over to us. 'Take 'em,' he said, 'and bugger off.'

There were enough shops within a quarter of a mile to serve all daily needs and they were open for twelve hours or more every day except Sunday. Older people and working women went no further, but mothers at home walked down town two or three days a week to save halfpennies and came back loaded like mules. On Saturday nights when the lamps burned among the market stalls we went to buy fruit and vegetables offered cheap at the end of the week. We sometimes got a load of bruised apples and stayed up late cutting out the brown bits and stewing the rest.

We knew the price of everything. We went to several of the same kind of shop to buy each item at its cheapest and we changed shops when the price rose. The grocer, seeing us pass with a rival's goods, would leap out from behind the counter and tell us to tell our mother the good news that his two-pound loaves had gone down a halfpenny.

At the worst times daily parsimony was extended to the Sabbath and we were given a halfpenny to put in the Sunday school collection. 'Give the best to Jesus,' we sang, and dropped him a halfpenny.

I got new clothes. My brother got my old ones. My father had the same overcoat and scarf from coming out of the army in 1919 until after the Second World War. Clothes that had to be bought we paid for by joining a club, either the Co-op's Mutuality scheme or the Provident Club which permitted the use of a larger range of shops and spared one the trouble of paying instalments at the Co-op grocer's. Bob Critchley came for the money on Friday nights in his bowler hat and bicycle clips. He was a nice man, flustered with self-consciousness, and he took an interest in what had been bought through his good offices. He made the best of things. If I was paraded in a jacket whose sleeves covered my fingers, he would comment, 'Nice easy fit, give him room to grow.' If we got anything too small, which rarely happened, he would remark on the 'snug fit – you don't want a suit you could get somebody else in as well'.

My brother, landed with my old clothes, usually got a new cap to embellish his appearance. My mother always took him to the same shop, where he was recognised as the willing victim of sport. They would fit him first with a cap that perched on top of his head, then one that fell down over his eyes. He made faces like Stan Laurel. More caps of deliberately hopeless fit were brought out. Everybody in the shop laughed. It was a time of simple pleasures.

Both Co-op Mutuality and the Provident Club were much more economical than the hire-purchase companies. Through either, things cost no more than their cash price. The shops that subscribed to the Provident Club paid the administrative costs, not the customer, and their goods were usually slightly cheaper than the Co-op's, though of poorer quality. But the Co-op paid 'dividends', a rebate on all purchases except funerals, paid quarterly and usually amounting to ten per cent. Most people subscribed to both the Co-op and the Provident for the permitted maximum and many to the dearer forms of hire purchase as well. Older generations in Lancashire prided themselves on 'owing nobody nowt'. For most in the 'thirties it was impossible to live without credit.

Bob Critchley came for many years. His cautious and apologetic manner made him better liked than heartier rivals. He prospered to the extent of acquiring an auto-cycle which led to further success by giving him an extra turn of speed.

The landlord came for the rent, a shy unemployed weaver who had been left the house and could get no more out of it than our weekly five shillings. We forebore to mention the rising damp and penetration water under the gutter that made the place permanently soggy and he for his part pocketed our two half-crowns with a nod to each of us as though we had contributed generously to his well-being.

There were landlords of a more sinister kind, as I learned at a friend's house when the rain burst in and poured down the inside of the window. 'Capitalist landlords!' his father shouted, splashing round and collecting vessels. 'They did our Polly in, they killed that bird.' He raced back and forth with bowls and pans and plant-pots and jerries. As each was placed at the foot of the window the cascade shifted to miss.

'Pneumonia finished that parrot and grandma's going the same way. Two hundred years old the bird was and I bet it had never lived anywhere as squalid as this.'

The ceiling at the top of the window darkened and crumbled and a powerful waterfall tumbled down, tossing the furniture about the room.

'That's capitalism,' he exclaimed, elated to see his point proved. 'That's what happens when the profit motive governs human habitation.'

The other regular visitor on Friday evening was the doctor's man, in readiness for whom the receipt book and coins were left on the sideboard. At first it was an exhausted old man who sought to distance himself from the medical

business. 'A sit-down by the fire and an aspirin will do more
good than any doctor,' he said disloyally.

Some weeks he bent over the book for a long time. We
knew then that he was not only entering payment but
inscribing the amount of a new bill as well. The moment he
left we rushed to see how much it was. The doctor's bill
was a regularly renewed debt which was not paid off until
we were grown up.

The old man was succeeded by his son-in-law, a cross-
eyed man with ginger hair *en brosse*, who as the doctor's
chauffeur had been trained to fling open for him in rapid
succession the door of his car and the door of the patient's
house. As a collector he proclaimed himself, not in the usual
way, by knocking or by shouting as he came up the hall but
by whistling loudly. He then entered the room juggling the
keys in his trouser pocket as though tormented by a bad
attack of crabs. My brother thought he had been demoted
because his crossed vision made him a danger at the wheel
and caused him to throw the wrong doors open. When the
collector entered our room Eric pointed to the wrong corner.
The collector nodded and walked unerringly to the sideboard
where the money lay, which confirmed Eric in the belief
that the poor man was best served by misdirecting him
ninety degrees.

Different insurance men came on their bikes; then came
one, a blond young man with a slight moustache and plus-
fours, who arrived in a motor car. He made it known that
he had motored to the South of England. He described the
expedition as though he had been up the Amazon. We were
left with a notion of wide roads and glass factories, lush
fields and woods, and of brisk people of sharp speech and
punctilious driving habits, living in green and spacious
towns. He rounded off his description by offering my
mother a cigarette from a gold case, which was flattering
but profoundly shocking.

The carts of competing tradesmen filled the terraced streets
all morning. The Co-op delivered milk in bottles before
seven o'clock. Around nine three farmers arrived in milk
floats. They ladled out a small extra measure with each pint,

and on hot days when milk went off quickly they came
again in the early evening. Four ice-cream carts passed in the
afternoon, magnificent vehicles styled like fairgrounds. Each
had a real Italian inside, moustachioed men with dark rolling
eyes who rebuked us in the language of the movies as we
shook on the raspberry vinegar: 'Ah you waste da razz, boy.
Mama mia!'

Before them had come the fish cart, heralded by the buzz
of its clouds of flies, coal men, and two greengrocers whom
we sometimes followed for the fruit the cobbles shook from
their carts. No tradesmen were welcome on Mondays when
washing was strung across the back street; coalmen were
prohibited by a convention stronger than law.

Chimney sweeps also had to watch their step. When things
went wrong they filled a room with floating soot in which
one saw the dismayed faces of the inmates moving about as
though in a clouded aquarium. In any case it was cheaper to
set the chimney on fire, though it was illegal and the yellow
rolling smoke by day or the flying sparks in the darkness
would bring a policeman to the door. The householder
would affect surprise and concern. The policeman would
accept it as an accident that could happen to anybody's chimney. There would be no more chimney fires in the immediate
vicinity for a respectable period of about a fortnight.

A muffin man came round ringing a bell. A knife-grinder
in a sombrero made sparks fly from his carborundum wheel.
A greengrocer abandoned his shop for a couple of hours
to peddle kippers. In a straightforward way he shouted,
'Kippers.' The firelighter man addressed himself to a select
class. 'Now, you firelighter buyers, two bundles for three
ha'pence.' He did not do too well with firelighters – why
pay 1½d when you could start a fire with a broken box or
screwed-up newspaper? – and he carried other lines, buttons,
pins, dolly blue, on his handbarrow. It had a single wheel,
revolving in a slit in the centre of the deck. He leaned it
against the wall to make a sale.

Delivery boys came from the Maypole dairy pedalling
low-geared bikes with a rumbling box over the front wheel.
Sleeker youths came very occasionally from the posh shops
where you did not need to bear away your parcels but could

command a time of day (the same day) for delivery. The Maypole boys whistled snatches of tunes, and so did all the tradesmen who had no cry of their own. Everybody whistled – bus conductors, postmen, craftsmen at work, everybody. As possession of wireless sets spread, they all whistled the same tune in any one week. Why does nobody whistle now?

The rag and bone man sang the terms of the transaction, 'Rag and bone – rubbing stone', in an old voice. Rubbing stones were white or yellow sandstones used to embellish doorsteps. The rag man rarely spoke but he was a man of some repartee.

'What art thou so mournful about, Jimmy?' another old man asked him.

'Business is bad,' the rag man replied.

'Have folk got no rags?'

'Aye, but they're wearing them.'

At noon he knotted the donkey's reins, sat on the back of the cart, his boots dangling, and started to spoon down bread and milk out of a blue can. We stood in a half circle watching him. My brother asked: 'Is that all you've got for your dinner, pobbies?'

The old man did not speak for a long time, then he replied: 'I dine in the evening.' He stuffed a pobby into his mouth, swallowed it and added: 'At eight.'

'Do you have a right dinner?' Eric asked, 'at eight.'

'Sumptuous repasts. Haute cuisine.'

He lived with his rags in a ramshackle shed by the railway. His donkey lived the other side of a half partition. But he had given hints of his high life for years, it seems. It was said that he was of a rich family and had come down in the world through gambling or bereavement and that he worked and spent nothing and had a small fortune stuffed away under his rags. But when he died one night in his sleep nothing was found in the hut but the rags and the donkey.

At one time his business had been threatened briefly by high-powered competitors. Two men parked outside school a big motor van, crammed full of treasures – football jerseys, wickets, white cricket balls, a huge fort manned round its castellations by red-uniformed soldiers, small sewing machines, dancing shoes, typewriters, everything the heart might desire. The display was huge in quantity and power-fully banked up to the roof. The men explained that they wanted no money, only rags to exchange for trinkets and 'better clothes' for forts and cricket sets. Children dispersed fast. Many came back tear-stained having lost the struggle at home but others, particularly those whose parents were out at work, returned with dresses, overcoats, and linen from the sideboard.

One man on shift work awoke and found his working clothes gone from the chair and his Sunday suit from the wardrobe. He arrived angrily at school in borrowed clothes from which his fists stuck out of the short jacket sleeves like drumsticks.

The headmaster at assembly told the school that nothing more was to be brought to the van, and during the morning he went out and ordered the men away. Such was the power of headmasters that both the children and the men obeyed him.

For the old rag man it had been like the competition of a multi-national. It sucked up the rags of the district like a giant vacuum cleaner and afterwards there must have been a lull in trade. But evidently business picked up at least to a level to feed an old man and a donkey, even if perhaps it did not really run to haute cuisine.


One day my mother called me through the house to the front door. A beefy man with a moustache and a bowler hat was standing there with a large suitcase at his feet.

'Oh yes, I would know how to protect Ronald,' he began.

'Donald,' my mother corrected him.

'Donald,' the man agreed with an apologetic nod. 'I would know how to protect and succour Donald if we were benighted together.'

He said he had been telling my mother he had lived in many parts of the world, and appealed to her to confirm this.

'I've been benighted in the bush and in the tundra,' he said. 'And I've come through to salute the dawn.'

A dewdrop collected at the end of his nose. He flicked it off with a big red handkerchief.

'Now, Donald,' he said, 'if you were benighted, even in England's green and pleasant land but on a stormy night, would you know how to proceed?'

I said I wouldn't.

'You understand the word benighted?'

I said I didn't.

'Benighted – caught in the open, especially in a dangerous or inhospitable landscape at the fall of darkness with in places a precipitous drop in temperature.'

It was a contingency to which I had not given thought. I shook my head.

'But if you were with me, Donald, I should know what measures to take. If we were benighted together in a storm we would ascend into the foliage of an umbrageous tree, compose ourselves between cross branches and I would spread my raincoat to shield us on the windward side.'

My mother and I mumbled our thanks, which encouraged him to plunge into his bag and come up with an encyclopaedia in each hand.

'Knowledge,' he said. 'It's all in here.'

He had us baffled but he was on a hopeless wicket. Books in our house either came as Sunday school prizes or as gifts for taking a newspaper or not at all. We withdrew behind the closing door. He craned in for a final burst, gave up with a dismissive wave of his hand and bent to snap the catches of his suitcase. We heard his confident rat-tat-tat-tat next door.

Doorstep transactions were normally to be measured only in coppers. Poor people called with trays of matches and buttons and sewing cotton, and everybody bought something if only to help empty their tray and let them home. Some were twisted and lame, many were ex-Servicemen and at least one was unable to speak. He wore medals and a card hung round his neck bearing the name of his regiment.

Gipsies came, swirling their lace shawls and offering clothes pegs. They flattered the lady of the house by asking if her mother was in. My mother was moved by the story one of them told and lent her her Sunday blouse to attend a funeral. She was surprised that it was not returned. She could only think some misfortune might have befallen the woman. It seemed possible, in the light of our recent learning, that she had been benighted.

Tramps rarely came to the door, but every day an intermittent procession of them passed the school railings on their way to and from the workhouse. Most were destitute old men. There were few women alone but many old couples. They wore rags and carried all their possessions with them contained in broken suitcases or paper carrier-bags. They arrived at the workhouse before dark, fed and slept, ate again in the morning, performed some perfunctory job and were turned out to go on to the next town. Two consecutive nights in the same workhouse were not permitted, so the down-and-out were kept in permanent circulation.

For a time there was in vogue a romantic theory that people chose to be tramps because of atavism in the soul which caused them to regress to the earlier life pattern of nomadic man. Most tramps were in fact people of low intelligence who through bad luck or ignorance had lost their home and fallen out of benefit. Drink had done some of them down and it was widely believed that any alms given to those bold enough to beg at doors would be rapidly invested at the pub or in the methylated spirits account at the hardware store. Their tramping was not chosen but enforced by the remaining effects of the old Poor Laws which made each parish responsible for its own poor and thereby incited every local authority to keep vagrants vagrant. In earlier times constables whipped them across the boundaries.

The belief that tramps enjoyed the life or that it met an instinctive need was especially prevalent in hiking circles, whose members envied and admired them as weekend drivers respected the racers at Brooklands. The youth hostels, of which new ones opened every year for the encouragement of hiking and biking, were organised on exactly the same lines as workhouses – communal eating, night-time segregation by sex, some small job after breakfast, then out into the elements and onward to the next hostel.

It is true, though, that some tramps had actually chosen the open road or, having fallen into tramping, come to enjoy it. They were usually younger, bronzed and in good shape, greeters from afar, ever ready to impart the lore of the outdoors, the birds, the trees, the crops and seasons. My grandfather fell in with men of this sort when he was allowed out into the park as a rheumatism patient in Buxton hospital. They had their round, a circuit they made once or twice a year, infrequently enough not to sour their welcome at those houses, farms and pubs where they stood a chance of a meal and maybe some old clothes. They refrained from theft and did useful jobs. They slept by preference in barns rather than the workhouse.

Tramps of any sort were people apart. Nobody admitted to having one among his relatives. They belonged to a separate species. Our notion of them came not from life but from jokes of which, like waiters and lunatics, they were frequently the subject. It was a shock when one actually spoke to us.

'Art thou on t' road?' he asked.

We were taken aback. He repeated his question. We said no, we were collecting ladybirds from the hedge for our model circus. He did not get our drift any more than we got his. He told us the way to Todmorden workhouse. We realised too late that he wished to know in return how to find the workhouse from which he thought we'd come.

Thinking back on it, we felt rather honoured. We began to collect tramps. We noted the detail of individual styles. We spoke of them in the mock heroic. The expression 'knight of the road' came to our welcoming notice and then a poem, 'Christmas Day in the Workhouse', a noble and enduring work in the literature of defiance.

> In came the workhouse keeper
> And, as they sat round the grimy walls,
> He wished them a Merry Christmas.
> And all in one voice answered 'Balls'.

We knew through films and comics of the great race of tramps beyond the Atlantic, where they were called hobos and usually prevailed, though violently used. They were knocked into rivers and off scaffolding, flushed out with flame and steam, fired upon with shotguns, struck, thrown, hit with planks and custard pies and addressed only with two words: 'Beat it.' In the hobo misfortune was comic. Charlie Chaplin, with only the battered clothes he stood up in, was unheedingly deprived of his pullover by the blind girl who unravelled it in winding her wool.

Unlike ours, American hobos did not proceed on foot. They rode the rods, as the metal chassis of railway trucks was called. They also rode on the roofs and galloped back the length of the train as a bridge or tunnel was approached. Some were left swinging round signal arms.

In 1935 hobos migrated from myth to the news pages. From all parts of North America, from as far away as Nova Scotia and Texas, it was reported, they were riding the rods to Edmonton, Alberta, for a universal hand-out of twenty-five dollars. It had been promised in his provincial election campaign by a Baptist radio preacher, Bible Bill Aberhart, leader of the Social Credit party. He advocated a rudimentary sort of Keynesian system. Everybody was to be given twenty-five dollars, which would prime the trade pump. The money would circulate, the economy would revive and the slump would end.

The Reverend Aberhart won the election. For his inauguration as Premier of Alberta, Edmonton was besieged by the most enormous gathering of hobos ever seen, all waiting for their twenty-five dollars. If any has had the patience and sufficiently long life he is still waiting.

Bible Bill ran Alberta until his death in 1943, and his Social Credit pals for many years afterwards. Nobody got twenty-five dollars.

# 5 · SALVATION

In 1933 Pastor Jeffreys pitched his marquee on Burnley cattle market and opened a campaign to wrestle for the soul of the town. His congregation sat in the murky yellow light of the tent, and he held forth from a high square platform like a boxing ring. He softened us up with the sorrows of Jesus, uncomplaining and eager to forgive, and the choir crooned emotive hymns:

> Tell mother I'll be there, in answer to her prayer,
> O tell my darling mother I'll be there.

Or more pleadingly:

> Do not pass me, gentle Saviour, hear my humble cry,
> And while others Thou art calling, do not pass me by.

The pastor appealed for converts in a soft sad voice. 'Will you add to the suffering of the infinitely-loving Jesus or will you accept him tonight in your heart? Will you go the way of the world or the way of the Cross?'

Chairs scraped. People rose.

'Thank you, brother. Thank you, sister. Christ weeps in joy for you this evening.'

The penitents moved down the aisles towards the platform.

'Who else will join the saved? Who else will turn his back on sin? Who else will renounce Satan tonight?'

The choir sang warningly:

> Too late, too late will be the cry,
> Jesus of Nazareth hath passed by.

'O my dear friends,' Pastor Jeffreys pleaded to the still seated, 'His loving arms reach out to save you. Will you reject him? Will you make him suffer again? Will you delay too long? For the world will end in 1939, as He tells in this Good Book, and then He shall return to judge the quick and the dead. Allow this moment to pass tonight and your time may not come again before the Last Judgment.'

I sat there with my grandparents, moved by the singing and the voice, feeling the muscles of my legs taut with the urge to stand up for Jesus but aware, as I insisted to myself in order to stay seated, that we were in a tent on the cattle market with our feet on the cobbles and that this emotion would fade when we got outside, just as the tears and the laughter of the picture house disappeared on emerging into the street. It went on and on. Whenever the pastor seemed to have come to an end, he resumed his pleas like an auctioneer working long to coax out the last bids. He prayed over those assembled before his platform, 'Hallelujahs' burst forth from all quarters, and the saved passed in front of a desk where their particulars were taken down.

Pastor Jeffreys healed the sick. He laid hands on their bowed shoulders, prayed, then sprang back, crying, 'You are whole, brother' or 'You are well, sister. Go in peace.' The congregation shouted 'Hallelujah' again, the choir sang, and the healed person turned and walked back to his seat, sometimes raising a hand or joining in the hallelujahs. Of some the ills were not visible, so neither was the healing. But there were hunchbacks, the lame who went on crutches and those who were pushed up in wheelchairs. As they came back the choir sang:

> What a friend we have in Jesus, all our sins and griefs to bear,
> What a privilege to carry everything to God in prayer.

The congregation rose in their seats to see the healed

return. Those who had gone on crutches came back on crutches. Those who had approached in wheelchairs were trundled back. Hunchbacks returned bent, though some of them punched the air and shouted: 'Thanks to Christ I'm whole again.'

Healing evidently did not mean what we thought and nobody ever argued that it might legitimately mean not making well but reconciling the sick person to his condition. The pastor had the beaming face of goodness and nobody, as far as I know, ever accused him of being a quack. We accepted uncomfortably that there must be something we failed to grasp.

My grandmother approached the healing hands. Like many women of her age she suffered from a painful but undiagnosed malady which caused pain in the stomach and back. Doctor's medicine did her no good and neither, it had to be confessed, did Pastor Jeffreys.

'Do you have faith?' the pastor would ask. 'Do you truly believe that He who saves can make you whole again?'

So if the healing hands failed it might be not through their lack of virtue but through a want of faith on the part of the supplicant. And this would apply in some degree to all who came. They included many who had been ill for years and tried everything, hypochondriacs and people suffering from nervous illnesses for which no effective treatment was then available.

When the visit to Pastor Jeffreys brought no improvement my grandmother confessed that perhaps there had been a deficiency in her faith. My grandfather would not have that She then thought that, as time at the platform was briefer than in the doctor's surgery, she had not conveyed the nature of her illness with sufficient accuracy, so that the pastor might have been misled as to the direction a cure needed to take. This seemed a satisfactory explanation. Pastor Jeffreys remained high in our esteem. My grandmother reconciled herself to her illness, just as Paul, she said, had to reconcile himself to the thorn in his flesh.

Sometimes on wet afternoons my grandfather and I patronised the hall which was established as a permanent tabernacle when Pastor Jeffreys and his marquee moved on.

Calvary Hall was a disused mill of red brick, up on the canal embankment near the town centre, a substantial building sound enough to see them through until the end of the world six years hence. My brother, who had trouble with his letters, misread the billboards outside as Cavalry Hall and hung around waiting to see the horses.

The permanent pastor, Mr Watson, until recently a coal miner in South Wales, was supported by a volunteer choir, largely of women in late middle age, and a regular congregation of small grizzled men, who were surprisingly powerful in shifting forms about the place and ferocious in prayer. One rose and, with hands clenched and the veins standing out in his forehead, called down vengeance on the wicked:

'Smite, O Lord, Thine enemies, pulverise them that mock Thee, shatter the iniquitous, sunder the erring, lay about Thyself, Lord God of Hosts, in every conceivable direction.'

'He's a blessed Saviour,' an old man bleated.

'Turn the face of Thy wrath, Great Redeemer, against them that war against Thy people, the Canaanites and the Hittites, the Jesubites and Moabites, the Sodomites and the Trotskyites. Dry up their wells, cause their fruits to wither, suffer them not to multiply. Bring down upon them flood, fire, famine and pestilence, and further incommode them, O Lord God of Hosts, with such additional measures as may occur to Thee from time to time.'

'Hallelujah,' the regulars in the congregation would shout.

'He's a blessed Saviour,' the old man bleated.

Pastor Watson wisely turned down the heat in his own orations, aware that the fervent were but a small part of his congregation. Most were idlers about town like my grandfather and me, who might find refuge from the rain elsewhere if harangued too vehemently. Moreover, performing twice a day, seven days a week, Mr Watson had to pace himself. My grandfather and other godly old men supported him in his sermon with a 'Humph' of agreement, the equivalent among the pious of 'Hear, hear', and Mr Watson for his part pitched his daily appeal for converts with little more emotion than that of a patient sergeant asking for volunteers. He chose the more rousing kinds of evangelical hymns.

Out of the mud and the mire, out of the mud and the mire
I have been lifted by Christ today,
Now I am singing along life's way.
Jesus lifted me up, out of the mud and the mire.

Pastor Watson led the singing in his resonant Welsh voice. He went on without pause from one hot gospel hymn to another so that even the indifferent were drawn in and warmed up before the big double doors were opened and spilled us out into the cold of the streets.

Faced with the competition of Calvary Hall, the Methodists bestirred themselves to bring in counter-attractions. They filled Fulledge chapel for several days with a top act, Gipsy Smith, then a brown and wrinkled old man who had made a fortune telling at such crowded gatherings the tearful story of his impoverished childhood in the caravan and of the compensation he found in the friendship of badgers and squirrels. My uncle Ben, who had not been to church since he was married, was put into his best suit and made to attend one of the gipsy's orations. I asked him what it had been like.

'It was proper painful, Donny', he said, 'listening to him slobbering about his old mother.'

The highlight of the gipsy's story was his mother's death, for which he wept nightly in the pulpit, softening up the less hard-hearted of the congregation for his appeal for converts. It was what would later be recognised as the brainwashing technique of reducing the subjects to an emotional state to make them vulnerable to suggestion.

By the time Pastor Jeffreys and Gipsy Smith had finished their mission half of Burnley, I suppose, must have been won for Christ. There were a few weeks of full churches, then people slid back or regained their balance, according to how you care to look at it, and the churches were as empty as ever.

A new minister at Fulledge chapel was behind some of these stunts, the Reverend Stanley Parker, a rich man from the South of England. He looked like a benign version of Comrade Molotov, who was then cautiously working his way up the Soviet hierarchy. No sooner had the caravan

rolled on than the Reverend Parker engaged a troupe who
called themselves the Negro Spiritual Singers. They performed with great attack and panache.

> And when I get to Heaven
> I'm goin' to put on my shoes,
> I'm goin' to walk all over God's Heaven.

Everybody came, even Roman Catholics and atheists. The
singers sang a wide variety of songs and played on different
moods without any intention of softening anybody up for
the message, and indeed without any intention at all except
to delight. The stolid congregation laughed and came close
to tears, and sometimes even clapped and stamped their feet
to the songs. The Reverend Parker went up to the stage
beaming like a beacon, announced the time of the next performance and pronounced the Benediction.

The singers were a quartet, two men and two women.
Nearly everybody adopted a favourite one as though they
were choosing between dolls. Nobody chose the business
manager, who was paler than the rest, tea-coloured, and
played the piano wearing spats. He had grizzled grey hair
and small eyes and would look up from the keyboard quite
wicked. It was quietly rumoured that before giving his life
to Christ he had played with jazz bands in brothels. Joy and
good humour shone out of the rest. We did not doubt that
they had a spirituality denied to white people. They sang
with fervour and conviction as though they had personally
participated in biblical events which for us were rather
remote stories.

> When Moses smote the water,
> All the children they passed over.
> O brother, ain't you glad the sea went dry,
> O brother ain't you glad you left that sinful army,
> Brother, ain't you glad the sea went dry.

The piano-player in spats shook his head sternly at 'sinful
army', which rather confirmed suspicions about his previous
occupation.

The peripatetic evangelists passed. The Salvation Army remained. One summer evening their band wheeled into our street followed by throngs of children, first the army's regulars perched up on a cart and beating tambourines, then a great ragged battalion of new recruits. We had no idea what it was about. We tagged on and marched in and out of the terraced streets collecting more children as we went, then across Todmorden road where the motors stopped for us, and straight through the wide-thrown double doors of the Salvation Army citadel. The bars clanged to behind us and in the darkness, to which our eyes were not yet accustomed, a choir sang:

> At the cross, at the cross, where I first saw the light
> And the burden of my heart rolled away,
> It was there by faith I received my sight
> And now I am happy all the day.

The choir were ranged in a semi-circle up on the platform

round a woman captain who wore small oval spectacles. She
was pointing with a stick to words on a big board similar
to the one from which we had learned 'Have you ever been
lonely?' at Blackpool circus.

'Learn a hymn tonight,' she shouted, 'and on Friday you'll
get a treat.'

'What will we get?' John Ingham challenged.

'Is that John Ingham?' the captain demanded, peering into
the gloom.

'No,' John Ingham shouted back.

'Chuck him out, George.'

George, a sixteen-stone Salvationist of simple faith, seized
John Ingham by the collar and the seat, kicked open in a
flash of daylight the bars across the door and pitched him
into the street.

'We are here to praise God,' the captain shouted. 'Them
that get chucked out can in no wise approach the Throne.'

Sam Hamer had a voice like a fog horn. 'What's this treat
we're going to get on Friday, then?'

'You'll have to wait to Friday to see.'

'Pie and peas,' Sam Hamer sounded.

'Is that Sam Hamer?' she shouted, peering.

'No,' Sam Hamer hooted back.

'Chuck him out, George.'

Sam went.

'Christ's kingdom is open to all,' the captain proclaimed,
'except them that spurn His love. God Himself was moved to
eject the rebellious angels from heaven into a pit of eternally
burning brimstone. So if you want to stay in and get your
treat on Friday night, just watch your step.'

She started the hymn again. Some boys instead of singing
'At the Cross' sang 'At the Cross Keys' which was the name
of a pub. She pointed and George threw them out. There
was some disturbance at the back and smaller bruisers were
called on to sort it out. Then came a ferocious banging on
glass and the shadows of John Ingham and Sam Hamer
appeared on the frosted high windows. George thundered
out after them. Uproar broke out all over the hall. Boys
danced on the seats, girls shouted that they wanted to go
home.

The captain faced the mutiny boldly, like Captain Bligh or the later Queeg. She shouted orders and threats and commanded that the hymn should be started again. The pianist struck the keyboard, the choir opened their mouths. But nothing was audible in the uproar. The captain capitulated.

'Let 'em out, them that want to go,' she ordered. 'Them that love the Lord can stay, and they'll be the only ones that get their treat on Friday.'

'Pie and peas,' the throng of children derisively shouted back.

They let us out. The bruisers at the door cuffed some as we passed. What the Friday-night treat really was we never found out. None who stayed would admit it.

# 6 · BARNACLE BENSON AND FRIENDS

They were known by their individual titles: *Adventure, Wizard, Rover, Hotspur* and *Skipper*. Collectively we called them 'books'. These publications of D.C. Thomson and Company were the only books we read by choice, twopenny magazines which filled the newsagent's shop with the smell of their bright red, blue and yellow covers. They often depicted a man with hair *en brosse* and a jutting jaw on the point of tackling some danger – an octopus or a grizzly bear or a death ray. The *Adventure*, which I preferred for what I thought its greater realism, favoured air fighting and Westerns; on the cover our man in a white sombrero, legs apart, huge hands poised over his revolver butts, confronted the dagos. You could tell them by their drooping moustaches and their conical straw hats with a bootlace chinstrap.

Some of the books had a page or two of coloured strip cartoons designed no doubt to wean readers from the *Beano*. The best-liked were 'Nero and Zero, the Rollicking Romans' and 'Nosey Parker'. Mr Parker, a tall sinuous man, stuck his nose into everybody's business and was invariably requited with violence. Blows on the head, admonished with staves or shovels, concertinaed his top hat and raised a bump surrounded by short vibrating lines of pain and a halo of stars. 'Ouch,' he exclaimed and came back for more next week.

Another hero was a burglar who climbed around chimneys under the crescent moon wearing a cloth cap and a mask and carrying a sack labelled $s. I foolishly thought that this represented his somnambulist breathing until some bright lad explained that $s were money, dollars. Evidently I was not alone in my ignorance. The sack was relabelled 'Swag' for the benefit of the unsophisticated.

Many of the stories were written by Americans and presumably first published in the United States. Some of the less familiar words and phrases were no doubt translated into English by Scots at D.C. Thomson's newspaper factory in Dundee, but most remained and were incorporated into our vocabulary as unheedingly as earlier words from nursery rhymes and the Bible. Americans were not foreigners. We knew more of American legal expressions than of our own and more of the fauna of North America, the moose, the caribou and the buffalo, than of our native wild animals, the stoat, the hare and the badger, which we never saw.

We carried the books about pushed down our socks and swapped them to the point of tattered illegibility. One of the rewards of being gravely ill was that you might get several books in a single week, possibly the lot if you were at death's door. D.C. Thomson thought of a cruel scheme to bind our custom even closer. With each book you got four pictures of motor cars; when you had collected a set of, I think, sixty-four you sent them in and D.C. Thomson sent you a football by return of post. It did not cost him much. Collection seemed at first simply a progression. All you had to do was to buy a book for sixteen weeks, collecting cards and changing the odd duplicate ('Swap your doubles with a pal') and you joined the tousled lad in the illustration grinning over a football. The replications piled up; everybody had the same. But some cards nobody had, for the good reason that they were issued in very small quantities, just enough I guess to escape accusation of fraud and to permit publication of a weekly list of 'lucky lads'.

The disappointment did nothing to put us off the books. I have the annual of one of them, *The Skipper Book for Boys*, awarded to my brother for regular attendance at Sunday school in 1936. It revives the ghost of an old pleasure. All the stories are remote from any kind of life we knew and several of them set in foreign parts. Other races are regarded as inferior, but there is no general animosity towards them. When they are the subject of the story they are heroes and their racial characteristics are commended, as with Hugh Hottentoch, son of Sitting Moose, but now a doctor at a hospital in Chicago, who after perilous adventures persuades his fellow Omaha Blackfeet to stay put on their reservation and to refrain from the pastime of nipping into the city and scalping people.

Foreigners in minor roles are usually villains. Most villains are either fat or weedy. All of them in the end get a pasting.

One author had it in especially for Dutchmen, one of whom when the story opens is about to take possession at Batavia of a British ship whose owners have gone bankrupt. 'With a smirk on his fat yellow face he waddled 'forward, his enormous paunch shaking.' The British skipper, Barnacle Benson, is a different physical type – 'a powerful hawk-eyed, hawk-nosed man with a barrel-like chest'. The Dutchman sacks him and the crew: 'It'll come cheaper to run it with native labour with some Chink as skipper.' His further observations prove 'too much for Barnacle Benson'.

A mauler of a fist shot out. It caught the Dutchman on the third button of his waistcoat, doubling him up like a jack-knife and driving the breath from his lungs like the sound of the bursting of a balloon. As his head shot forward Benson's open hand clumped on his right ear, knocking him sideways. The palm of his other hand cracked on his left ear. Right and left Barnacle slapped him, till he was swaying about like a rudderless ship in a breeze while he howled with pain and fury. Barnacle lifted him into the air and stamped across the deck with him. With a heave that had all the weight of his body behind it he threw the Dutchman into the filthy water of the harbour. Van der Steen struck the surface with a splash like the bursting of a shell.

This was only the beginning of the admonishment Captain Benson saw fit to hand out. The Dutchman came 'waddling' back with armed native policemen whom the skipper assailed in such a forthright manner that 'almost in less time than it takes to tell he had the deck littered with their stricken bodies'. He kicks one who tries to shoot him ('the native's wrist snapped like a rotten stick'), scatters police reinforce-

ments 'like chaff' and strikes through a detachment of soldiers 'like a cyclone'. But they are quick on his heels. 'They
gave the skipper the race of his life. Indeed it seemed that
he would be overtaken, for the heat affected the Britisher
much more than it did the natives.'

He is picked up and whisked away by two white men in
a car. They appoint him to the command of another ship.
At sea he has occasion to reprove a seaman.

Did you hear me, you lubberly rat?' roared Barnacle,
flushing with anger.
      The man had a revolver. 'Hit me and see what happens
to you,' the ruffian jeered. 'I'll fill you so full of lead that
you won't need a weight on your legs when we pitch you
overboard.'

It is not the only weapon on board. The ship, of which
Captain Benson innocently accepted command, turns out to
have a cargo of munitions which it is running to a Dyak
chief called Bogu.

'By thunder!,' gasped Barnacle. 'White men giving guns to
savages to kill other white people.'

Barnacle puts a spoke in their wheel. He seizes hand gren-
ades and from the bridge threatens to toss them into the hold
unless the ship is sailed to Sarawak. There 'every man jack
aboard' is arrested and Barnacle suitably rewarded. The British authorities give him the ship.

Most parents did not care for the books. My grandfather
called them 'penny dreadfuls'. Adult sentiment in those years
was mildly pacifist. Fisticuffs and gun play were deplored.
Contempt for foreigners was contrary to the spirit of the
League of Nations. They would have liked us to read other
books. But there were none comparable. We occasionally
saw the *Magnet* or the *Gem* but their perennial serials had
little appeal, not because they were about public schools but
because they were written (by one man turning out 50,000
words a week for thirty years) in a verbose repetitive style
in which the story made slow progress. In Mr Thomson's

books development was rapid and direct. It was formula fiction: a strong quickly-drawn central character, development of a problem, a crisis and resolution.

So here we have the heavyweight boxer Hamface Gibson within one fight of the title but vulnerable because of his vanity.

> Draped in a dazzling dressing robe that made other folks'
> eyes blink and smart, he stood in front of the mirror.
> Painfully he was screwing his homely and rugged features
> into what he fondly imagined was a fascinating smile. At
> the same time he was carefully parting his ginger hair with
> the help of lashings of lavender-scented brilliantine.

Hamface's vanity is spotted by two 'shifty-eyed' men who come to his gymnasium – Foxy Martin, the manager of his opponent Slug Maginty, and Educated Edwards, 'a notorious confidence-trickster and ex-actor'. They so play on his fear of losing his good looks that he concentrates on defending his features and almost loses the fight. It is a draw. Before the return contest Hamface's manager hits on a plan to disillusion him. He fixes a series of humiliations and finally a film audition which Hamface fails.

> 'I'm not saying you haven't got a film face,' said the casting
> director quite kindly. 'You've come to the wrong section,
> that's all. They'll probably jump at your services in the
> gorilla and horror section, where they're doing *The Terror
> of the Mountain.*'
> 'Haw, haw, haw,' guffawed the studio hands.
> This was too much. At long last Hammy's stupefied brain
> registered that his looks were being grievously insulted. His
> huge hands shot out to shake the casting director like a rat.

This leads to a general punch-up with the studio crew in which numbers eventually prevail. Hamface suffers 'a terrific battering'. His good looks are gone, his illusions destroyed. All that remains is the happy ending.

> To the pop-eyed horror of Foxy Martin and Educated

Edwards, he sailed straight into their man in his usual
hurricane style. With never a thought about defending his
battered face, he slogged Slug all over the ring for the first
two rounds and put him down in the third with such a
terrific right-hander that Maginty had to be carried to his
dressing-room on a stretcher.

The Thomson books, published after the First World War,
were characterised by fast-moving adventure stories,
although all of them, especially the *Hotspur*, still carried some
stories about boarding schools whose style and assumptions
were Edwardian. They were probably written by former
boarding-school boys now in later middle-age and using, at
least in their writing, the vocabulary of their early years.
No doubt D.C. Thomson's sub-editors, state-educated, born
into the proletariat and likely to remain there on the wages
he paid them, could have translated into the vernacular, but
they left well alone as they did with the stories of American
origin. We learned the lingo of fiction's boarding schools
like a second language, though we did not imitate it in speech
because it sounded soft, unlike American which sounded
tough. Writers of school stories knew who the customers
were, and exercised themselves to admit proletarians into
the action.
   In 'The Scorer of Westfield', Joe Smith the porter's son is
the central hero who, brought into the school cricket team
in emergency, saves the match. In looks, as the illustration
makes clear, he is of a different race, 'a tousle-haired, snub-
nosed boy' among the refined-looking young gentlemen.
   'Bunk down to the pavilion and get my cricket boots like
a good fellow,' one commands him. It is a characteristic of
Joe that he proceeds by 'bunking' or 'scudding'.

   The porter's son was the scorer for Westfield. He sometimes
   thought how wonderful it would have been if he could have
   been a pupil himself and perhaps played for the school but,
   as that was not possible, he found contentment in serving
   the eleven as a humble 'Handy Andy'.

The school captain Eric Winston is a snob and tries to

prevent Joe from climbing aboard the charabanc, a real open charabanc, as the illustration shows, with doors all along the side. Sam Lawson, 'the blunt big-handed wicket keeper', successfully puts in a word for him. 'Joe's earned the trip. He's scored and played valet for us all season.'

> Swiftly the miles of leafy lanes slipped by and at last the grey turrets of Moreton rose against the blue summer sky. . . . The team trooped into their dressing-room, followed by Joe Smith laden with bags.

He is kept busy, bunking and scudding and massaging the bruised bowling arm of Devereux, the 'dependable vice-captain'. Another member of the team is not so dependable. He collapses at the toss. Joe is invited to play, much against the judgment of Eric Winston, the captain. The two miss a crucial catch by colliding, and Moreton make 193. West-field's batting collapses. Then Joe takes the crease and sets about the bowling.

> 'By Jove, I take back what I said about young Smith. He's keeping his end up like a trump,' exclaimed Eric Winston admiringly.

There is a heart-stopping moment when the old bat Joe has borrowed gives way at the splice and breaks his wicket. But it is a no-ball, and Winston is moved to send out to Joe his brand new bat given him by his uncle, 'the old Test player', and signed by Jack Hobbs, Don Bradman and Maurice Tate.

> 'Don't say No or I'll think you bear malice for my unpleasantness,' said Winston steadily. 'It was caddish of me to behave as I did. Take the bat and keep going – for the sake of Westfield.'

Joe obliges. Westfield win. Winston awards him the bat.

And that is how Joe Smith the porter's son realised his dream of playing for Westfield – and how he won a staunch

friend. For, from that day forward, Joe had no better friend
in Westfield College than Eric Winston.

The intention of the story was no doubt to pander to boys
of humble origin who were the books' main readers. In our
case the effort was misdirected because we would identify
with school porter's sons no more readily than with public-
school boys. In fact we would not have known what a school
porter was. The only porters we knew of were railway
porters and 'natives' who carried boxes on their heads. We
were not really clients for a story designed to take the edge
off class-consciousness; we had none because we hardly met
other classes. There was no servant class amongst us and of
the better off we knew only doctors, teachers and parsons,
who owed their living to working people and refrained from
asking us to bunk or scud.

None of the school stories I remember were about elementary schools like ours, nor indeed would we have welcomed
it. We did not cherish school. It was not central to our
thoughts. It had no corporate life. It stood for daily imprisonment. We counted the years until we might leave. When a
later headmaster adjured us to strive for the honour of the
school nobody knew what he meant. We did not want to
read about elementary schools.

Boarding schools on the other hand we imagined to be
institutions of freedom and independence. There were stud-
ies in which feasts could be held ('We sent down word to
Matron that we sha'n't be wanting regular school tea') and
'dorms' which served the same purpose after 'lights out'.
There were school teams (we had none) which travelled to
away matches in charabancs and played cricket in white
flannels and soccer in proper 'footer togs'. There was above
all the absence of parents. For us it was a joy whenever our
parents left us in the care of aunts or grandparents. To get
rid of them and their rules and strictures for a whole term
at a time would have been a boon beyond imagination. It
did not occur to us that boys like those in the stories might
be lonely or that underfeeding might lie behind their
obsession with food and the many stories of ruses to lay

hands on 'tuck' parcels in defiance of the school authorities.
We knew no hungry children.

Boys in school stories were fourteen to sixteen, some
seven years older than most readers, which was necessary to
give them the command and independence we envied. The
adventure stories, which we preferred and which predomi-
nated, were not about boys but about men. They lived not
in a social hierarchy but among equals and observed a rough
code of conduct quite different from the conventional moral-
ity of a boarding school.

In the *Skipper* annual Steelfist Hogan, a menagerie
employee, is allowed to commit a crime and get away with
it. What is more, he is allowed to hate an animal, Samson
the gorilla, the 'ugly brute' he has fought with a pitchfork
in the circus they both serve on the outskirts of San Francisco. He warns the proprietor, Mr Whalen, that Samson must
be put down before he kills somebody.

> 'Rubbish,' snapped the circus boss. 'I'm not going to destroy
> an animal that cost over five thousand dollars.'
>     Hogan drew himself up. This was more than he could
> stand and his hot temper flamed. He shook a great fist at
> Whalen. 'You rotten little money-grubber,' he roared.
> 'You're so mean it's a wonder you feed the animals.'
>     Mr Whalen jumped to his feet with a screech of rage. He
> pointed a trembling finger towards the door. 'Get out,' he
> shouted. 'You're fired.'
>     Hogan took a step towards the man but he realised if he
> hit somebody so undersized he was liable to kill him. He
> swung round and walked out.

Later he returns to the caravan and robs the safe of twenty
thousand dollars, not for his own gain but to 'punish the
miser'. He donates it to 'one of New York's most deserving
hospitals'.

Hogan gets a job in a warehouse at Salem, Oregon, under
the name of O'Rourke, but is traced by a private detective
hired by Whalen, one Bloodhound Wilson, arrested and
taken in handcuffs to the train for San Francisco where he
must stand trial. By coincidence his old enemy, the gorilla

Samson, is on the same train, caged in a van. Hogan, sticking
to his story that he is called O'Rourke, pretends not to
recognise him, but Samson escapes and comes down the
corridor rapidly preceded by a 'negro conductor whose eyes
rolled until only the whites showed and his teeth chattered
with terror'.

An enormous creature appeared in the corridor blocking it
from side to side. Through the train echoed the drum-like
rumble of the clenched fists beating on a mighty chest. . . .
The red-rimmed eyes were shrewdly intelligent and Hogan
knew that the thing had recognised him.

Samson is driven out through a window by bullets from
Bloodhound Wilson's revolver. He climbs along the roofs
and flings the driver and fireman from the cab. ' "I'm going
after it," Hogan said. He lifted his manacled hands and his
clenched fists descended with terrific force on the detective's
head.' The train is accelerating downhill and running, as
the negro conductor 'babbles', towards the Oregon express
coming up the single-track line. Edging along the outside of
the carriages, Hogan reaches the tender.

The gorilla was prancing up and down on the footplate,
clinging to the throttle with both hands. . . . Blazing with
anger, Hogan launched himself forward, striking with his
powerful fists at the hideous head of the ape. He felt his
knuckles crunch home and gave a grunt of satisfaction. All
his pent-up feelings were being released. Between him and
the lives of several hundred people was the raging killer of
Whalen's Circus.

They fight a titanic battle on the footplate as the train roars
on at 80 m.p.h. Hogan, 'bleeding from terrible scratches',
eventually manages to get handcuffs on the 'gibbering monster' and secures it to a rail in the cab. He halts the runaway
train less than a yard from the cowcatcher of the stopped
Oregon express, then jumps for freedom into the wilds of
the surrounding Indian reservation.

Bloodhound Wilson half raised his gun. Then, with a sudden

determination, he returned the automatic to his pocket. He
turned his back on the running man. 'O'Rourke is his name,'
detective Wilson said.

The best of these stories were expertly written, firm in
structure, and strong in narrative drive; the backgrounds
and the technicalities were convincing. They were strongly
influenced by films and so close in form that they would have
made film scripts with little adaptation (though Hollywood
would not at this time have been in the market for another
ape story). The heroes were winners and on the side of
right. They were strong, courageous and in their rough way
honest. Vengeance was as strong a motive with them as with
Shakespeare's characters. They were short-tempered and
violent in word and deed.

It was behaviour we understood. We fought all the time.
In the school yard we scuffled, not like the mighty punchers
of the books but by endlessly tugging and shoving each
other about. In passing and without ill-feeling we would
catch a smaller boy in a headlock and throw him over our
flank. In a community of squat people boys with long necks
were thrown all the time. We went out of our way to
incommode people. We stepped into their path when they
were in a hurry. We deliberately trod on their heels marching
into school. We stuck chewing gum in each other's hair.

How much this was the gambolling and tussling inherent
in young creatures and how much the effect of the books I
do not know. We certainly modelled our speech on them.
'You skenning rat,' we would yell at somebody who had
earned mild opprobrium. 'I'll beat you to a pulp.' Like them
we admired bad temper. 'He who loses his temper loses the
argument,' my uncle Frank, a patient Communist, used to
say. But this was not so in the school yard. The boy who
lost his rag, got his monkey up and sailed in with his tongue
gripped between his teeth was unstoppable among us desul-
tory scufflers. A small boy blockaded in a doorway would
fly out in desperation whirling his coat round his head,
flailing his tormentors with the buttons. They would break
and run. He would be well thought of for his temper.

My mother, having been brought up in a country family

of girls, deplored violent language. She commended some
children of her own early years who wore sailor suits and
said to each other by way of reproof, 'I'll give you a pocket
full of posies' or, at an extreme and raising a chubby fist,
'I'll put five on your nose.' She would quote from the Bible,
'Provoke not thy brother's wrath', which my brother echoed
by complaining, 'He's provoking my rocks again.' She disliked the word fool. 'He that calleth his brother a fool is in
danger of hell fire.' This seemed a bit extreme measured
against the vocabulary of what we could and did call people.
My father had a copious stock of words of abuse which he
directed at us: thundering fool, blockhead, thickhead,
gobbin, piebald monkey, mug, mugwump, tup. He would
reprove some mild offence by saying, 'You're rotten, lad.
You're rotten to the core.'

What eventual effect the books had on our characters is
hard to know. Possibly they helped to toughen us mentally
for the years of the war, through which the more faithful –
'here or on far distant shores', as the song said – continued
to read the books whenever they could lay hands on them.
But in the end we proved a pacific lot. The civil peace was
never more assured in Britain than in the mature years of
the generation brought up on Thomson's books.

# 7 · THE SILVER SCREEN

Cinema films reinforced the message of the books but with a much stronger transatlantic influence. They carried us to the discovery of an America where life was romantic, heroic, comic and free-moving, lived in picturesque shacks or palatial houses, and where the individual and what happened to him was of great importance.

The power of films to move people in the mass exceeded that of any art known before. Audiences came out laughing or contemplative or with tears in their eyes. My brother had to be held back by the collar to prevent him from somnambulating into the traffic.

'Dream palaces', they called the cinemas, and so they were with their plaster colonnades and grand names (Royal, Imperial, Empire, Palace, Majestic). Films were the best opiate of the people, an escape from everyday dullness and a balm to the wounded spirit of the unemployed, of whom, it was reckoned, more than ninety per cent went to the cinema at least once a week. The only big buildings I remember going into in Burnley in the 1930s were the employment exchange, built to cope with the flood of custom, and the opulent Odeon. At sixpence for three hours it was something everybody could afford. A pint of beer cost as much.

Films were put on with some ceremony. Continuous performances came in only in the later 'thirties and then only in the big cinemas down town. There were three 'houses' a day. The place filled up to music, then there was a ceremony of raising the curtains in front of the screen, which in the Odeon became a performance in itself with its curtains rising in intricate fan shapes. The adverts were shown, still mainly local ones on slides, the curtains closed again, music played, then the curtains lifted and the certificate came on the screen to a great collective shuffle at adult performances and a deafening cheer at children's.

But this would herald only some short film, 'interest', as it was optimistically billed, usually some tap dancer rattling away at a marble floor. I suppose in the early days it was a sound sharp enough to be reliably picked up by the old insensitive microphones while the subjects were flinging themselves about.

The newsreel had no sound problems. Apart from occasional quavering statements by politicians dressed like undertakers, it was shot mute. Effects and music were added, along with a hectoring commentary relieved by excruciating quips. Horses raced, footballers with sleeked hair and long shorts scored flickering goals, liners sailed, aeroplanes took off. It had all happened weeks ago by the time the newsreels got to the small cinemas, but even so the print had suffered nothing like the scratching of the main features which had been going the rounds for years and it was almost free of the incessant rain which fell across them. The newsreel often ended with an item about cute animals and from this developed a small industry of talking horses and wise-cracking dogs. The little picture which followed was quite often English-made and stagey. The speech, Actors' Upper Class, was foreign to our ears which had become accustomed to the gritty crackle of American voices.

The curtains closed, the lights went up, attendants with trays of ice cream and sweets walked the aisles, music played, half the audience went and relieved themselves, then everybody settled down again and the curtains parted for the big picture.

While my father was still a Co-op branch manager we all went in winter to the early evening show. Tuesday, which had been half-day closing, was the night for superior kinds of shop men and their families. They paid. Monday was the free day. In the evening they let in local journalists and owners of pubs and chip shops who exhibited their play bills. The afternoon was free for old-age pensioners who returned the kindness by telling everybody what a rotten show it was. The small cinemas changed their programme halfway through the week, but prudently did not invite a second free visit by pensioners.

What sense my brother at three made of the films I do not know, but he watched wide-eyed in the darkness and by the age of five he spoke fluent American in the voice of a scratched optical sound track. 'Wise guy, huh? Scram, Buster, beat it, step on the gas, and I don't mean maybe.'

The rising star was Shirley Temple. 'Sparkle, Shirley,' her mother was reputed to say, just before the camera turned. Shirley sparkled, and danced long complicated routines on a single take. It was a performance of astonishing virtuosity and rather grotesque, like a monkey on a bicycle. Some mothers dressed their little girls like Shirley Temple and put them through dancing lessons, which if they had sparkled enough would have been a good investment. By 1932 Shirley was reported to be among the ten highest earners in the United States.

Gracie Fields was also making a bob or two with her cheery optimistic films. Her fee reached £40,000 a picture, which was about 800 times the rate she would have earned if she had stayed in the cotton mill. George Formby, the other well-known Lancashire comedian, also prospered. I never heard from adults anything but admiration of their talent and wealth; they were too remote to envy.

The stars of our children's Saturday afternoon shows were the American journeymen of the industry, who worked six days a week and were sorely knocked about: Laurel and Hardy, of course, who made a twenty-minute two-reeler every week, the cowboys Tom Mix and Buck Jones, and hosts of others whose names were long forgotten until television began to dig out the old film archives. They spoke curtly through slit mouths like ventriloquists and they moved fast, usually in pursuit of each other. They chased round corners, across scaffolding and along the roof of trains, they pursued each other on horseback, in stage coaches and by motor car, they admonished each other with planks and with hurled custard pies and bags of flour, and when they were really annoyed they shot each other off rocks and tall buildings. In the epic battles of the screen I believe the extras all clung on to life for as long as the director would stand it; once killed they were out of the picture and off the payroll. There were in every sense only two kinds of actors, the quick and the dead.

We liked best Laurel and Hardy, who created a different order of being, a state of the spirit superior to and remote from the dull logic of workaday life. They were hobos, casually and invariably disastrously employed, but men of enduring dignity with their bowler hats and Oliver Hardy's fastidious manners and expressive gentle hands. He and Stan were defeated at every encounter but their spirit triumphed over the world of calculation and commonsense, a victory of the simple-hearted.

At children's matinées the old films broke often. Sometimes they broke clean and the screen flared blinding white. More often they ran down, the sound sinking to a low warbling groan and the picture visibly melting and burning. Either way children howled. They banged seats and drummed their feet, they pounded on the wall of the projection box, they flung pop bottles over the balustrade of the circle into the demonstrating mass below.

The dazzling light of the projector was cut off and house lights, dismal by contrast, came up. Voices lowered, then the uproar broke out again when the manager appeared on a small balcony by the screen. He addressed mute words to the mob who, modelling themselves on the heroes who had just disappeared from the screen, yelled and shook their fists and looked round for a rope to lynch him. His message was that the show would only resume when the noise ceased. Unlike the Salvation Army citadel across the street, the Pentridge pictures employed no bruisers. Apart from the projectionist, who locked himself in his booth, the manager had only a small staff of lady attendants who were cast in so sexist a mould that they never advanced to become bouncers.

The uproar eventually blew itself out, the smell of burning passed, the film resumed at the next reel. We knew we had missed a chunk but it did not matter. Action pictures did not depend overmuch on consequent logic. The special children's films based on fairy stories, we were glad to see sped on their way. Adults who by error or as guardians got into the children's show departed with pounding headaches.

It was generally held in those days of epidemics that cinemas were unhealthy places, which they were but no more than schools, and that their influence on the young was to be deplored. Schoolteachers were hard on new Americanisms in speech without suspecting how much their own English had already been modified by American usage. We persisted in trying to model ourselves on screen heroes. We drawled. We narrowed our eyes. We attempted wisecracks but rarely got beyond an elementary exchange. 'Sez who?' 'Sez me.' 'Oh yeh?' We knew the next move was a sock on the jaw, but we could not bring ourselves to hit people in the face and in any case our punches were too feeble to put an adversary down. A scuffle was not an answer to a wisecrack.

We imagined that court procedures in Britain, which we seldom saw on the screen, would be like those in America with the gavel much used, the DA leaping up to say, 'Your honour, I object' and the judge responding, as he turned in his seat, 'Objection overruled.' We supposed bad hats everywhere were sent to the electric chair.

From films we acquired the background knowledge to take an intelligent interest in newspaper reports on gangsters. The most famous was Al Capone in Chicago, about whom the film *Scarface* was made in 1932 with an inserted speech by an acted politician who urged that selected Italians should be sent back to where they came from. We followed reports of the jailing in New York of Legs Diamond, Dutch Schultz and the Mafia boss Lucky Luciano. We knew their hierarchies better than that of the kings and queens of England. My brother at five regularly died like a gangster, reeling and clutching his chest. 'They got me, Charlie. Look after the wife and kids.' If some visitor gave him money he would toss me a coin. 'Buy yourself some candy, Louis.'

When we played with guns we played cowboys or gangsters, rather than soldiers. The Great War, about which returned combatants seldom spoke, was more remote from our experience than the American underworld and the Wild West. The violence was charade. We had no sense of its reality. Goodies did not die and cowboys did not bleed. But

I remember the day when it came home to me and the sick feeling at the squalor of violent death depicted in a newspaper picture of the warm and bleeding body of the gangster John Dillinger shot dead as he emerged from a cinema in Chicago. The body was put on show by the FBI, and people dug up as mementos the bricks of the road where he had fallen. It was not like that in films.

Nearly all the heroes and heroines of the cinema were single. They breezed into town alone. Few had a steady job. Their freedom and independence was an essential part of their character, men and women alike. We inferred that life was over at marriage. Pictures often ended with people on the brink, which was regarded as desirable, but without actually taking the plunge into what we saw as a dull and rather demeaning state. We were not alone in this. Marriage was in reality the end of freedom to move about and throw money around, and young married men must have envied the single heroes free to come and go and seldom down to counting the small change. Women on the screen were more likely to be found as part of a family but there were also many independent young women who lived alone, earned their own living and knew their own mind. Most of them were dancers in honky-tonks or schoolteachers.

American films, like the 'books' and the Bard, endorsed vengefulness. Apart from that they were on the side of good. They upheld courage, the virtue that makes other virtues possible. They favoured honesty, truthfulness, industry and courtesy to women (but not necessarily to fellow men, who could be seen off with a wisecrack, a punch or a burst of gunfire). They communicated easy-going tolerance, good humour, and respect for and pleasure in the variety of human character.

Above all, they were about free people, living in a vigorous nation. Most of the adults we knew were not free. They were stuck in the mud of economic stagnation and of their own conservatism. Films were among the influences that helped them a decade later, at the end of the war, to revolt against the dowdy life.

For some of us, exposed in childhood, they did more

than that. With their handsome men and pretty women, the sunsets and the music behind the dialogue, they implanted romantic notions from which we remained incurable for life.

# 8 · UP IN THE WORLD

One Sunday in the summer of 1934 my parents came back in great excitement from an afternoon walk. They had discovered a house to let up the hill above Towneley wayside station, where the town ended and the countryside began. Removing was a working-class hobby. Few owned their own house. Searching for a better place, tramping through empty houses, was a regular diversion, and moving almost an annual event. By the age of ten I had already lived in six houses. The one up Moseley Road, high above the town, was to be the seventh.

It was in a terrace of old stone houses on a steep hill and opposite hen pens. From the back yard, steps ascended to the back door and descended to the cellar. The back window looked across the long low gardens of the opposite houses to Towneley park, the bluebell woods and the moors. 'A most salubrious situation,' the agent said, throwing open a window and letting in a gale. 'A prime residential district in upper-class occupation.'

The rent was really more than we could afford and, with my grandparents almost permanently resident, these were to be the most straitened of our years. The move had been made to restore the health of our mother, who had frequently suffered from influenza in the low-lying damp of Fulledge. It succeeded in that and it conferred on my brother and me one of the greatest boons of childhood, the proximity of fields and woods.

We seldom went away for a holiday again and that year the resources were put into the removal. We had a motor van instead of a coal cart and the usual ceremonies of removal were thoroughly performed. We scrubbed out our old house, which the new occupants would scrub again before moving in, and we scrubbed out the new house, which had already been scrubbed by the departing tenants. My grandfather turned up in his starched front and bowler hat, as usual on these occasions, to superintend the administrative and social aspects of the move, engaging delivery men, meeting the man to turn on the gas and making himself known to the neighbours. He was rather rattled by a deaf old man who was in the habit of putting his trumpet to his ear when he spoke and lowering it when people replied.

Efforts to keep grandfather away from the paint failed. He found an old tin of sticky blue in the cellar and set to work on a big slab of slate which screened an area about six feet square where there had been an old-fashioned iron range. The range had included a fire grate and an oven which had been converted to gas. The proximity of flame and gas proved unfortunate, and the range and some earlier residents departed through the window at the same time. The blue paint my grandfather applied looked lugubrious even to himself. He sought to relieve it by buying white paint and tickling in oblique shafts over the whole surface which left the impression of perpetually falling snow.

In bed, in the unaccustomed darkness of a new room, we heard the chuff and clank through the night of slow trains of empty wagons returning to the Yorkshire coalfield. It became a sound without which it was difficult to fall asleep.

The residents were not quite so upper-class as the estate agent had claimed, but most were white-collar workers and there was one who was a manufacturer, George Wilkinson, who made buckets. Our immediate neighbours were Teddy Pickles, who kept a lock-up tobacconist's shop in town, and Charlie Seddon, a coal miner.

The Pickles, seen out together, were a contrasting couple. Teddy was little, sombrely dressed and inclined to mournfulness; Millicent a big handsome woman decked out in bold colours and fancy spectacles. She descended the steep road at a half trot, sweeping along like a galleon in full sail. She laughed a lot and in her excitement spoke in explosions of sibilants. Her son Norman, who had inherited her lively nature, she kept within bounds by clubbing him with the rolling pin.

Norman took his father's midday dinner down to the shop, and when Norman was away on holiday I went. Mr Pickles brightened at the arrival of the dinner basin, a high point in the twelve-hour stretch he did each day behind the counter waiting for customers. It was a sad change, he lamented, from the old days in his father's time when the population was bigger and better off, and people fought to get into the shop. To spoon up the mush from the basin he squatted on a low seat, his head just above the level of the counter. By being in attendance sixty hours a week he just about made a living until the war came and put paid to the business. He then got a job as a clerk at the colliery. It was socially a step down but it took years off him.

Charlie Seddon, our neighbour on the other side, had an altogether luckier life while it lasted. Moustached, grizzled and approaching old age, he came home black from the colliery which then had no pithead baths and, rather than muck up the newly-installed bathroom at home, he had his wife scrub him down by the sink at the kitchen window. She decked him out with his union shirt overhanging his trousers, stuck his clay pipe in his mouth and exhibited him on the front door step.

It was generally felt that he was not an ornament to the district. Overnight he became its richest man. He won £8,000, a fortune, on the pools. They brought him up the shaft of the pit to tell him and he never went down again. When he received his winnings he repaired to the Butterfly hotel just below the station and slapped a large wad of notes on the bar. 'Tell me when we've drunk that up.'

He and his mates did not quite succeed in drinking their way through his fortune. He was brought home up the hill in a taxi every afternoon at closing time. One afternoon they delivered him back dead. After that, police inspector Hebden and his comely daughters moved in next door. It was regarded as a social improvement.

The immediate vicinity was known as 'our back'. It comprised about thirty houses whose gardens flanked the back street, which was steep, unpaved and deeply rutted where tradesmen's carts had churned through in winter. At the bottom it turned a right angle into a wider flat stretch bounded on one side by houses and on the other by an overgrown pen containing a couple of huts used as garages. This flat stretch was our playground when the fields were wet, our cricket and football pitch, and the place where for short seasons we played with girls a game of throwing a ball against a slated house wall.

We had thought at first there were no children, for none was about when we arrived and my brother and I spent the afternoon while the scrubbing was done watching the trains go by and dropping bricks into the jinny tubs of the narrow-gauge colliery line that ran parallel to the railway. The next day they all came out like flowers after rain, the children who would be our friends and companions for the remainder of our childhood and until we went to the war.

We were welcomed in a shy and slightly aloof way by the most popular boy, Harry Ryder, who was to become a Spitfire pilot and an executive of Barclays Bank. He had just been informed that he had passed the eleven-year-old examination and would go to the grammar school in September. Ralph Thomas, still to arrive as we pitched the wickets, had not passed. We were told this with some malicious glee, but all the same everybody was waiting for Ralph. It was as though the day could not begin without him. 'He's here now,' shouted Norman Pickles who was by way of being Ralph's right-hand man. 'Hi, Ralph.'

Ralph came down the back street carrying his bat under his arm, a big fat boy with pink knees and gold-rimmed spectacles. He wore a tweed jacket such as grown men might wear at weekends. His family had come recently from Shipley in the West Riding. Ralph approached in the robust manner of his father, a successful insurance superintendent who in a peculiar Yorkshire way was friendly, quizzical and bumptious at the same time. Ralph nodded acknowledgement of Norman's greeting.

'This is the lad that's come to live next door to us,' Norman said, 'Donald Howard.'

'Haworth,' Harold Lever said.

'Is it Howard or Haworth?' Ralph asked.

'Haworth,' I said.

'Take care with folks' names,' he said to Norman. He grasped and pumped my right hand. 'Ralph Pilling Thomas.'

'And this is his brother Eric,' Norman said.

'How old are you?'

'Seven.'

Ralph flicked the air with a chubby forefinger. 'Go and play with your own age.' He turned to me: 'Are you a bowler or a batsman?'

I wasn't sure. He had the bat. 'A bowler,' I said uncertainly.

'Are you an all-rounder, then?' he challenged.

'A bowler.'

'Toss me a few up.'

He took off his tweed jacket, revealing an adult diamond-patterned pullover, brushed aside whoever had been ready to bat and took his leg and middle. My aspiration, like that of all boys in 1934, was to become a demon bowler in the steps of the good Larwood but, cowed by Ralph's presence and the glint of his gold-rimmed spectacles as he faced me, I faltered at the end of my long run and lobbed up a short slow ball. Ralph's bat flashed and missed. The ball trickled on the wicket with just enough force to dislodge a bail.

'Brilliant,' Ralph shouted, flinging out an arm to commend me to all the watchers. He advanced down the pitch, his hand extended, and caught me in a grip of congratulation. 'Yorker, pitched right in my block hole. You'd play for Yorkshire if you'd been born t'right side o' t' Pennines.'

Ralph made me his protégé. He showed me secret paths over Crown Point moors and shallow river crossings in the bluebell woods. He guided me to the monks' well hidden deep in the trees of Thanet Lee wood and he said that one day we would come back with some gunpowder made from his chemistry set and blow it up. We speculated about blowing other places up. He thought we could bring down the Towneley tunnel and block the railway line, and that if we could lay hands on an extra phial or two of carbon and salt-petre we might be able to mix enough gunpowder to wreck Burnley Wood school. Having failed the scholarship exam, he would have to spend another year there before he could go on to a fee-paying grammar school. It was, he said, a dismal academy staffed by dead-heads who had done nothing to help him catch up after he had been off for several months with pneumonia. This was no doubt true. My brother had the same experience when he lost the best part of a year in hospital. Classes numbered fifty or more. Teachers taught every period of the week without relief. Anybody who fell off the wagon was left to run behind or give up, as he chose.

Ralph had me in to play on their miniature billiard table, which was a privilege he said they wouldn't extend to gobbins who ripped up the baize. He let me have a go on his mouth organ and switched on their Murphy wireless and invited me to listen to its 'mellow tone'. I became his second. Whenever he got into a fight he gave me his tweed jacket and his gold-rimmed spectacles to hold. His challenging manner provoked combat in the school yard and with lads from other gangs we encountered down by the river or up on the moors. Sometimes there was a general mêlée, but more often champions fought each other in ritual wrestling matches. The aim was to down an opponent and sit on him until he gave in, which was hastened by throttling him or hovering over his face with drooping spittle. Few who went down under Ralph's weight resisted long, and on the few occasions he was worsted he surrendered promptly before the wet of the ground could strike through his diamond-patterned pullover and bring on his cough.

The gang got along together with a harmony I had not previously known among boys. They decided what they were going to do by discussion and majority vote, seldom splitting and going in different directions. As we all got into trouble for coming in with muddy shoes, we took it in turn to filch a shoe brush from home. Harry Ryder brought the hat brush from the hallstand on his way out and returned it when we had done. He described his father brushing away with widening eyes as a coating of mud spread across his bowler hat.

These boys by uniting in a joint effort were able to win a football from D.C. Thomson's 'books', the only people I ever personally knew to succeed. Ralph, of course, had custody of the collection of cards to which they all contributed, and in due course announced that the ball had arrived and at what time he would appear with it in public. We hung round his back gate at the end of the garden. The ball was small but of a clean leather colour and dubbined by Ralph's father to the stickiness of a lollipop. We marched up to the field behind Ralph. He threw the ball in the air and booted it. 'I'm t' first to kick our new football,' he said. 'Carry on.'

Everybody wanted to be on Ralph's side because he maimed opponents. He knocked people down like a bounding boulder. He was particularly menacing at rugby, which he insisted was a more manly game, taken up in preference to soccer by his brother Jack who at sixteen wore plus-fours and parted his hair in the middle. Only Ralph knew the rules. He would wheeze along, his pink knees pumping, and ram his fingers into people's eyes. 'I've handed him off,' he replied to cries of protest as a blinded boy reeled into the fence clutching his head.

On summer evenings we practised cricket down at Burnley cricket club at Turf Moor, where some of us were members, or in nets ranged along the stream in front of Towneley hall. A groundsman came round to collect a penny from each of us and usually stayed on and gave us a bit of coaching. There was a marvellous smell, which strengthened at twilight, of the river and cut grass and sheep dip. We walked home across the darkening golf course, idly throwing the wickets in front of us like spears.

On winter nights we went down over the level-crossing into the terraced streets of Burnley Wood, where girls played games within a small compass in the light of corner-shop windows or swung sitting in the loop of a rope which wound and unwound spirally round the upright of a gas lamp. Boys sat on walls. We had no social night area in our own district because there were no shops to cast a light. The welcome we got varied from indifferent to hostile.

But I did make a mark one night with a cart lamp which

I found in a rut in the back street. Under the rag it came up shiny black. It had a clear magnifying glass at the front set in an opening door, and a red lens at the back. The source of light was a candle stuck into the base. The heat was diffused through a grille that formed the top. I made a string handle.

When my school pal Arthur Holden saw the lamp he drastically changed his plans. He lived down in Burnley Wood and usually came up to play on Saturday mornings. But the daylight, he divined, would be no good for the lamp. He would come up at night and we would go down together to Burnley Wood and show it to those gathered round shop windows.

We made quite a stir. Children clustered round to see the front glass opened and to warm their hands in the trails of tallow-smelling smoke that rose through the top grille. We permitted trustworthy boys to take the lamp off into the darkness, where its full power would show. They played its beam on walls and cats and passing pedestrians. One lot shone it through house windows into darkened parlours, bringing indignant inmates to the door. Everybody said it was a grand lamp.

But by the next night the interest had worn off. 'What is it?' a girl said. 'It's only a lamp.'

We could not deny that. I don't know what we had expected of it. Nothing definite. But it was a thing of beauty, unimagined as a possession. We had vaguely expected that it would impart an altogether finer quality to our lives, and the success of the first evening had seemed like a promise of that.

At the level-crossing we turned on to the station platform and sat down by the waiting-room fire. We often went in for a sit and a warm on cold evenings. There was never anybody else in. Only one passenger train stopped all evening and only two or three people got in or out. But the station was kept lighted, with a porter on duty who banked the waiting-room fire with great shiny cobs of coal from the wagons on the siding. Holiday posters brightened the wall. The gas light sang. It was a cheerful place.

The porter spotted our lamp standing on the centre table

and, thinking it might be railway property, came in and inspected it. I told him I had found it on the back street.

'It's the tool of somebody's trade,' he said. 'You don't want his horse blundering into a wall in the dark, do you?'

I said no.

'You must give it back. You mustn't make off with property. That's theft.'

It was quite normal for any adult to rebuke any child for anything, particularly those in authority like the porter. I told my grandfather. He agreed with the porter. That made a consensus of judgment I could not oppose. My grandfather undertook to return the lamp to its owner. But none of the tradesmen he accosted at the back gate had lost a lamp, and when he left it standing on the wall top nobody claimed it.

I kept it. It eventually proved quite useful when the black-out arrived and torch batteries were scarce, but in the meantime it was nice just to have it standing on the shelf in the cellar. Like a familiar painting it gave a slight but sure pleasure whenever one passed.

From early October we went out at night to collect wood for the Guy Fawkes' bonfire. We dragged fallen branches out of woods and broke up sagging fences, of which there were many round abandoned fields and allotments. We knocked on doors and asked for wood for burning, adopting an unctuous manner in the hope of distinguishing ourselves from those who toted round a guy and sang for money. Householders who gave us broken furniture or wood from their garden were exempted from having loose planks rived out of their huts or staves kicked out of their fences. One year our oily manner impressed an old lady sufficiently to order her Irish gardener to thin out their bit of woodland and saw up the branches for us. He even lent us a trolley made from pram wheels to transport them up the steep lane home.

We stored our wood in the overgrown pen which seemed to have no owner along one side of the flat part of the back street. Once the heap grew we took turns to stay behind and guard it against raiders. It was a cold boring duty. One year we passed the time by ragging the man who lived in the end house by the pen. We knocked on the front door, then immediately afterwards on the back door, then at the front again. We had him belting back and forth through the house, wrenching doors open and making short sallies into the night, where he stopped and stared round through lopsided spectacles.

He changed his tactics. Instead of racing about he quietly quartered himself in the front vestibule ready to fling the door open the moment the knocker sounded. We outguessed him. We lit an explosive firework, a demon, and posted it through the letter box. The detonation resounded. The flash filled the confined space with brilliant light. Our victim shouted in terror.

We ran up the lane and turned on to field paths. 'Did you hear him yelp?' somebody shouted. But by the time we regained our breath what we felt was not jubilation but contrition. We had gone too far; it had been a mean trick. It was not even as though we had anything against the man. We had picked on him because he was handy and also slightly odd. He and his wife were too old to have children our age and they kept themselves rather apart from other adults. But that hardly amounted to enough offence to put somebody in mortal fear. It might even be that the pen where we stored our wood belonged to him. Walking back, we agreed we should make some reparation. We thought we might call and invite him to the bonfire, but when it came to it nobody had either the courage or the effrontery to go and knock on the door again.

The fire was expertly lighted by Mr Marshall. Seen coming home in his greasy overalls with his bait box under his arm he could have been mistaken for an ordinary worker. But he was in fact an aristocrat, a cotton-mill engine man, in sole and absolute charge of the shuddering room shiny with oiled steel where the giant pistons reciprocated and the great flywheel revolved. The floor was not to be crossed except with his permission. On Saturday at the end of the week when the place had been cleaned and wiped and polished nobody, not even the mill manager, was allowed in.

Mr Marshall deigned to light our bonfire but he did it in his own good time. His daughter Mona, who was our age,

said he would have his tea first and she could not be per-
suaded to go in and hurry him. Boys climbed on to the wall
and watched his progress through the kitchen window. 'He's
just knocked t' top off his second egg. . . . He's reaching for
t' jam.' Then an outraged, 'He's settling down wit' paper.'

We appealed to Mona. 'Light it yourself if you're in a
hurry,' she said. She knew we had neither the skill nor the
greasy rags which he brought home for the job.

So everybody stood in the November night and waited.
When Mr Marshall emerged we sprang back to make a
passage for him. He thrust in his rags and set light to them.
Flames leapt out at the side. Mr Marshall watched until the
fire took hold. Then he went back in and closed the gate
behind him. He spoke to nobody.

The night was usually dank and the back street churned
to mud in the area where people moved round the fire. We
scorched on one side and froze on the other. Matches got
wet and we picked brands out of the fire to light fireworks.
Smaller children had pretty fireworks which were set off
first. We had nothing but demons. The aim was to engage
somebody in conversation and then give him heart failure
by dropping a lighted demon behind him. As everybody
had the same intention it never worked and the evening
passed in the more artless way of tossing demons into each
other's path.

A fat boy, somebody's school friend, came up from
Burnley Wood wearing a pair of very light baggy flannels.
Ralph was immediately fired with the ambition to blow them
off him. But he bodged it and succeeded only in burning a
hole through the backside.

The fat boy ran home clutching his seat, which was
received with mediaeval merriment, but returned with his
thin mother, which wasn't. 'Where's Ralph Thomas?' she
demanded.

'Gone to join the Foreign Legion,' somebody in the outer
darkness said.

'I'll attend to you later. I know where he lives.'

She sloshed up the muddy back street. We saw the bar of
light as Thomas's back door was opened to her. We learned
later that compensation had been negotiated, Mr Thomas

trying to keep the price down with affable observations about boys being boys.

We had turned our attention back to the potatoes blackening on the floor of the fire and her return out of the darkness took us by surprise.

'Now, who's the one who said he'd gone to join the Foreign Legion?' she demanded.

'That lad's gone too,' Norman Pickles said.

She swung and clopped his ear. It was a creditable blow for so small a woman but Norman, brought up to withstand the rolling pin, scarcely juddered.

'They were brand new trousers,' she said, 'and it's seared his rump. That's grievous bodily harm.'

'It weren't us.'

'You're all accessories before the fact. You're all rotten on this back street. You'll go down to hard labour. I'll tell the policeman.'

We didn't think she would or that we could be jailed for merely witnessing the scorching. Old Mrs Dent brought out baked potatoes done more evenly in the oven than ours in the fire and my grandfather brought out a tray of toffee. We were relieved that when the policeman came he made no allusion to the evening's misdemeanours. He warmed himself, wolfed three potatoes and departed with a mouthful of toffee, happily unaccompanied.

Harry Ryder's father's car, which was of a pale daffodil yellow, hibernated in a lock-up garage somewhere down in Burnley Wood and came out with the early flowers at Easter. It puttered up the hill, a portent of summer days, crunching under its wheels the last of the cinders the corporation had laid on the steep road against the snow in December.

The car had black mudguards. The running boards carried on one side the spare wheel and on the other a petrol can, an oil tin and a fire extinguisher. The headlights were mounted at each side of the radiator on a spindle; when they were dipped both nacelles nodded gracefully in a bow to the approaching car.

Mr Ryder, a senior bank clerk, was in a social class of his own, which was signified by his contrary choice of headgear, a bowler hat on weekdays when most men wore cloth caps and a cloth cap on Sundays when they wore bowlers. He put on a suit of tweed to take the wheel.

The car was licensed for the warmer six months but stayed in its garage on weekdays the whole year through. Mr Ryder, who came home to lunch, walked the mile between his home and the bank four times a day. When rain fell he took the bus. There was nothing to prevent him from using the car; he could have parked all day on Manchester Road outside the front door of Martins' bank, but it would have seemed ostentatious if not eccentric. No pleasure-motorist of normal prudence would think of using his car every day or leave it standing out in all weathers.

On Saturdays when he had cashed up at the bank and eaten his midday dinner Mr Ryder put on his cap and walked down to the garage in Burnley Wood and let the car out. Harry and his brother joined in washing and polishing it. They kept it immaculately. The engine compartment, which spaciously displayed all the separate organs, shone as though it had just been assembled. There was a wonderful smell of petrol and polish and leather. They pumped up the narrow tyres and lubricated the stays of the folding canvas roof. The car then went back into its garage for Saturday night.

On Sunday Mr Ryder walked down again and drove it up and they all climbed aboard. Mrs Ryder sat in the front and the boys in the back. Enviously watched, they chugged up the hill and out of sight.

Motorists enjoyed a strong sense of motion. Most of the roads, especially in towns, were still cobbled, and the vibration was transmitted through the cart springs and the steering column. Passengers shook and the driver sat upright to wrestle with the writhing steering wheel. He had a lot on his plate. He had to keep the engine on song with the mixture-control and ignition advance-and-retard levers and, lacking a synchromesh, he had to double-declutch to make a gear change; it sounded like the start of a speedway race. Everybody on board was exposed to fresh air. Perhaps because motoring was regarded as a summer sport the top was often down or the split windscreen opened horizontally. The wind carried in flies and engine fumes. A low, swirling draft whistled through the holes in the floorboards through which the control pedals operated.

It was a sport for the hardy and for the brave, claiming as many victims then with far fewer vehicles on the road as it does now. Roads were poor. They narrowed abruptly, surfaces changed, adverse cambers made bends dangerous. Children played and animals wandered on village streets. Slow carts lumbered along. Pedestrians had not all learned to jump, and drivers had been fatally taught when a hazard appeared in their path to sound their horn; their panic reaction was to close their eyes and grasp the bulb in the hope of honking out of existence the danger that loomed ahead. The brake, even if they had the presence of mind to think of it, could not be applied hard without inducing a skid of the narrow tyres on wet cobbles.

Motorists who survived became devil-may-care fellows, retailing their narrow squeaks in detail and with bravado. Where two or three were gathered together it was like a reunion of the Dawn Patrol. Belisha crossings were laid across the streets in an attempt, largely unavailing, to give pedestrians an even break.

Harry Ryder, an unusually modest boy, was not to be drawn on their near escapes or the pedestrians they had winged, but he could not conceal his pride at the distances they covered.

'Do you go to Blackpool?' my brother asked.

'Better places than Blackpool,' Harry said.

My brother asked my grandfather where could be better than Blackpool. My grandfather couldn't think.

'We want to get a car,' my brother said, 'then we'd find out.'

It was not even a remote possibility. When we persisted in asking for things my grandmother would chide us: 'I want, I want, I want. I want a carriage and pair but I can't have one.' The impossible aspiration brought up to date would have been a motor car. Of the thirty or so households along the back street Ryders' was the only one to own a family car.

But there were also a couple of old wrecks owned by two young men and handily garaged in the huts on the back street. Bill Marshall, a mechanic, had a little green car, squat like himself and with wire wheels and tiny brake drums. Rodney Clough was tall with crinkly hair and he also had a car to match his style, a fawn Italian job with doors rounded at the bottom like those on horse carriages and a self-starting button which could be used instead of the handle. Both cars dripped oil and smelled heavily of petrol and were almost permanently under repair. There was much vroom-vrooming of the engines. One summer Bill and Rodney developed a passion for erecting poles and hoisting out the engines on chains.

When they set out for a road test we leapt on to the running boards. Usually they brushed us off in the hedges but when they were in a good mood they let us hang on and ride at speed down the new arterial road. Torn at by the wind, we watched the needle of the speedometer in delight and terror. It was quite dangerous. The doors to which we clung did not lock (why should anybody want to lock a car?) and it was all too easy in resisting the centrifugal force of the bends to turn the handle one was gripping.

The only reliable transport in daily use on our back street was Stanley Ashworth's pony and trap. He was severely lame and climbed up on to the step in a writhing movement that was painful to see. But once aboard, he took total command and drove everywhere at a furious pace. His whip cracked, the pony lifted its knees high, the big, slim wheels bounced over the cobbles. He had a pork-pie hat crammed down on his head and steely grey eyes under ginger brows. He grinned in challenge, showing his teeth. Nothing pleased him more than to pass motor vehicles broken down at the road side. He hurtled by with a pirate's laugh and a crack of the whip in the air above his head.


One April, drawn by the sunshine, we went up into the fields and pitched our wickets. Soon the sky darkened and a blizzard swirled across our pitch. A young cat, little more than a kitten, followed us home through the snow, disappeared somewhere, but ten minutes later jumped up on to the window sill. We begged to let her in until the snow stopped. She washed herself by the fire, stretched out and slept, and stayed for the rest of her long life.

She was barred, but fawn and brown rather than ginger, an unusual colour, good to look at. Everybody liked her, even my grandfather, though he shooed her away from the place on the rug where he toasted himself at the fire. She retaliated by springing on to the table and snatching the meat from his plate. A few days later she came back over the coal-place roofs carrying somebody's Sunday joint. She was thin. Evidently she had lived wild and learned to forage. The habit disappeared with regular feeding but reasserted itself when she had kittens. She would come over the wall with some-body's fish in her mouth or drag a string of sausages up the yard.

She added to the interest of the house, more than a wireless would have done and more than another human being since we already had a full set. Her presence helped to make the peacefulness of the evenings.

I never did any good at Burnley Wood school. I was put in Ralph Thomas's class, which he implied he had brought about by having a confidential word with the headmaster. The class was ahead of me in having done decimals. Miss Sharples tried to compress several weeks' tuition into two minutes. I didn't get it. 'A half is point five,' she said with some exasperation, 'a quarter is point two five, so what are three quarters?' Boys and girls bounced in their seats impatient to answer. 'I'm asking him,' Miss Sharples said. I made a guess. She rolled her eyes. The class jeered. I was mortified. I had never been the class dummy. Ralph threatened the jeerers with a pasting.

The headmaster, Mr Sutton, was more than six feet tall and grey from top to toe – grey suit, grey tie, grey face, grey hair cut to a stubble. My grandfather, with the authority of an amateur barber, surmised that he adopted that style, which was uncommon outside prisons, to keep his scalp clean. He guessed Mr Sutton would dunk his head in the washbasin and scrub his stubble as soon as he got home from school.

He may have been right. The headmaster was obsessed

with cleanliness. His distaste for smells was visible on wet mornings when three hundred of us assembled in the central hall. Through the rising steam of our seldom-changed clothes he would remind us that the body was the temple of God and that we had an obligation to keep it clean for His habitation no less than the caretaker's to swab the floors. The school was festooned with pictures of beetles above the caption 'Where there's dirt, there's danger.' Mr Sutton warned us about black finger nails and deadly epidemics and we sang:

God be at mine end and at my departing.

Some mornings without notice Mr Sutton held a clog inspection. A buzz of alarm passed through the hall as he announced it and we all teetered on one foot, like a zoo full of storks, trying to polish each upper on the back of the opposite stocking. He always rooted out the farm boys who tramped in samples of the cow byre and anybody else whose clogs had not seen polish or black lead that morning. They had to parade after the next day's assembly for further inspection.

I suspect he got at his teachers about their appearance. They were an exceptionally well scrubbed and turned-out staff. Mr Pilling was the most spruce, with dark hair and moustache like Clark Gable, horn-rimmed spectacles, and occasionally the bow tie sanctioned by his office of music teacher. His ankles in light socks were neat on the pedals of the piano, his long fingers delicate on the keys. He was a precise and fastidious man, surprisingly the favourite and indeed the hero of Ralph Thomas, who was proud to remind us that his own middle name was Pilling. Their common love was music. Pillings were famed as musical stock throughout Yorkshire, Ralph told us. He himself was learning the violin. He had already mastered the piano, the mouth organ and the Jew's harp. He sang us bursts of opera. 'We run 'em in, we tell them we're the bold gendarmes.' Suiting action to word, he seized a small boy by the collar and the seat of his trousers and ran him, feet scarcely touching, the length of the school yard.

Ralph was quick to proceed from music to violence even in Mr Pilling's class, where he was called out, bristling with the honour, to sing solos. The musical tradition was stronger in Yorkshire than in Burnley. What to Ralph was an honourable performance in the arts was comic to the rest of the class: the fat lad behind the sheet music, singing 'Cherry ripe' or 'Where the bee sucks' while Mr Pilling tickled and pedalled out the accompaniment. Ralph would stop at the end of a line, halt Mr Pilling with a word, and threaten anybody who dared to laugh again. More than once he sailed up aisles and shook people in their seats. Mr Pilling said there would be no more solos if they were going to lead to disorder. Only Ralph felt it would be any great loss.

These musical interludes with Mr Pilling, which were tedious at first, became a welcome break, an oasis in the week, when we were promoted from Miss Sharples' class to that of a man whom, not to speak ill of the departed, I will call Mr Belper. He was a welter weight, weighing in at about ten stone eight pounds, with a solid left lead and a stunning right cross, a stocky little bruiser with a grizzled sunburnt face and crinkly grey hair parted in the middle.

He started by warning the new class of what they were in for. 'You've had women teachers up to now. Well, that's come to an end. You've finished with petticoat government. From now on you're in a class without girls and you're going to be treated as lads.'

We knew from older pupils what that portended. Passing through his class was a six-month sentence. 'You blockhead,' he would growl. 'I'll knock you over, you dummy.'

He would advance up the aisle, lash out, and over would go chair and pupil. He had fingers missing. Some said he had lost them in the war but we preferred to think he had carelessly lopped them off in the guillotine which stood there for our education in book-binding. He clubbed us with the stumps.

He never punched Ralph. 'If he thumps me I'll thump him,' Ralph said. He would, too. He had already retaliated before I arrived against a male student teacher. His mother's solicitude after his illness made him pettish and easily resentful, and at eleven he was as big as small teachers.

Mr Belper also spared a few favourites, those with a marked talent for handwork, which was the only subject he cared to teach. Handwork in other classes was a diversion, a subject for the last hour of an occasional afternoon. Mr Belper ran his own curriculum. Handwork could start in mid-morning and go on all day. The room stank of the glue that bubbled in pots along the wallside bench. Jelly graphs for making copies and marbled end-papers stood about. There was the guillotine and a wooden press. In one corner several trusties chiselled away through all the periods of the day at large model ships or cut lino for screen printing. The rest of the class bound books. All the books for the school were bound in Mr Belper's class, whose transformation into a bindery must have been condoned by the headmaster.

My mother, seeing the flow of bound notebooks and needle cases I brought home, grew anxious about my diminishing chances of passing the eleven-year-old examination. She waylaid Mr Belper on his way home. He frankly confessed that he was very dubious about my prospects. My mother asked if I couldn't be given homework. He said it would do no good.

He would brook nothing that would upset the handwork, and indeed he regarded boys who hoped to pass the exam as deserters. More than half of the class had already failed and were too old to sit again. They would stay on at Burnley Wood to the age of fourteen and for periods each week come back to him from higher classes, long-term clients for handwork. He knew where he stood with them. They belonged. He was more at his ease with them and punched them more often.

Some parents got at the headmaster, who seems to have pressed Mr Belper to make a gesture towards preparing exam candidates. He did it reluctantly and in a bad temper. He started by reading some general knowledge questions from a paper. He asked me one.

'Why are children allowed to travel half-price on buses? Is it because a) they earn no money? b) they take up less room?'

I couldn't think.

'You'll fail, lad.'

I said I didn't think it was for either reason.

'So you're cleverer than the examiner? You're brighter than the authorities, are you, you blockhead?'

I asked him what the answer was.

'He doesn't know,' he sneered, raising a stump that called forth deep-voiced laughter from his ageing book-binders.

'Which is it?' I asked.

'Isn't it obvious to you yet, lad?'

'No.'

He led the book-binders in another jeer.

'It's because they take up less room. That's obvious to everybody but you, lad.' He appealed to the class: 'Isn't it?'

'Yes, sir,' they chorused.

I said children in buses didn't take up less room. They might in trams where they could be crammed tight along the bench seats but not in buses. A seat for two held only two whether they were childen or adults or one of each.

'Are you arguing with me, you dummy? I'll knock you over, you blockhead.'

He gave me another try. He read a few lines from Shakespeare and asked me what they meant. I said I didn't know. He read the lines again, very slowly, chopping each word off separately as though by the blade of his guillotine. I still didn't know. He raised an exasperated hand to his head. The book-binders chortled.

'What does it mean, sir?' I asked.

The question took him aback. He stared at the page then, recovering, thrust his head down at me so I got the full force of the spittle.

'Shakespeare's deep, lad. Nobody can plumb the depth of Shakespeare.'

The only compensation for being promoted into his all-male class was that football, an hour a week, became part of the official curriculum. We had enviously watched senior classes marching off to Fulledge recreation ground but, as we discovered, Mr Belper's was seldom amongst them. He abhorred refereeing football even more than teaching academic subjects. If rain fell, however lightly, there would be no game. He cancelled it likewise for any misdemeanour, usually one trumped up in the half hour before we were due to go. We did not play more than two or three times in the six months of his régime.

In fairness, football was no treat for teachers. We played on cinders with coats for goal posts, without proper strip and boots, and with little skill and order. Everybody shouted and flocked round the ball like crows.

The first time we actually got to the recreation ground I was sent back early. I had been put to mark Kenneth Tattersall, a popular boy and one of the few in Mr Belper's favour. We collided and fell. Mr Belper, standing on the imaginary touchline, lagged against the cold with his mac over his overcoat, awarded a foul against me. After a further clash he came on and marched me back to his side of the pitch. 'Play right back, you blockhead, where I can keep a close eye on you.'

We were so close that in jumping to head a ball I came down on top of him. He rose hopping on one leg and grasping at the opposite foot. 'You dummy, get out of my sight. Go to outside left, you blockhead.'

I went diagonally across the pitch. Whenever I was in a tackle he blew for a foul so, to avoid contact, I shot as soon as I got the ball. The only thing I had learned in life up to that point was to kick a ball a long way, the pitch had been made very short so Mr Belper could keep all parts under surveillance without moving, and most of these pot shots sailed past the goalkeeper. Some were inside the 'posts' and some outside. Mr Belper called them all out. The other boys growled at me as we waited while the goalie ran to retrieve the ball. Then I mishit one that struck a window mullion in one of the houses that flanked the rec. A woman appeared in the door. 'Shift your coats,' she shouted. 'Go and play over by the river.'

She spotted Mr Belper, squat as a snowman under his coats. 'You're old enough to have more sense,' she shouted. 'Get 'em shifted.'

'Right,' he said, 'pack up. We're going back to school.'

There was a howl of outrage so violent that, besieged on all sides by indignant boys, he dithered for once. 'It weren't all of us, sir. It were only him.'

'All right. Shift the goals, and you, you blockhead, go back to school and report yourself to the headmaster.'

Mr Sutton came out of a classroom and asked me why I was waiting at his desk.

'I've been sent off,' I replied, 'by Mr Belper.'

'Come to the boys' cloakroom and I'll attend to you.'

I had read about schoolboys in the last century having to climb posts like those in the cloakroom to be birched as they clung there. But Mr Sutton had no such design. He brought disinfectant and lint, ran a bowl of water, and told me to roll down my socks. 'What happened?'

I said I had kicked a ball that nearly hit a window. He showed no interest. 'What happened to your knees?'

They were scratched with cinders and bleeding a little. Everybody who played on the rec had scarred knees. 'I fell over Tattersall,' I said.

Mr Sutton bathed my knees. He said he hoped some day we would get a field to play on instead of the rec, then, improving the occasion to turn on his favourite theme, he said there was danger in dirt. Germs in cuts, if neglected, could make it necessary to have a leg off. My boots, he observed, would need a very good polishing before I came to school the next morning. He gave me the rest of the afternoon off. It was only ten minutes but I enjoyed a feeling of great privilege walking with stiff clean knees up the empty road while everybody else was still at school or marching back with Mr Belper.

He seldom took us to play football again and made little further effort to prepare anybody for the scholarship examination. But he did provide the vital motivation to pass, the determination to escape to some school where one would have done with book-binding.

There is one more thing I ought to say about Mr Belper. A friend who knew and worked with him in later years tells me he was esteemed as a charming colleague and a kindly man. It is disquieting. It makes me wonder how differently the characters of these chapters might be remembered by others who knew them. I had better press on before doubts cramp my hand.

Incidentally, Ralph became a vicar.

# 9 · ERIC AT SEVEN

The fever hospital, on a hill to the north of Burnley, filled each winter with children infected with scarlet fever or diphtheria. The hospital had its own ambulance. We were warned not to go near when it stopped in the street lest we pick up germs from the child who was being carried from the door of his home. Most recovered from scarlet fever. Diphtheria was a killer. The serum that attacked the disease also attacked the heart, so children could be cured of the infection but dead.

Drains were suspected. We were taught to pass bad-smelling ones holding our breath. At home the drains and the tippler lavatory at the bottom of the small garden were treated with disinfectant from November, when the epidemics began, and we were made to gargle with Condy's fluid, a brew the colour of raspberry pop made by dissolving crystals in water. Headaches or sore throats caused searching inquiry by parents. Children, feeling they were being blamed, at first denied symptoms, then tearfully admitted them.

One morning in the January of 1935 my brother Eric, then seven, woke with the symptoms of a cold heavy enough to keep him off school. He had his breakfast in bed, then got up and sat looking at books by the fire. In the afternoon he became more ill and was put to bed. When I got home from school towards dusk my mother and grandmother were discussing whether he was bad enough to justify disturbing the doctor. I asked what was the matter. Neither of them could bring themselves to pronounce what they suspected. They decided they ought to call the doctor, and my mother walked down to the telephone at Towneley station. Snow was falling heavily. Dr Dixon angrily asked her if she couldn't see the weather. He would come first thing in the morning.

When my grandfather arrived home it was apparent to him that the morning might not be soon enough. He tramped down to the surgery and asked the doctor to come at once. Harry Dixon, a heavy man who wheezed through Turkish cigarettes, normally had a soft spot for him and addressed him as 'grandpa', but faced with an expedition up the hill in snow, he swore. How could he get up there in his car? Why hadn't they sent for him in the morning? How could he turn out and leave the waiting-room full of patients? They argued back and forth, my grandfather, according to his own account, saying little.

'Anyway,' Harry Dixon concluded. 'I'm not turning out tonight. I'll come in the morning.'

'Very well, doctor,' my grandfather said. 'And if the boy isn't with us in the morning –'

He left the question unfinished and walked down the passage and out into the snow. Behind him the doors were yanked open. 'Grandpa,' Harry Dixon shouted, 'I'll come.'

The doctor made the last part of the journey up the steepest part of the hill on foot and arrived wheezing and angry. He clumped upstairs, shedding clots of snow. He complained of being called so late. He complained of the dismal light in the bedroom. He rammed a dessert-spoon handle into Eric's mouth and said so fiercely I could hear him downstairs. 'Come on, keep your mouth open. How do you expect me to see?'

But when he could see he calmed down. 'It's diphtheria,' he said. 'I'll send for the ambulance.'

My father came home from work. The ambulance men carried Eric out to their vehicle wrapped in a big red blanket. The last boy I had seen carried into the fever ambulance had cheerfully called to onlookers. He died within three weeks. My brother was carried out worse. His head lolled. He was incapable of saying anything.

The ambulance slid and slewed down the snowbound

road. We sat late by the dying fire without speaking. My mother looked old.

Next day, a Saturday, was visiting day at the hospital. Children were not allowed to visit at all and adults were not allowed beyond the matron's office for fear of contracting the disease. A catwalk had been built round the outer walls which parents mounted to shout in through the window to the patients. It sounded like a market. But my brother was too ill to respond with more than a faint smile. When they came home I could see they thought he would die.

A bulletin from the hospital was posted each day at noon outside the bus office in Burnley town centre, and we got the same information earlier by telephoning the hospital from Towneley station. It amounted to little. The patients were placed in three categories: seriously ill, ill, and making satisfactory progress. Nobody would divulge any more than that.

My brother remained on the 'seriously ill' list. We followed the bulletin each day, dreading the disappearance of his number.

Then one day in February he was out of the top category and listed among the 'ill'. It was as though the spring had arrived. But it was a false blossoming and soon he was back among the 'seriously ill'. It was not a relapse so much as the onset of a secondary malady. The serum had attacked his heart, and now he had to lie for weeks with the foot of his bed raised on blocks. Death claimed many at this stage. He made progress, then relapsed. He was four months in hospital before the battle was won.

When the ambulance brought him home he looked different. He was fat. He could hardly walk. His wildness had disappeared. He was quiet and subdued and seemed to speak in a different way.

There had been a heart-rending moment every week when visiting time was up and parents shouted their last words through the hospital window before turning to go. Children cried out in abandonment, unconsoled by the visitors' gifts of books and jellied chicken which nurses brought to their beds. Eric's teddy bear had been taken to him early, the most cherished of the family of stuffed toys he habitually took to bed with him. He did not bring it home. Much later he said that other children had laughed at him for having a teddy bear at the age of seven and he had given it away. We felt the anguish that loss must have caused him.

I went out and bought him a 'book' and some chocolate and sat opposite him across the table wondering whether he would become like himself again or whether this pale chubbiness was a permanent mark the illness would leave.

Fresh air and exercise were prescribed. My father took us for long walks over Crown Point moors, carrying Eric on his shoulders when his legs tired. It was May by then. The moorland flowers were out, the hawthorns in blossom, and birds rose calling from the new grass. Eric's agility began to return and his cheeks reddened.

My father stuck at the exercise with good humour and patience. He had spent little time with us of recent years. Boot-repairing in the cellar occupied much of his leisure, but in any case he showed no great wish for our company outside the home and we preferred to go with boys. So these charmed weeks, a couple of months perhaps in all, remain in memory as the last time in childhood when, bound by a sense of loss closely averted, we all three enjoyed each other's company and found it sufficient.

Riding on father's shoulders, Eric sang lilting cowboy songs he had picked up in hospital – 'Old Faithful', 'Home on the Range', 'The Cowboy's Farewell to the Prairie' – and sometimes he rendered in a blithe and cheerful way the morbidly apposite song that had been a warm favourite of the children in hospital:

> If I had wings like an angel,
> All the way, all the way I would fly.
> I would fly to the arms of my dear daddy,
> And then I'd be willing to die.

He had a big repertoire learned from the wireless: 'Gipsy Tearoom', 'The Isle of Capri', 'Smoke Gets in Your eyes', 'Did You Ever See a Dream Walking', 'The Wedding of Mr Mickey Mouse', 'Night and Day', 'Who's Afraid of the Big

Bad Wolf', 'Home, James, and Don't Spare the Horses', 'Red Sails in the Sunset' and, new that year, 'Easter Parade'. He rounded off his performance, on the moors or in bed at night, with Henry Hall's sign-off tune, 'Here's to the Next Time'.

His stay in hospital had made him an aficionado of the radio and, as he would spend quite a time in the house in convalescence, my father decided to buy a set. It could not be a modern one because, apart from the cost, we had no electricity to plug it into. It would have to be a battery set from Accumulator Joe. Joe was a heavy, jovial old man draped summer and winter in an ancient brown greatcoat. Water seemed to drip permanently from the brim of his battered hat and from his nose end. He always sounded to have a cold.

'Dis is dot bodern plywood rubbish,' he said, stroking the elderly cabinets in his shop, 'Dese sets have stood de test of tibe.'

His shop was by the canal bridge at Finsley Gate. The windows were opaque with dirt and faded cardboard advertisements. The inside was a cavern of darkness, relieved only by a low-power electric bulb dangling on a wire and the twinkling small lights of the accumulator-charging board. The floor was deep in dirt and wireless parts, the walls festooned with spiders' webs and wires.

'Dese sets dote succube when de bob ruds out in de beter. Dey go od gaily playig in de dark.'

He set them going in the shop. They did, as he said, play gaily in the dark.

We bought one on legs, a cabinet of two compartments. The bottom one housed the batteries, the top one the coils and condensers and valves that glowed when the set was switched on. On the front were mounted a couple of bakelite tuning dials which when twiddled produced oscillation in sets in neighbouring houses. Mother, ever anxious and having read of a family electrocuted by a wireless set, taught us to step back smartly when we had pulled the starting knob. All precautions were taken. The set was earthed through a cable for which Accumulator Joe bored a hole in the window frame so outsize that the wind whistled in and

billowed the curtains. The aerial we detached on retiring at
night and at any threat of thunder lest lightning might pulverise the wireless and set the room on fire. The set cost £2,
and for that Accumulator Joe threw in new batteries and
delivered it in his ancient car.

Sales were an occasional windfall to him. His regular trade
was in recharging accumulators, the wet batteries on which
the sets depended. They ran down in two or three weeks.
As the signal faded my brother moved closer to the cabinet
until, braving all warnings of electrocution, he finished with
his ear pressed into the speaker. Nobody else in the room
could hear the faintest sound but we never sent for Accumulator Joe until even Eric pronounced the set dead.

It cost sixpence to recharge accumulators, and at that price
you had to get full value. Not that Joe was begrudged his
money. For economy he had to restrict the use of his car to
shifting wireless sets about. The accumulator business he
did on foot, walking to the customer's house, replacing the
battery in the set with a smaller one on loan, carrying it
down to his shop, from us nearly a mile away, putting it on
his trickle charger and carrying it back. He was rebuked
when his ancient sets expired on somebody, but nobody
ever accused him of profiteering on the accumulators.

The batteries were heavy. Accumulator Joe carried them
one-handed in a collapsible metal frame with a wooden
handle. He changed hands frequently and came along in his
thick overcoat like a slow hulk listing first to port and then
to starboard. One day when he called, his collapsible metal
frame collapsed and could not be disentangled. He could not
contemplate making the distance carrying the accumulator
against his chest. 'Hab you a cord,' he asked, 'or a thick
piece of strig?' We produced some string. 'It's too thid,' he
said.

'Plait it,' my brother said. 'Tie it on the railings and plait
it.'

'I can't sped be day plattig strig,' Accumulator Joe
expostulated. 'What do you thick I'b od, you youg bonkey?'

He shook the rain from his hat and wiped the dewdrops
from his nose end. He relented. 'I'b glad to see you back on
forb,' he said. 'We all thought you were a godder.'

As well as popular songs Eric accumulated in hospital a large collection of broad jokes, most of which he did not understand. Once started, he rattled on until he had run through the whole repertoire. He gave his peak performance at a family tea at the home in Bacup of grandfather and grandmother Haworth with Uncle Frank and his family present. It was a big occasion to mark Eric's survival and his eighth birthday. His jokes ran non-stop through the meal and set everybody laughing helplessly not at the punch-lines but at his relentless delivery.

'Stop it,' uncle Frank said, tears in his eyes, 'I can't stand any more.'

'Then there was this looney looking over the wall of the asylum who saw a gardener shovelling up horse muck on the road. "What are you doing that for?" he said. "To put on my rhubarb," the gardener said. "Come inside," the looney said. "we have custard on ours."'

Laughter rose higher.

'Stop him,' my mother said.

'That'll do,' my father said.

'This chap went into a newsagent's shop and said to the woman, "Do you keep stationery, miss?" "Sometimes I wriggle about a bit," she said.'

'Stop it,' Uncle Frank pleaded. 'Stop it.'

'Stop it,' my father growled.

'This woman went into a butcher's shop and said, "Do you have a sheep's head?" "No, madam," said the butcher, "it's the way I part my hair." This chap went into a res- taurant –'

Everybody, laughing, shouted at him to stop. Uncle Frank rocked back and forth between his bowl of stewed fruit and the wall behind him. He caught his breath, breathed calmly, then burst out in uncontrollable snorts, half-slipping off his chair and pulling the table cloth with him. Dishes clattered to the floor.

' "No, sir," the waiter said. "I don't have frogs' legs. I bound because my shoelaces are tied together." '

'Stop it,' everybody shouted. 'You've put uncle Frank on the floor.'

Eric stopped and blinked and looked at the blighted scene

as though he was seeing the room for the first time. On the bus journey home he said they liked good jokes in Bacup. My mother said some of the stories were not very nice.

That was July. In September Eric was taken back to the fever hospital with another attack of diphtheria. It was unheard of. Diseases were believed to immunise the patient against a recurrence. My mother was in anguish that some oversight of hers in hygiene had harboured the infection. She feared that, weakened by the earlier attack, he would not survive this time. But the disease was milder. He never approached close to death and he came home again in ten weeks or so.

It did not take him long this time to get his strength and agility back, but he had lost through hospital and convalescence nearly a year's schooling and that he never made good. The headmistress promised that he should have special tuition, but with classes of fifty it was not possible.

He became one of the backward children who through absence or changing schools or initial lack of intelligence were bigger and older than everybody in their class but still bottom. He lost interest in school work and confidence in his ability to do it. My parents' disappointment that he would stand no chance of passing for the grammar school got through to him. He thought they thought him a failure and at the age of eight he thought himself a failure. Nothing was expected of him and he exacted nothing of himself. I had read aloud to him stories from boys' magazines when he first came out of hospital and that continued for several years before he was able to read fluently enough to enjoy it.

It was not his nature to brood. He went to school cheerfully, but he was not interested in the work, and nobody had time to try to engage his interest. He became one of the group of oversize children who had an unspoken compact with the teacher to cause no disturbance in return for being left undisturbed. He was quite happy and full of tales, he had a sharp intelligence for spotting and mimicking personal traits and characteristics, he won races in the sports. But it was not until ten years later when he joined the air force that he became confident again in his ability to learn anything.

Everybody believed that life was determined at the age of eleven. You took your ruler, pen and pencil and sat for a school examination lasting two days. If you passed you went to the grammar school with the prospect of a good job, migration perhaps, or, if you chose to stay, membership of the town's superior caste, the grammar-school old boys. Failure sent you down the pit or into the cotton mill or into those indeterminate jobs where workers shoved handcarts about the streets or slid home for their dinner oozing oil. No parents wanted their children in manual jobs; those were the ones from which workers were most readily dumped on the dole.

Through the grammar school it was possible to go on to university, but few of the parents of the boys admitted at eleven had any intention that they should stay beyond sixteen. A school certificate was enough to land a 'good job'. Dallying longer in education, still to be under instruction as one approached adult years, seemed effete. Most parents thought they'd done enough by forfeiting the income a child would have earned if it had continued at elementary school and left at fourteen.

There was a half-way stage between elementary schools and the grammar school, Todmorden Road Central School, which gave its students a smattering of culture, some French and music, but trained them for the lower rungs of office work. Those admitted had passed the written examination for the grammar school but fallen at a second hurdle, an oral examination conducted by the headmaster, Mr Fletcher. He was a Cambridge graduate, chubby, genial and in his early thirties. His speech seemed especially quick by contrast with the slow monotones of the candidates he confronted across his desk. We trooped in, six at a time, and read aloud in turn from a book. He pressed us on the meaning of the text, fanned brief discussions and asked questions of general knowledge. How far was it to Bacup? Who was the President of the United States? The interview for each batch lasted about twenty minutes and on the strength of this, Mr Fletcher, poor man, had to decide whom to discard.

I expected to be let in. My cousin Stanley Kerry, although only four months older, was already there. So were most of the boys with whom I played on our back street. Up there in Towneley district boys were expected to pass for the grammar school and girls for the high school just as down in Fulledge most of them were expected to fail. I was always lucky, just as my brother was unlucky, and I did not doubt that my luck would rescue me from Mr Belper's bookbinding and pugilism.

At the grammar school, a Victorian gothic building perched on the high bank of the river Brun opposite the parish church, a different kind of eccentric lay in wait.

Like most cranks and crackpots, Johnny Vaughan put himself forward as a man of infinite common sense. He it was who had the job of knocking each new lot of entrants into shape. He did not use his fists, which was a pleasant change, but rather scorn and sarcasm.

On the first morning the second form, which was the entry year, assembled for him in a dungeon of a room guarded outside the window by two Russian cannon captured in the Crimea. The rest of the school assembled for the headmaster in a room high in the building overlooked by the picture of an old boy with a grenade in his hand who had won the Victoria Cross in the Great War. Johnny Vaughan conducted the segregated assembly for the second-formers throughout their first year. Now at the outset he dished out the hymn books. I missed getting one and applied. 'Can I have a hymn book, sir?'

Johnny Vaughan was in his fifties, dressed always in

brown down to his polished shoes. He had spectacles and heavy chaps and a strand brushed across his pate.

'A boy here wants a Nym Book,' he announced resonantly. 'What's your name, boy?'

'Donald Haworth,' I said.

'Is it indeed? Donal Daworth wants a Nym Book,' he informed the throng. 'Articulate, boy. Sound consonants and aitches. No, there are no Nym Books left.' He thrust his wide eyes towards me, 'You have missed the bus, boy. You have failed to be alert.'

Unlike the other masters he did not wear a gown and it was spitefully said that he had been a woodwork instructor who seized his opportunity to stand in on the academic side during an influenza epidemic and hung on by staying one hop ahead of pupils through correspondence courses in science and scripture. If so, he showed no signs of his humble origins. He was completely self-confident. He sang loudly at his assembly, circulating through the desks and directing his voice at any boy who faltered in the song of praise. He insisted on correct speech and firmly rejected some accepted usages. In his science lessons we were not permitted to say that acid 'turned' litmus paper red.

'To turn, boy,' he said, 'means to make a rotary motion, to change direction or to bend. Did the litmus paper make a rotary motion, change direction or bend?'

'No, sir.'

'Then don't say it did, boy. It *changed* to red.'

Anybody who thereafter wrote 'turned' was not subjected to public ridicule in the ordinary way but invited for a private talk which Johnny reserved for hard cases.

He favoured deep breathing and spritely walking. He drew in the foetid air of his dungeon like a powerful vacuum cleaner and discharged it in a long whistle. He demonstrated a spritely walk, first striking the floor with his heel, then rocking on to his toes. He passed back and forth in front of the class, rising and falling like a camel. It might look exaggerated, he confessed, in the confines of the room, but against the wider panorama of the public streets it would be seen as a dignified and healthful mode of procedure. He invited us to observe him at any time on his way to or from school and in particular to obtain a rear view so we should see how he kept the waist of his shoes polished no less than the uppers.

I saw him put out only once. Some boy had gone fumbling through his school bag and his desk to find a book. Johnny said everything should have its place; he himself could go directly to anything he carried with him. A boy asked him to produce his folding scissors.

'Folding scissors,' Johnny echoed. His hand fluttered and alighted on a waistcoat pocket. The scissors were not there. He tried another pocket, then a third. He patted himself all over like a man afflicted by fleas. 'I don't have them with me, I've lent them to a colleague,' he said. The class roared with laughter. Johnny was sitting on a stool. 'You think you're pulling my leg, boy,' he said to a big lad. 'All right, come out here and pull it.' He raised his foot exposing the polished waist.

The lad grinned awkwardly.

'Well, come on, pull it.'

The lad shook his head. People jeered. The lad half subsided in his seat, then dashed out, seized Johnny's foot and dumped him on the floor. A gasp went through the class. Nobody laughed. Johnny picked himself up, walked to the blackboard and continued the lesson.

We did not exactly like him but it was no pleasure to see him humiliated. He was a harmless man in whom sarcasm was a habit rather than an expression of malice. He did not pick on particular boys and I think, looking back, he avoided assailing boys who were in one way or another weaker than the rest. He did not send anybody to the headmaster or to detention, and he restored at the end of term sweets he had confiscated in class. He took pleasure in the memory of one boy whose sticky toffee had so deteriorated over the couple of months it was kept in the cupboard that he brought a spoon to eat it when it was given back at Christmas.

Johnny also bore well with a boy in our form who wrecked his experiment with the boiling point of water. We boiled a flask down at school and took the temperature, then formed into a column and marched through the town and up to the moors. Johnny took a can of water and a primus stove and we were to heat the flask again to demonstrate that water boils at a lower temperature under lower atmospheric pressure. We cowered by a dry-stone wall while, bending low, he slopped about with methylated spirits and pumped up the stove. The wind was whistling through the chinks and the stove took a lot of starting. When it was going Johnny held out a hand for the flask. The boy carrying it, caught by surprise, made too hasty a turn and smashed it against the wall. Johnny breathed deeply, composed himself, then delivered a lecture in the gale in which he laboured our duty to the public to pick up all the bits of broken glass and passed on to speak of the nature of scientific proof and the unsatisfactoriness of taking anybody's word, even his, on the boiling point of water without the verification of having boiled our own up on the moors. We would return another day.

He was adept at drawing morals in any situation. Through his quirkishness and his vigilance to reprove he did the job he was intended to do with the first year. He made people smarter, cleaner, more alert and more methodical. It was a useful job.

Going to the grammar school meant appearing in public in distinctive clothes, the cap with three chessmen on its badge, symbolising I know not what, and the blazer with the same badge and the scrolled motto, 'Palmam qui meruit ferat', which, we would learn, meant: 'Let he who deserves it take the prize'. There was a black pinstripe suit for winter, blazer and flannels for summer, a raincoat, tie, shirts, socks and sports gear. It was the biggest kitting-out I had between leaving the pram and joining the air force. It had to wait until after our first day at school when Johnny Vaughan, having dished out the hymn books, divided us between the four houses of the school which would determine the colour of the football jersey we required.

The new school year was a bonanza for the clothing shops, particularly the Co-op and Weaver to Wearer Thirty Shilling Tailors, which supplied on credit. Ninety small boys from the grammar school and ninety small girls from the high school milled round with their parents, most of whom would feel the weight of this spree for a long time to come. Indeed, a few parents refused a place because they could not manage the initial outlay. My grandparents were shocked to silence by the pile of parcels my mother and I brought home.

I tried things on to show them, then got away upstairs with the prize of the collection, a football jersey, the first I had ever had apart from one my father had brought back from the army which fitted me like a woman's dress. I had chosen Ribblesdale as my house because its colour was light blue and its football jersey identical to those of Manchester City, Cup winners and champions at that time. It now occurred to me, looking at myself in the mirror, that the 'good jobs' for which the grammar school qualified people did not include professional football, the career on which, though with waverings towards aviation, missionary work and cow-punching, I had set my heart. Footballers started in the lowly stages of their career when they left school at fourteen. People leaving grammar school at sixteen were too elderly. It was clear I had missed my way. Spurred on by the general momentum, my parents' anxiety and my distaste for book-binding, I had gone in a false direction. Now that all this gear had been bought it was too late to rectify the error. I had not missed the bus, as Johnny Vaughan had averred, but heedlessly boarded the wrong one.

Grammar school masters had a job for life. In my five years at Burnley grammar school the headship changed once and an old chemistry master retired and was replaced. Nobody else on the staff moved. Teaching was a greatly prized job, the prime aim of many undergraduates, and grammar-school masters were highly respected, even by the landladies with whom the bachelors among them lodged. They walked to and from school in pairs, like policemen in a rough district, ignoring pupils who crossed their path. They did the walk each way twice a day, disdaining, except in the heaviest rain, to take one of the line of buses that parked at the school gates to run people home for the midday break. They were aloof, authoritarian, and in class brisk and vigilant.

Little Wilfrid Stuttard, the English master, was around thirty-five, neat, smart and hardly higher than his desk. He could spot a misdemeanour at the back while his head was down reading a poem. Glancing up, he would incorporate his rebuke into the verse. 'Angels are still bright, you silly fellow, although the brightest fell'.

He insisted on clarity of understanding and of expression. Nobody in his classes bumbled on about their half-coherent feelings. He took a text line by line and demanded to know what each line meant. 'This has meant something to generations of educated people,' he would rebuke a silent, frowning boy. 'If it means nothing to you we must assume the deficiency is in you, not in the author'. He would accept a rough paraphrase as a start and progressively refine it with volunteered contributions from around the class. Only when he was satisfied would we move on to the next passage. It was slow, exacting work, but from it sprang the exhilaration of reading a difficult book a second time and finding in it not only meaning but pleasure.

Wilfrid Stuttard opened the way to the enjoyment of literature to four decades of students. However well acquainted with texts, he made a practice of reading through them again the night before they would be read in class. As the years passed he began to look forward to retirement and the large amount of free time he would then have at his disposal to read widely and as fancy took him. But by the time he gave up work the urge was spent. He seldom opened a book but passed the years of his retirement watching television.

Back in his best days he and other grammar-school masters were rather encouraged to see themselves as characters and to cultivate minor eccentricities. Little Willie walked head back, pipe in the air and hands clasped behind his back. Walter Bennett, who dug up the moors for miles around looking for the flints of Ancient Britons, wore his tie in the Victorian manner with a loop above the bow, a fashion we followed, hoping to dismay him by presenting thirty caricatures of his style. Bert Evans, the younger maths master, always affected not to know what page of the text book we had reached and got everybody's name wrong.

But they remained somewhat impersonal. Only old Tommy Whitehead, the senior maths master, who looked like an affable German pork butcher, ever mentioned his private life. He frequently allowed himself to be carried off course into marine navigation, which as a yachtsman was a favourite subject. He would tack back reluctantly to the syllabus. 'I suppose we must concentrate,' he would say. 'You've an exam to pass and I've an expensive family to keep.' He lived in an outlying village and performed a winter act when the snow came and the buses stopped of walking to school along the wall tops. He presided over a small circle of half a dozen country boys who stayed at school and ate their sandwiches at dinner time. They brewed up from a gas water-heater in the physics laboratory.

There were two genuine eccentrics. Mr Burgess, our form master, was a tubby little man with strong spectacles who had managed to qualify as a gym master. He was also the music master and unfortunately did not have time to change properly between lessons. He turned up at the piano in the dungeon which Johnny Vaughan used for his morning assembly as though he had been dressed from a jumble sale. He wore the jacket of a brown suit over an open-necked white shirt and white flannels usually smeared with soot from the outside walls. His shoes and his gown were black. Thus apparelled, striking many wrong notes on the piano, he goaded us through a music text book of paralysing boredom. We sang on rising and falling scales:

Crystal palace, Crystal palace,
Café au lait, café au lait.

All kinds of words were sung. Boys buzzed and whistled like oscillating wireless sets. Mr Burgess leapt angrily from the stool. He had been born without much sense of humour and reared in a Church of England choir school in East Anglia. 'I don't know,' he would say, specs steamed and hands on the hips of his brown jacket. 'It's all confusion. I simply can't understand the attitude of some of you people.'

In my first week at the school I enrolled in the choir of which Mr Burgess was the master. I enjoyed singing in bed with my brother and, knowing nothing about school choirs, I expected they would sing the same kind of popular songs – 'Old Faithful', 'Red Sails in the Sunset', and 'The Isle of

Capri'. We started rehearsing 'Sigh No More, Ladies' and
'Of Delicacies so Dainty'. This was in free time after school,
which Mr Burgess seemed to resent as much as we came to.
He was always in a bad temper. After a couple of weeks the
whole choir wanted to resign. We were made to stay until
Founders' Day evening, when the rehearsed numbers were
sung for an audience of parents, then until Christmas. Mr
Burgess permitted us a sea shanty.

> A cannon ball knocked off his leg with a bump,
> He merely said ' – ' and fought on on the stump.

By convention, Mr Burgess instructed us, the dash would
be sung as 'Hmm'. He sang it to us several times, poking
the notes on the keyboard. By prior arrangement between
ourselves we sang the dash as an explosion of expletives.

Mr Burgess rose in rage. He prowled to and fro across
the front of the choir, hardly able to keep his fists to himself.
He settled on his stool. 'Hmm,' he said. 'Hmm. That's
sufficient to represent the sentiment. Hmm. I don't know.
I can't understand the attitude of you people.'

He couldn't, and we couldn't understand him. He
belonged to a different culture, gentler, of greater propriety,
more solemn, more conformist. Few of us had known anybody from more than fifty miles away.

A fifth form which he taught history undertook the promotion of his popularity. They formed up along the high
wall of the school and cheered his approach all the way to
the door as though he was a batsman who had made a
century returning to the pavilion. They ran a campaign with
slogans chalked about the town to have him elected mayor.
They greeted his entrance to the classroom with applause
and lit paper bonfires of celebration in the lids of their desk.

Eventually he left and returned to his choir school, where
no doubt he was better understood and appreciated. His
time in Burnley, he told his colleagues, had been years of
purgatory. Many who went through his musical tuition
hadn't enjoyed it much either.

Charles Arthur MacNess also belonged to a different
world. He alone of all the masters had a motor car. He was

reputed to be rich. He wore fine checks with spats. He was old and bald with small eyes and a clipped moustache, very much like the villains of English films. He played up to the reputation of being permanently drunk. It was said that he had broken his wrist by driving into his garage with his hand still out of the window to signal the turn and that he had given himself up to the police as a notorious murderer then on the run.

We would see his shadow very slowly approaching along the interior frosted windows of the corridor, and our noise would cease as though a switch had been thrown the moment he reached the door. He abhorred noise, which assaulted his hangovers and betrayed his long absences from the classroom when he made expeditions to the staff room, to fortify himself, we believed. It was a long way, he walked very slowly, the journey took a long time. He would try to catch us making a noise by going only a few steps down the corridor and then turning and coming back. The noise always stopped the second he reached the door. He did not seem to have rumbled through the years that his shadow gave him away.

Occasionally he taught us. He would dictate notes on the position and importance of the towns of England. 'Stoke. Position: between Manchester and Birmingham. Importance: pottery manufacture.' We filled a notebook on England and then moved on to other countries, but we did not get far across the world before geographical instruction ended. The subject had long since been judiciously dropped from those offered for school certificate.

More often he left us to copy a map while he read the *Financial Times*. The slightest noise jarred his nerves.

'Who made that noise?' he would demand.

No reaction.

'Who heard it?'

Hands shot up.

Peering round the room through narrow eyes he would ask like a subtle sleuth, 'Is there anybody with his hand not up?' There never was. 'Then who made the noise?' he would ask again.

A frightened boy would raise his hand and Mr MacNess would advance upon him.

'How did you do it?'

'I moved and my desk creaked, sir.'

'Do it again.'

The boy wriggled and made a creak. Mr MacNess growled, punched his head, dragged him out and caned him with a short baton like a policeman's truncheon.

He was the only assistant master to resort to violence. The headmaster used the cane, but infrequently, and almost always for smoking. Most boys owned a cigarette which they kept in a secret place, usually in a tin in a niche in a wall, and smoked a few drags at a time over a period of about a fortnight. The moors or park shelters on weekdays were the recognised places for smoking, but bolder spirits lit up on the back seat of buses and in the school lavatories.

The caretaker, Albert Smithers, looked like an animated potato. He was called Joey by staff and boys alike and he did his best to make an institution of himself, a sort of unofficial sergeant major. He took it upon himself to stop the playing of football with cinders in the yard, and he prowled through the school looking for skivers from morning assembly or from the drill periods the whole school was put through after break. But his greatest ambition was to catch smokers. He would haul them up to the headmaster's study and say in a sanctimonious voice, muted by outrage: 'I catched these boys Smoking in the Lavatories.'

The headmaster got out the cane and Joey doffed his cap. It was the only time anybody saw his matted grey head.

He ran a racket in lost property. Any books or kit left lying about he impounded and locked up in the cubby-hole where he kept his brooms and buckets. You got it back for a penny, which he was supposed to pass on to some good cause. He was over-zealous. He refused to observe any distinction between what was lost and what was left. Every evening the queue of boys waiting to redeem things from his cubby-hole stretched the length of the corridor. He shouted them into line as though they were on jankers, dished out brushes and gave them classrooms to sweep. Any who dissented he threatened to haul up in front of the headmaster. I think he imposed himself no less on the masters. One, by birth a country gentleman, abominated Joey's righteous insubordination. He delighted us by coming away from one of their frequent encounters growling: 'The man is intolerable!'

Unlike the masters, once away from school, Joey mixed in. When my cousin and I met him in the street he took us to his allotment just outside Turf Moor football ground and gave us potatoes and peas and flowers to take home. But on Monday morning he was as hostile as ever. Boys who toadied to him by volunteering to sweep up or to help him in selling the bottled milk at morning break were usually double-crossed in the end and taken for a caning.

# 11 · PARTICULAR FELLOWS

Brooklands Road Methodist Sunday school was built in the twilight of the age of faith. Then came the Great War and the general abandonment of religion, so that the church which was to have stood on the adjoining paddock was never built. The school was fitted out as a chapel and served both purposes, which made it a lively sort of place in use for one thing or another almost every day of the week. We went there for Band of Hope evenings, we took part in plays, we made rugs with crochet hooks and bits of wool, we raced about in the body of the chapel cleared of forms in the games of social evenings, we sat through lantern lectures.

The most frequent of the lantern lecturers was a bald pacifist in tweeds who, standing beside the screen, clicked a tin frog when he wanted the slide changed and required this to be done with military precision. He sharply reprimanded the volunteer operator for errors, which sometimes panicked the poor man into a flurry of mistakes in which to the general merriment some slides were shown upside down. The lecturer raised his voice to drive home his message, which was of gentle manners and peace to all men, especially Germans. His favourable view of the German race had been formed as a reaction to official propaganda while he was in prison as a conscientious objector and reinforced by agreeable visits to the Fatherland, including one which gave him special reason for gratitude. Going down with fever, he had been sustained by patient nursing, revived by conversation in Esperanto and restored with strengthening broths. He scornfully rejected any suggestion from the audience that Germany had possibly changed since he was last there. He blamed everything on the Treaty of Versailles and international financiers, which tended to put him on the same wavelength as the Führer.

On Sunday mornings we endured the less entertaining locutions of local preachers. Some were middle-aged men who had pondered their message and who won from the congregation the praise of being 'thoughtful', but a surprising number were old hillbillies, strangers to logic, who trudged down from the farm bringing in the whiff of cattle and damnation.

The sparcity of the congregation did not deter them. At the foot of the pulpit sat the choir, consisting of five or six singers and an organist. The children, some fifteen of us, there to get a star stamped on our cards, occupied the forms in the body of the hall. Half a dozen old people listened with cupped ears from the pews at the side. One of them, a woman, caused a stir of amusement by turning up an hour wrong when the clocks were altered.

Local preaching was a job for exhibitionists. Most of them were deeply interested in themselves, held up their attitudes for admiration and were centrally present in the anecdotes they related. They relished those in which they had floored some sinner by a throw of moral judo. '"Will God forgive me?" he asked, "after all my years of wicked living?" That's what he asked, "Will God forgive me?" So I looked him in the eye and I answered him. "God forgives," I said, "God forgives the blackest sinner. But," I said, "but Nature doesn't."'

The preacher would then stand back from the big Bible on the lectern sorrowfully shaking his head. Nobody in the congregation reacted. Everybody was waiting for him to come to an end. We children passed the time quietly playing at guessing the dates embossed on each other's pennies brought for the collection. Some of the brighter girls made anagrams from the letters of an admonition, 'Enter into His courts with praise', which had been painted on the wall above the preacher's head and incompletely obscured by a later distempering. My brother was regularly told off from the pulpit. One preacher plaintively reminded him of the hours of study, writing and prayer that had gone into the making of his sermon and of the wisdom accumulated over a lifetime that he was offering without charge. 'So leave alone what you're playing with,' he said, 'and give me a chance.'

A suppressed titter ran through the several sections of the congregation, the phrase recalling to all a joke in which a similarly ignored local preacher appealed to 'th' lads at t' back to stop laiking wi' t' lasses and give me a chance'.

Such laughs were rare. Some preachers tried to tell jokes but spoiled the punch-line by adding the moral. They returned quickly to themselves and their attitudes. 'I came here this morning not to preach politics but to preach Christ crucified,' the preacher would proclaim, or, oppositely, 'I make no apology for preaching politics from the pulpit. If Jesus were here in my place and in this age Jesus would preach politics too.'

The old men in the congregation had no rigid views. 'Humph,' they would grunt by way of agreement with either sentiment. It was the only reaction all morning, apart from coughing and children shuffling about on the forms. The preacher would fling his arms apart at the small lolling knots of the congregation. 'Christianity is a religion of joy,' he would shout. 'Humph,' the old men grunted.

Some of the locals preached through a pad full of notes. Others prided themselves on preaching extempore, having no word prepared but allowing the Holy Spirit to carry them where it listeth. They would come out with a flow of tenuously related ideas that would have delighted a Freudian alienist.

'Oh yes, friends, they were happy enough in the ballroom of the *Titanic*, drinking, dancing, listening to profane music. But when they struck the iceberg that changed their tune. "Nearer my God to Thee" the band played as the ship went down. Contrition seized those sinful hearts as they bubbled under the cold Atlantic. Too late. It is never too late for God's forgiveness. "I have asked and my prayers have not been answered," a man said to me. "Yes," I said, "they have been answered and the answer is No." He raiseth the sinner from the dust and the beggar from the dunghill. We see them today, don't we, men and nations, ambushed on the road of life, ambushed. Oh yes, there's an iceberg waiting for each and every one of us. I saw a new earth and a new heaven. You can't hide from God, and all the politicians in the world can't lift themselves by their own bootlaces. Millions that day will be cast howling into the outer darkness, families divided to the end of eternity, the saved on the healing shore, the damned toppling through the gloom, your brother, sister, father, mother, uncle and aunts and grandparents, the whole bag of tricks of 'em who didn't listen, cast out not until tomorrow, not until next Christmas, but to the end of time. What a friend we have in Jesus.'

The sermon was the highlight, to which all other parts of the service were preparatory – the hymns, the address to the children, the announcements, which always included before the box went round a statement of what the 'offertories' last Sunday had 'realised'. Even the prayers were only really a limbering up for the sermon. They were equally formless, delivered extempore even by ordained ministers, and they differed from the sermon only in that God rather than the congregation was the object. He was reminded of what He had said and promised from time to biblical time and He was credited with knowing and sharing the preacher's views. 'Thou knowest, O Great Redeemer' prefaced opinions which usually surfaced again in the sermon. Lacking the eye contact with God which he enjoyed with the congregation, the preacher would sometimes dry up in prayer. He would then stand with eyes closed and hands clasped, head slowly shaking and body slightly swaying as though silenced by a profundity beyond speech. Then the stream of utterable thoughts would start again, increase in volume and come swilling past. 'Humph,' the old men would grunt by way of encouragement.

The conduct of the services must have been healthful for the preachers. They glowed as the congregation wilted, they came down and shook hands at the door with a wrestler's grip and they strode back to the hills on sprung heels. There were exceptions, rabbity little men, thunderous enough in their sermons but losing confidence when they descended from the pulpit and apt to address people by the wrong name. Most of the preachers were old men. They were able to look back with rueful satisfaction at sixty or seventy years of moral decline.

As a small chapel we saw little of the circuit minister but we came to have a share of a half-trained pastor from the Wolds of Lincolnshire whose rudimentary tuition had at least inculcated the golden virtue of brevity. Pastor Holton was a big man in his sixties, with a heavy moustache and a silver quiff, whose shifts of weight to ease the discomfort of his heavy-booted foot made the pulpit creak. He had been knocked off his motorbike and lamed too badly to return to his job of farm labouring.

'But the Lord was there,' he said. Unlike our slow locals, he spoke in rapid chirpy phrases, bouncing slightly with each word. 'The road to Horncastle where I was spilled was for me the road to Damascus.'

He had long been a church worker, regretful that his early lack of education had prevented him from becoming a minister. Now a bachelor without ties, unable to drive the cows and follow the plough, he took the plunge he had long contemplated and applied to become a pastor, a sort of full-time NCO in the Methodist ministry. He was sent on a short course and posted to Burnley. He was not only mercifully brief, so brief that some of the old folks complained of having to wait about for the twelve o'clock bus, but also, exceptionally for a Methodist, he was uncensorious.

'We have done some dark and shady deeds in the past week,' he would rattle out by way of prayer, 'and we've stooped to some low tricks and no doubt we shall again, but we ask forgiveness and we know that whatsoever we ask in Thy name will be granted, so we can all go home for our Sunday dinner, O Lord, with the slate wiped clean and hope not to accumulate black marks as thick and fast in the future as we have in the lamentable past.'

One afternoon in Burnley centre I came upon Pastor Holton and my grandfather ogling the stills of fan-dancers displayed outside the Palace theatre. 'A disgrace,' my grandfather was saying, 'corrupting to those of impressionable age and an affront to respectable citizens of all generations.'

He and the pastor bent for a closer look. 'We must not

pass by on the other side,' my grandfather said. 'We must make the voice of Methodism heard.'

They raised the scandal at several church meetings and, although several of the brethren readily agreed to go and investigate the matter, the voice of Methodism spoke quaveringly in a resolution directed nowhere. My grandfather decided to make a démarche to the civil power. He took Pastor Holton to call upon Councillor Jack Yates and enjoyed the delicate diplomacy of conveying to him the full impropriety of the display without scandalising the prim Mrs Yates who remained present.

Nothing came of it. Pastor Holton as a countryman was unpoliticised and uneasy about becoming further embroiled with the council. He was quite tolerant and no doubt thought of watching the acts of fan-dancers as among the minor 'dark and shady deeds' for which he regularly prayed for forgiveness of Sunday mornings. Furthermore, he did not like to be out and about more than he had to be. His leg was often painful and he had comfortable lodgings with a big fire blazing in the grate and apple pies on the sideboard.

Councillor Jack Yates was politician enough to sympathise with the Methodist concern and he undertook personally to call the theatre management to task. But his heart was not in the protest. He himself had trodden the boards as a blue-nosed comedian before he settled for a job with the Co-op and a seat on the council, and in the theatre office plastered with playbills and with the whisky bottle on the table his purpose faded. He was introduced to the artistes and the evening ended convivially with song.

My grandfather for his part had exhausted the agreeable dramatics of the protest and in any case lacked the time to pursue the matter further. As a Liberal and a man of peace he had become caught up in all sorts of Popular Front organisations. One of these was a shop in the town centre where he did a voluntary job several days a week of taking in gifts to send to the Spanish Republicans. It was opposite the Palace theatre. His initiative had come to nothing for the time being, but he was able to make it his duty to sally across and keep the changing displays of photographs under regular scrutiny.

The Band of Hope, a rallying of forces against the Demon Drink, was founded in Leeds in 1837 by Anne Jane Carlisle who, as an Irishwoman, had a close acquaintance with the problem. Bands sprang up everywhere and amalgamated into a national union. They and similar societies could claim some measure of a victory. The reeling drunkenness of the pre-1914 years was no longer to be seen in the 'thirties. Bands of Hope continued to flourish in Sunday schools.

Ours met on Monday evenings in winter and was attended by boys between twelve and fourteen, most of whom did not go to Sunday school. We arrived early and joined in a sprawling fight in the darkness of the paddock before we were let in. A bar of light appeared at the door. A voice called us in. We clumped into a vestry, dried out and stank.

The proceedings began with a hymn from an evangelical book. James Reynoldson played the organ and sang above everybody in a fine tenor voice. He was a gentle old man, as fresh-faced as though he had never left the Yorkshire dales to work in a Burnley factory. He would stand and sing a verse solo, spectacles at the end of his nose, shoulders rising and falling, glowing like a coal. He then asked for a volunteer to sing with him but seldom got one. Most of the boys had come for the pleasure of fighting outside and the comfort of keeping warm inside. They thought singing ridiculous, and indeed regarded the whole proceeding with derision.

They expressed it at their peril. Mr Reynoldson, although a Sunday school superintendent, was only a minor official, the musician, at the Band of Hope. The main men were George Timpson, the thin-lipped chapel caretaker, who gave the lesson, and Sam Steer, a tough impassive little man with bristly hair who arrived to pump the organ in his boiler suit and clogs. He was the chucker out. While Mr Reynoldson sang in shining innocence Mr Timpson and Sam Steer scanned the audience with sharp eyes, alert for any misde- meanour. It would be requited once Mr Reynoldson had gone. One week when he called for a volunteer to sing somebody proposed Joe Mo.

'Which is he? Which is Joe?' Mr Reynoldson asked.

'That's him,' everybody replied.

'Come out and sing, Joe,' Mr Reynoldson invited.

A cross-eyed snotty-nosed lad with men's trousers cut short at the knee was shoved out by his neighbours. Mr Reynoldson pressed the keys and sang. Joe Mo stood beside the organ, head down, growling to himself.

'Come on, Joe,' Mr Reynoldson encouraged him at the end of the verse. 'Let them hear you at the back.'

'I can't bloody sing,' Joe snivelled.

'Come on, Joe, I know you can.'

Joe made an effort and let out a long expiring moan. The vestry exploded with laughter. Mr Timpson watched with clenched fists. Sam Steer scuffed the floorboards with the clog of his kicking foot.

Fighting in the paddock was resumed after the meeting. When Mr Reynoldson had gone home, Mr Timpson came to the door.

'Who said Joe Mo could sing?' he asked into the darkness.

'Fred Murphy,' Fred Murphy said.

'Where's Fred Murphy now?'

'Gone home,' Fred Murphy said.

'I'll see him next week then.'

Mr Timpson half turned back, then changed direction, quick as a rat.

'You'll do in the meantime.'

He slapped Fred Murphy's head. Sam Steer shot out and clogged him.

They worked well together on nights when Mr Reynoldson was absent. Their aggression was smoothly phased and more or less continuous. We would usually get through the opening hymn and a prayer without violence. Then Mr Timpson would announce as though it was something that had not happened before: 'Now, tonight we're not going to stand for any messing. We'll lay into you.'

Sam Steer rolled his shoulders.

Mr Timpson's instruction was barely interrupted by the succession of chuckings out. As he spoke he would nod towards some boy and Sam Steer would seize him. Two pairs of clogs receded down the corridor, the door opened, the boy shouted as Sam kicked his backside and the door closed. Sam clumped back into the vestry and settled on his stool like a menacing cat.

The lesson was seldom about the social effects of drinking, perhaps because much of the audience needed no telling, but rather about what alcohol does to the body. There was a sort of league table listing beverages in ascending order of harmfulness. Green Chartreuse was at the top. Nobody knew what it was but everybody was determined to have a slug of it some day.

Once a year we signed the pledge, undertaking to refrain from all alcoholic drinks except when prescribed by a doctor for strictly medicinal purposes. The Band of Hope also condemned, though less prohibitively, tea of which we drank gallons and coffee which we seldom saw. The OK Nonconformist drink was cocoa from the Cadbury plantations, in days of course before it was reputed to be an aphrodisiac. There was little choice about signing the pledge. Any who demurred were cuffed by Sam Steer. The few who persisted in resistance he clogged into the outer darkness.

Sunday school was kindlier. Everybody wore their best

clothes, there was no fighting in the paddock and the teachers refrained from sailing into us. Afternoon Sunday school filled the building. Nearly all children were sent to Sunday school even though their parents seldom went to church, and young men attended in large numbers to qualify to play in the cricket team. They were vigorous, well scrubbed and brilliantined. The volume of their singing rattled the lamp fittings in the chapel and roused people dozing under the Sunday paper in the surrounding terraces.

After the hymn and a prayer we dispersed to our classes. Our first teacher, Arthur Hargreaves, worked at the pit and shone with an extra burnish that came from rasping away the coal dust. He specialised in jokes which perhaps at some time had been used for illustration or relief but which, as his repertoire increased, came to occupy the body of the lesson.

'A little man went into a restaurant. "Do you serve shrimps?" he asked. "Yes, sir," the waiter replied. "We serve anybody. Sit down."'

'Two flies were playing football in a saucer. One said to the other, "You'll have to do better than this next week. We're playing in the cup."'

We occupied the small gallery overlooking the main hall and when Mr Reynoldson, the most benign of superintendents, was on duty we made little effort to hold back our laughter. Sometimes he would come up smiling, happy to see us happy, but holding up his hands for restraint. Arthur would then read out an uplifting passage from the teachers' instruction book. Mr Reynoldson would make some comment upon it and go back downstairs. After a cautious silence the jokes were resumed *sotto voce*.

We passed on to the class held in a vestry under the tuition of Wilfrid Bird, a hawk-faced man in his early thirties who had been recruited to the Sunday school as a fast bowler and in a generous-spirited way had volunteered to be a teacher when one was needed. He lacked a stock of jokes but he had been to Australia and, having successfully related his adventures to some Sunday school meeting, he seemed to imagine they were suitable subject matter for all occasions. We got his yarns every Sunday afternoon. The superintendents became concerned. They took to arriving in mid-lesson.

Mr Reynoldson would intervene with tact and imagination to bend to the gospel the current part of Wilfrid's saga. Another superintendent, Herbert Pratt, a bald Co-op grocer, simply cut across it with some moral advice of his own. He was a shy man of rapid speech, embarrassed to interrupt but determined to do his duty. He rattled out his message, blushing to the top of his pate, and shot out of the door. We returned to the creeks and billabongs.

The third superintendent was a more formidable church officer. Harry Hesling represented authority. Voices were lowered and rough or playful behaviour ceased whenever he approached in the Sunday school or even in the street. He was of middle age, stocky and chubby, and on Sundays he wore a blue serge suit and highly-polished boots of light brown. Head held slightly back, he looked down through his horn-rimmed spectacles with a smile of watchfulness and tolerance which did not disappear on the occasions when he found it necessary to put into words the rebuke that was latent in his look. His chastisement was brief but, coming from Yorkshire, he was more robust and forthright than the local brethren. He was a winding man at Towneley colliery and permitted no bad language from the miners who rode in his cage. Any lapse on their part he requited by letting the cage hit the bottom with a crash that jarred their bones. He now turned his attention to our class and Wilfrid Bird.

For several weeks he creaked in his bright boots into our vestry, sat silent and smiling at the end of the bench seat and creaked out again. Then one Sunday he sat at the table by Wilfrid and, opening the teachers' instruction book, asked us questions arising out of the previous weeks' lessons. We could answer none of them.

'They could tell you a tale or two, though,' Wilfrid said.

'A tale or two is not what we come to the House of God for, Mr Bird. You seem to have drifted into the wrong latitude. The Holy Land is where their thoughts should be directed, not the antipodes.'

'It's a new country, Mr Hesling. There's a lot to be learned from Australia.'

Harry Hesling frowned and said nothing. He was a keen cricket supporter and the bodyline controversy had added

Australia to the long list of persons, institutions, practices and countries of which he disapproved. He pointed to the pictures round the vestry walls of whiskery church elders. 'What view do you think they'd take?' he asked.

'I was just about to embark on a story with a high moral,' Wilfrid said, 'that'd suit them old chaps.'

'Set in Australia?'

'In the Outback.'

Wilfrid, as a seasoned bowler, was not easily knocked off his length. He went on with growing ease to tell a rather rambling story of an emergency journey that had to be made at night through trackless country. None was confident of finding the way by the feeble light of lanterns, then they remembered a blind sheep-shearer and engaged his help. Without any light he guided them twenty miles across country to their destination.

There was a silence when Wilfrid finished.

'Yes?' Harry Hesling asked.

'It just shows you,' Wilfrid said. He appealed to us. 'It just shows you, doesn't it?'

We all agreed it did. Harry Hesling rose, still smiling, and creaked through the door. The next Sunday Wilfrid was back in the body of the young men's class, and Mr Hesling introduced our new teacher, Arthur Plane, a bent and noisome old man called back from retirement to undertake our instruction. A bachelor, he was reputed to have been something of a dandy in his youth but now, living alone and scraping by on the old-age pension, he was hardly capable of looking after himself. When the blackout began some years later he trudged to chapel lighting his way by a candle in a jam-jar.

But with him we did at last get some kind of Bible teaching. He was aloof. He learned none of our names and, coming long ago from the South, still spoke in a posh accent at odds with his tramp-like appearance. His spectacles were held together by Elastoplast and his old Bible by a thick elastic band. But he knew it well, turning worn pages to refer one part to another, and we should no doubt have learned from him if only he had given the characters their names. But he didn't. Jesus he spoke of as 'the Lord'. All others were referred to as 'this here partickler feller'. This here partickler feller being of short stature clambered to a roof to see the Lord, this here partickler feller had the good fortune to be raised from the dead, this here partickler feller tried like the Lord to walk on water and bubbled under for his pains.

Thus we finished three years of Sunday school with a battery of jokes, a stock of anecdotes set in the Outback and a slight knowledge of the biblical world peopled not by the known and named but by a multitude of anonymous particular fellows. I am still hard put to it to be sure who was who.

Sunday was a day of habit even for those who did not go to church. Everybody wore best clothes. Most ate a Sunday roast at midday and tinned salmon and tinned pineapple at tea. Nobody disturbed the quiet. Even round home conspicuous or noisy work was taboo. Nobody worked up ladders or hammered or sawed. The bowling greens and the tennis courts lay vacant. Sheep grazed on the playing fields. The permitted exercise was walking.

Nearly everybody who attended Sunday school went afterwards to Towneley park. The object of the girls was to be seen in their Sunday clothes, the object of the boys to observe them. The girls walked with linked arms. The roads and the lawns surrounding the Elizabethan hall resembled a great mannequin parade in which new fashions were displayed twice a year, in spring and in autumn. Youths were merely spectators or, in the case of the more bold, commentators. They lacked any sort of competitive peacockry in their drab suits and coats which lasted for years.

But one Sunday we toured the park with a young man in an ensemble so distinguished that everybody looked round at him. Fred Hesling, son of the Sunday school superintendent, had taken a step to fulfil his father's aspiration by being admitted to Cliff College to train for the Methodist ministry. He came home in the regulation dress, pinstripe suit and bowler hat, the like of which was never seen in Towneley park except on ex-officers on Sundays when old soldiers marched to the cenotaph. He wore it well. He was a stocky youth with a shining open face. He had learned at college

the practice of discussion and he strode along teasing us with
Socratic questions, feigning surprise with a movement of his
umbrella, turning the conversation from side to side of the
group and generally treating us as equals rather than his
juniors.

For our part we were proud to be seen in his company.
We enjoyed the curiosity our passing raised among the strol-
lers. We warmed towards the ministry. Out of respect for
his cloth we refrained from smoking our Woodbine.

My brother and I enjoyed another afternoon at the centre
of attention in the park. We had lost our barred cat Tibby.
For six weeks we had searched for her, shouting her name
in the woods and in the gardens of empty houses, and we
were sadly becoming reconciled to the thought that she had
been killed or taken away when one Sunday dinner-time she
came back, leaping across the coal-place roofs and jumping
up on the window sill. Even my father, who usually took
little notice of her, was delighted by her return. She was
thin. My mother cut meat from the joint for her. She curled
up on the rug. When we left for Sunday school my mother
told us to go our usual walk afterwards and leave the cat to
sleep for the afternoon.

A couple of hours later we were astonished to spot her
making her sinuous way past the feet of the crowd outside
Towneley hall, which was a mile from home. My brother
gathered her up. The park-keeper came to see what was
going on. 'What do you think you're up to?' he asked.

'We're taking us own cat home,' my brother said belliger-
ently.

'Right,' the parkie said. 'You can take your own kittens
home while you're at it.'

He led us to the potting sheds. The kittens were on a bed
of sacks in a corner. The cat climbed in amongst them. It
was her first litter and for some reason she had gone into
the park and given birth under a rhododendron bush. A
park-keeper had come across them and the gardeners had
made the rough bed and fed the cat. The parkie, a man of
gruff authority, ignored our thanks. He handed us the kittens
in a paper carrier bag. 'Look after your cat better in future.
We want no more kittens here.'

On the way back everybody wanted a peep in the carrier. Girls made soft and gentle noises. The kittens created as much of a stir and reflected nearly as much glory on us as Fred Hesling in his pinstripe suit.

On two Sundays of the year, Armistice Sunday and Mons Sunday, we lined the main thoroughfare of the park to watch the parade of men who had served in the Great War. They marched in fours behind the bugle band of the Boys' Brigade to the white marble cenotaph which overlooked a small ornamental pond. Many were poorly dressed, their medal ribbons striking the only colour in the drab ranks. The maimed came behind in wheelchairs and on crutches. There was a ceremony we were too distant to hear. The Last Post sounded among the trees. They formed fours and marched back through the park.

To us children they looked like old men, though most had not passed forty. They belonged to a time before we were born and had shared an experience of which we knew next to nothing. But we did know it had been an occasion of much sorrow, and we had seen inside the hall the memorial tablets on which the names of thousands of these men's friends were listed. Our school teachers spoke of their war as the final event in history. It was the war to end wars and those men with their dark suits and their chinking medals were the last of the world's warriors, ageing marchers from a time that would never come again.

# 12 · COMMUNISTS AND KINGS

On 20 January 1936 King George V died. Father of the nation, the newspapers called him. Grandfather more like, grey-bearded, and older than the head that was printed on stamps. He talked to us on the wireless on Christmas Day in a kindly guttural voice. We were sorry to see him go. Even my grandfather, like most Liberals an anti-monarchist since Queen Victoria's contretemps with Mr Gladstone, made no criticism of the deceased King. He had been a model of personal and constitutional rectitude and he had set an example in 1915 by renouncing alcohol for the duration of the war, which the government followed up by closing the pubs for everybody most of the day. My grandfather illiberally approved.

I myself in earlier childhood had thought of the King as a benefactor who provided generously for all his subjects. I read his name on pennies, 'Georgivs', to mean 'George gives' and supposed him to be the fount of coins for the whole nation, a donor to the realm rather than what he actually was, a collector from it. But in 1935 we had, without fanciful error, a real cause for gratitude; as part of the jubilee celebrations of the twenty-fifth anniversary of his accession we were given a day off school and a mug with the likeness of the King and Queen painted on it.

We hardly knew he was ill before it was all up with him. The voice of Stuart Hibberd, the BBC's senior announcer, came gravely through the wireless speaker: 'The King's life is moving peacefully to its close.' Then he was gone.

The newspapers reported his last words: 'How fares the

empire?' We thought that appropriate. Later it got around that he had said something different. A doctor had sought to encourage him by speaking of his favourite watering place. 'You will soon be fit for Bognor Regis, sir.'

'Bugger Bognor Regis,' the King replied, and expired. That we felt did him even more credit.

The new King we thought lacking in regality. In our notion kings rode rearing horses into battle, swords raised against the clouds, Richard the Lionheart with the badge of the cross at his shoulder or Henry the Fifth leading the troops once more unto the breach. Our civilian kings in their bowler hats and drooping overcoats were a sorry reflection of drabber times. The old King had at least the regality of a beard. His son Edward with his pinched face and dark clothes looked like anybody you might meet at a funeral. We heard very little about him.

But there was concern at a high level, it later came to light, from the earliest days of his accession. First it was his clothes. He was by no means content, it seemed, to go everywhere in his bowler hat. On the contrary, he aspired to be a natty dresser. In youth he had been rebuked by his father for wearing trousers with turn-ups and now, with the old King hardly settled beneath his stone slab, Edward was seen in flannels and sports coat and then appeared in newspaper photographs in plus-fours and floppy cap.

This caddy's outfit moved the Chancellor of the Exchequer, Mr Neville Chamberlain, to protest. Himself always impeccably dressed like an undertaker in dark suit and winged collar, he was so put out that he extended his criticism to Edward's work, of which he didn't do enough, and his comments on slums and unemployment, of which he made too many. Mr Chamberlain made his observations in a memorandum which the Prime Minister, Mr Baldwin, never one to disturb the peace, dropped into the filing basket.

But Edward's wardrobe, it transpired, was by no means the greatest cause of concern. Along with unsuitable clothes he had acquired an unsuitable lady friend. Wallis Simpson was a gay and witty socialite, about Edward's age, forty-one, and very apparently to all who saw them together a happy companion. But she was American, a commoner, and a married woman already once divorced. Obviously she would not do. While she was only a friend the Cabinet could not protest; but in late October she obtained a divorce from her second husband and would be free to marry. Edward wished to marry her and remain King. Mr Baldwin insisted it would have to be one or the other.

The population at large knew nothing of the affair in the period of nearly a year that the King and Mrs Simpson had been going about together. In those days secretiveness was practised as a sort of principle. In schools, works and church vestries doors were pushed to and voices quietened to prevent the lower orders from hearing. In the home adults would stop their conversation when children entered the room. The newspapers felt more deeply the obligation to conceal for the comfort of the establishment than to disclose for the interest of their customers. They published nothing about the King and Mrs Simpson. Wholesalers intercepted imported foreign papers and cut out any reference.

So the country remained in ignorance until the story broke on 3 December 1936. Two days earlier a provincial bishop had pronounced that the King was in need of God's grace. He knew nothing about the affair. The remark was made in all innocence, a rebuke aimed at most at flashy clothes and the late hours' dancing. But the secretive whisperers in London, imagining unknown enemies as devious and conspiratorial as themselves, thought their cover was blown. The game was up, the guilty secret out. The press barons broke their self-imposed silence. Mrs Simpson appeared on the front page.

Mr Baldwin, who could be both energetic and tough when he roused himself, flitted between Downing Street and the Palace. A choice had to be made, he insisted, between the lady and the throne. No compromise could be considered. A decision must be made quietly and quickly. He invoked the constitution. Since Britain has no written constitution, the constitution in new circumstances is what the men of power say it is. Edward was overawed by it.

All who disliked Baldwin and the old Tory order were on the King's side. Churchill and the press barons, Rothermere and Beaverbrook, became unexpected allies. In demonstrations against the government Communists and Fascists marched together. And in our household my grandfather for the only time in his life came down on the side of royalty. He did not condone late-night dancing, and indeed he added yachting to the morally dubious pursuits of which the King had been guilty. Divorce of course could never be condoned. We knew nobody who had been divorced. It was a disgraceful thing arrived at through court cases reported in the papers where partners vied with each other in accusations of deceitful and squalid behaviour. It was unsuitable for the King to have any connection with that sort of thing.

On the other hand he had had a thin life. Mrs Simpson, the papers said, made him laugh. Until he met her he had little to laugh about. He had been at odds with the old King, who, it was revealed, had been a stern and authoritarian father. He had grown up without love. He was lonesome and lacked confidence. He looked dismal. Why should he not in middle age find his happiness where he might?

Moreover he seemed to have his heart in the right place. He had worn uniform during the war and got as close to the front as the generals who fluttered round him would permit. He patronised ex-service organisations and showed concern for the poor. And why shouldn't he wear whatever he fancied? He had as much right to sport his caddy's outfit as the lugubrious ministers of state to wear their undertaker's clothes.

But general sympathy did not enable the King to defy Mr Baldwin. On 11 December little more than a week after the news broke, Edward went.

We heard his abdication speech over the radio in the Pentridge cinema. The film went off, the house lights came up and the manager appeared on a small balcony by the screen where at the children's Saturday matinée he shouted for quiet and order. Behind him on the wall was an illuminated panel incorporating a clock and the words of an advertisement: 'Get that hat at Bourne's milliners.' He made an announcement in a voice we could not hear.

'Speak up,' somebody shouted.

The manager tried again. 'We are about to hear a speech

from the Throne,' he bawled. 'Ladies and gentlemen, His Majesty the King.'

The speaker bumped and whistled. The voice of Mr Reith, the director general of the BBC, boomed round the auditorium. Turned down, he was completing his brief introduction of the King. Some people stood up, then those next to them. The raising of seats rippled across the house still everybody was standing.

The King said in a shaky voice that he could not go on without the woman he loved, at which there was a sympathetic murmur. He said goodbye. The speaker went silent. A man in front of us started to applaud. 'Don't clap,' his wife said.

'I thought he did very well,' the man replied. People around said yes, they thought he did very well. The man defiantly resumed clapping. A few people joined him. Then all the seats banged as everybody sat down. The house lights went out, the film resumed and the constitutional crisis was over. Children that Christmas sang a lament:

> Hark the herald angels sing,
> Mrs Simpson's stole our king.

Edward's brother, the Duke of York, was a much more suitable incumbent, quite without fancy clothes or fancy women. He was much photographed in naval uniform, which he had worn at the Battle of Jutland. He had a charming wife and two small daughters and, to judge by newspaper pictures, was liberally found for dogs and horses. He was crowned in May 1937. We got another day off school and another mug bearing the likeness of the King and Queen, the second in two years.

While all this was going on our cousins, the Kerrys, hit the jackpot.

One evening late in the year uncle Ben and auntie Abbie came over in their Sunday clothes to announce that they were leaving Burnley. He had got a job in an aircraft factory, A.V. Roe at Chadderton, Manchester, which would pay double what he earned making cheap furniture and give scope for the high skill he had learned in his apprenticeship and nurtured in his years in the Royal Flying Corps.

My grandfather was delighted, any compunction he might have felt as a man of peace being assuaged by the stroke of fortune rearmament had brought to the family. My grandmother grieved. The family had always lived in the same town. Now the Kerrys would be twenty-five miles away. Months would pass without seeing them. She could not have been more distressed if they were going to New Zealand.

Uncle Ben was put to exercise his skills in the manufacture of the Avro Anson, a twin-engined monoplane, which flew in Coastal Command at the outbreak of war and was later used as a navigation trainer. The family rented a semi-detached house on a new estate in Droylsden. They bought new carpets and furniture and installed a big new wireless set whose dial lit up with the names of the cities of the world.

When they came back to take me on holiday there they were dressed, as my brother admiringly said, like a million dollars. Their house was sumptuous. Everything smelled new inside and out. My cousin Stanley and I rode up and down in the Manchester trams, we went to inspect the new school at Audenshaw to which he had been transferred and we fished in the canal at Daisy Nook. Down town at Lewis's auntie Abbie bought me clothes and loaded me up with presents to take home. We got our hair cut. We pushed into the lift and rose to the top-floor restaurant for cream buns and pop, passing crowded floors where tills rang and money whistled along overhead wires. I gathered that this high living went on all the time.

It lasted for about a year. Then the Air Ministry decided it wanted the Avro Anson made in metal, and uncle Ben and hundreds of other wood workers got their cards. The hire-purchase company carried off the large wireless and some of the new furniture. Uncle Ben, unable to find another job, came back to Burnley believing he might have a better chance in an area where he was known. He stayed with us. My brother was moved into the bath to sleep. Uncle Ben shared our double bed with me.

He was then in his late forties, a wiry, dark man beginning

to go grey. He knew that he had had his stroke of luck and that it would not come again. He would do well now to get a job as good as the one he had left to go to Manchester. As he did the rounds of furniture factories without success his confidence sank and a secondary worry emerged: that even if he got a job, if it was piecework, he might not now be able to go fast enough to earn a living wage, having been at his age out of practice for a year. 'Anyway, Donny,' he said as we turned our backs to each other to go to sleep, 'I can't go back without a new set of tools.'

Apparently it was the custom in cabinet works for workers to supply their own hand tools, but not in aircraft factories. The prospect of working with worn-out tools seemed some nights to oppress him more than any other part of his bad luck.

Then one afternoon he came home jubilant. He had landed a job somewhere that was not quite a cabinet-making works but similar enough for his skills to bear. He spoke of looking for a house and getting his family back. Gathering momentum, he said it was an ideal sort of works with a very friendly lot of fellows, some of whom had nodded to him. They would live close by in a new district which he reckoned was the best part of Burnley.

He always smoked his pipe up to the moment of getting into bed. He would turn out the gas light, knock out his pipe and climb aboard. He enjoyed the luxury of lying silent for a couple of minutes, especially on days when he had walked a long way, then he launched into conversation. This night it was extremely cheerful. There was nothing more to be said about his new job and the prospects it opened; that had been enthusiastically turned over by everybody all evening in the living-room. So he launched himself, as he usually did in his brighter moods, into telling jokes and stories of his days in the Flying Corps in Ireland when he flew with a peg-legged pilot. He went to sleep happy.

He had been interviewed by the boss of the firm where he was to start work. Next day he saw the foreman, who had been away, to sort out details. An urgent order had come in and they wanted him to start without delay, but there was a problem: the recognised union in the shop was not the cabinet-makers' but the wheelwrights'. Uncle Ben said he was willing to join. The union representative telephoned the union. That would not be good enough, he told the foreman; they must not take on anybody who was not already a member of the wheelwrights' union. The boss had now arrived and protested that they had been unable to find anybody. The union representative repeated what the union had said. The foreman said it wasn't reasonable but they were better to work short-handed than have the whole shop out. The boss offered uncle Ben his apologies and saw him through the door.

Nothing much was said about it during the evening. My father when told was on the point of exploding but fell silent at a gesture from my mother. Uncle Ben was more than usually breezy, treating his misfortune as a minor setback and possibly the changing point in his luck; it showed there were jobs to be had if only one persisted in looking. But in bed, when he had turned out the gas and knocked out his pipe, he allowed himself to state the irony that when the National Union of Gas Workers and General Labourers was formed in the 1890s it chose as its motto 'Love, Unity and Fidelity'. How many unions today, he asked, would have the effrontery to include 'love' in their motto?

The incident did in fact mark a change in his fortunes. He had encouraging interviews at two or three places, then Layfield and Lee on Trafalgar Street offered him a job. It would be precarious for a time – firms operated a 'last in, first out' policy – and it would pay less than half of what he had earned at Avro's and less in fact than he earned before he left to go there. But it was not piece work. His euphoria increased by the hour. The firm, he said, was superior to others in every conceivable way. He sang, he made jokes, he drew on his pipe until the bowl glowed. He was a man reprieved.

Once he started work he rose early to savour the coming day. It was winter and the gas light was burning in the living-room. By the time I got down he had finished his breakfast and was sitting by the fire smoking his pipe and reading the paper while kittens played round his feet.

The family returned from Manchester and the furniture

van arrived loaded rather lightly with such of their effects as had not been repossessed. They had rented a big end house in Abel Street whose gable windows commanded a view of the gasometer and the fields and Pendle hill. Uncle Ben celebrated moving in with the pronouncement he made on all their older houses: it was an excellent domicile, ideally situated, the residence until recent years of the best of the aristocracy. Such a grand abode, he said, ought not to be cluttered up with too much furniture.

As the threat of war increased, a variety of peace organisations sprang up whose meetings preserved my grandfather from the boredom of sitting at home in the evening. He supported all of them. His friends ranged from members of the Communist party to the old-fashioned pacifists of the Peace Pledge Union.

Their discussions usually made a good long evening because most of them were teased by contradictions they refused to acknowledge. They wanted to condemn totalitarianism without condemning Russia. They wanted to 'stand up to the dictators', Hitler, Mussolini and Franco, while still opposing rearmament.

These conflicts and the more abstruse ones between the different organisations did not trouble my grandfather in the least. He himself never scrupled about expressing irreconcilable opinions. He took pleasure in hearing people's views and even more in having them listen to his. He was much given to quoting his father and Lloyd George. His ample leisure he put to the preservation of peace. He manned the shop taking in gifts to send to the Spanish Republicans. He carried messages about town and into work places between the organisers of meetings. He brought home boxes of envelopes and set my brother and me to address them on winter evenings for the distribution of 'literature'.

When my cousin and I were fifteen or sixteen he took us to a meeting of the Burnley branch of the Left Book Club. The national membership of the club never reached 60,000, but in the absence of an intellectual rival it was highly influential in setting the agenda for public discussion. It had been started in 1936 by the fellow-travelling publisher Victor

Gollancz with a staff of Communists and in support of the party line of promoting a broad alliance of left-wing organisations into a 'Popular Front against Fascism'.

Gollancz was an unpredictable paradox of a man – Christian Jew, capitalist socialist, bellicose pacifist, family man and amorist, skinflint employer and benefactor of all mankind. He started with a bad own goal by issuing against his better judgment *The Road to Wigan Pier* in which George Orwell, overdoing his role of devil's advocate, offered an earnest analysis of reasons why socialism repelled 'so many normal decent people'.

> The very word Socialism calls up on the one hand a picture of aeroplanes, tractors and huge glittering factories of glass and concrete; on the other a picture of vegetarians with wilting beards, of Bolshevik commissars (half gangster, half gramophone), of earnest ladies in sandals, shock-headed Marxists chewing polysyllables, escaped Quakers, birth-control fanatics, and Labour Party backstairs-crawlers.

Gollancz, criticised for permitting so unflattering a description of the club's heroes and customers, never wavered again. He made sure that writers, with a few exceptions for the sake of appearances, understood his editorial policy that 'while there is a grand atmosphere of impartiality which nobody can attack, the readers inevitably draw the right conclusion'.

The readers then met in groups to discuss the right conclusion. My grandfather, unable to afford the half-crown subscription required for each of the monthly books, was never acquainted with the text under discussion but did not allow that to deter him from contributing. He brought home discarded copies and could have jogged along one step behind the more affluent comrades. But he was always too restless to read anything more demanding than the paper. He had a jackdaw instinct and the pleasure of acquiring the orange-backed book was sufficient in itself.

The intelligentsia was present in force at the Left Book Club meeting to which he took my cousin and me. Miss Howard, headmistress of the Girls' High School, and Miss

Chew, the history mistress, sat in the front row, flanked by the curate of the parish church and Fred Brown, secretary of the Burnley branch of the Communist party.

There were other school teachers, including an unlikely recruit, the big and genial Bill Sparks, son of a country manse, captain of infantry, and now teacher of a class that had been formed to pass the time of unemployed school-leavers. Mr Sparks' job was not so much to instruct them as to keep up their spirits and confidence, and he did much the same thing at the Left Book Club, saying little himself but beaming on speakers, laughing at their jokes and frequently tapping the back of the seat in front of him by way of applause. Most of those who spoke deferred to the Communist style of referring to the German National Socialists not as Nazis, which was the expression in general use, but as fascists. The Communists, used the term to describe any and all of their opponents, and indeed the earnest members of the Labour party now assembled in common cause had been derided as 'Social Fascists' until the line changed to the 'Popular Front'.

Fred Brown, the party secretary, was a cabinet-maker who worked with my uncle Ben, small and neatly dressed in a fawn suit and highly-polished brown shoes. He had dark eyes and a nervous manner and was at pains to prevent a big man called Jim from speaking. Jim, the only obvious proletarian at the meeting, had once been a folk hero. In a confrontation between strikers and the police he had leapt pick-a-back on to the shoulders of an inspector and had clung there making a speech and emphasising its points by pounding with his fist on the top of the inspector's flat cap. But he lacked the resilience to change with changing times and the party expelled him as a left-wing deviationist. He now rose and made what I gathered was his stock speech.

'We shall hang the bourgeoisie from the lamp posts,' he proclaimed.

'No, no, no,' Fred Brown demurred as though he knew of better places to hang them from.

'The rivers of England,' Jim pronounced, 'will flow with capitalist blood.'

'No, no, no,' Fred Brown protested.

'Come, come, Jim,' my grandfather tutted.

Bill Sparks grinned. Miss Howard and Miss Chew put on the prim face with which they checked any unseemliness among the girls. If that sort of thing was going to happen they were sorry they had paid their subscription.

Councillor Jack Yates rose with more moderate observations, followed by Dan Duxbury, a journalist on the *Manchester Guardian* with an apologetic manner. Both exceptionally stuck to the text of the book under discussion and, also exceptionally, made a few jokes. Bill Sparks haw-hawed. Fred Brown looked uncomfortable.

Then it was his turn. He neatly worked in references to the book in the course of his tight-lipped run-down on the current stage of the anti-fascist struggle, a ranging review which brought together many strands and revealed the inter-related significance of events in many parts of the world. It was quiet, fluent, mesmerising soliloquy, the end of the evening, a secular benediction.

We rose, my grandfather picked up a discarded book he would never read and we went out into the night.

Times improved. By 1938, under the stimulus of rearmament, the economy began to flourish again. The main benefit was felt in the newer industries of the South-East, but for us too things looked up. My father got a new suit, and his weekly ration of cigarettes was increased to twenty Senior Service in a white packet. I got a trench coat with flaps, hooks and football buttons bought for eighteen shillings, the residue of my holiday earnings on farm work. My brother as youngest got his usual raw deal in the shape of my old school mac.

The squeeze of the bad years had hurt my father most. He was depressed by a sense of failure and was the more frustrated because he had an invention in mind which he believed would make us rich, but lacked the money to make it. It was a device for the efficient soaking of thick leather to make it workable, and it would indeed have been a great improvement on the crude and sloppy methods devised in the Middle Ages and still in use in the shoe repair business. He drew plans at night on the dining-room table, adding refinements and sometimes going back to basic changes. All the scrolls finished on the high top of the sideboard waiting for the modest funds required to make a prototype.

He turned, as half the population did, to competitions in the newspapers as a means of breaking out. The crosswords were so simple a child could have done them, but the preferred solution to a few of the clues would be far-fetched, though differing from the obvious answer only by an odd letter. Every week millions of competitors missed the big prize by a couple of letters and were thus encouraged to believe that all that was needed for success was persistence and a bit of luck.

Crosswords were only a beginning. Beyond, as the habit took hold, lay a wretched word game started as 'Bullets' in *John Bull* and now run under different names by several publications. You were given a word or phrase and you had to propose a four-word punning echo of it. To the phrase 'If we want peace' a competitor replied 'Let meek greet meek'. He was rewarded with 4,500 guineas. 'Every morning' inspired the riposte 'Let marmalade recall orange-blossom'. 'Starving' was righteously and profitably echoed by 'Disgrace to all unconcerned'.

An industry sprang up round these competitions. A new profession arose, solutionists, who for a consideration would supply lines and, if successful, take a proportion of any winnings. One solutionist signed himself 'Professor'. Another was photographed wearing a mortar-board. A whole family set themselves up as solutionists; in their advertisement they were pictured in oval frames each with a quality of the mind or the spirit printed below, Wit, Subtlety, Humour, Satire, etcetera.

My father was not in a position to engage these services and he saw no point in them. If the solutionists could turn out winning lines why did they not send them in and collar the prize? He did, however, invest in a magazine called *The Leader* which reprinted the competitions from many publications and suggested solutions. He took it to work with him and studied it while they sat around waiting for the van to return with some shoes to repair. When he hit on a good solution he would come home beaming. We usually spoilt it for him. We could never properly grasp the aim of the competition, let alone understand what his line was getting at.

'I see,' my mother would say, doing her best but puzzled. 'What does that mean?' Or she would guess at the meaning and be wrong.

He responded by trying to explain. 'Yes,' we would say, pretending to have twigged it. 'Yes.'

Usually he would leave it at that but sometimes, perhaps when our incomprehension echoed his own doubts, he turned away in temper and said, 'All right, then, if you don't understand.'

My mother, who could never let a complaint pass, would reply with bleak righteousness, 'Well, we don't understand.'

'All right,' he would say, 'there's no encouragement for anything here,' and bang out of the room.

His persistence through the years was rewarded by a single win, a consolation prize of six handkerchiefs.

We were rescued from the competitions by the acquisition of a garden. My mother spotted a house to let a hundred yards down Moseley Road from where we lived and out of curiosity went in to look. She was enchanted. The house, which was built of stone, was in a terrace which stood behind small gardens above the level of the road. It had leaded windows and a small french window to a paved yard at the back, from which a large garden rose to the horizon of trees. As a home it exceeded any ambition my mother had ever had. The lady who owned it said on the spur of a generous moment that she could have it for the rent we were then paying.

It was not worth getting a removal van for the distance. We got our relations and neighbours instead and humped the furniture down after work in the dark. Everybody was a practised expert at removal. We had the carpets laid, the beds set up and the furniture in position by nine o'clock and we sat down, our family and all the humpers, to a happy supper of fish and chips.

It set the mood of the place. We all loved it. The garden transformed my father. It was overgrown at first but a rewarding place to work, having been established, so we were told, before the Great War by a rich old couple who spent every possible hour on the soil. There was a pond where big goldfish survived the winters under ice, there was a sunken rose garden and brick paths and a small lawn by the pond with a seat under an apple tree commanding a panoramic view of the town and the countryside beyond.

My father, who knew nothing about gardening at the outset, learned from a sixpenny book. He dug and weeded and built. In summer he hardly gave himself time to eat his tea in his haste to get out to work. He became bronzed and happy. His patience returned. The house was full of plants and flowers.

In winter, with prospects now of paying back, he borrowed some money from his father and built his invention, the cabinet for soaking leather. Nothing came of it in the end because the war prevented its exploitation. But it looked good. The achievement was the more relished for having lain dormant so long.

# 13 · FARMER'S BOY

Thieveley farm stood 1,200 feet up on the moors above the valley road to Todmorden. From the village of Holme in the bottom one crossed a bridge over a turbulent stream and climbed up through woods to a boundary wall where the moors began and the path rose steeper. The steading, built in a hollow in the rise of the moor, came into view again as one climbed: first the chimneys against the clouds; then, from the crest of the rise, the whole house and the barn and the overgrown yard. The buildings, of whitewashed stone, crouched against the wind which was fresh even in summer, whistling through chinks in the heavy barn doors and wafting about the smell of dung and nettles. A three-hole lavatory above a cess pit stood by the yard gate.

It had been until recently a place of resort at weekends and bank holidays when families with small children struggled up the hill. The front room served as a shop. The stock had to be carried up in crates and boxes on somebody's back and they felt justified in adding a halfpenny to the price of pop or crisps. But even with that enterprise the place was too small and unproductive to support a family in a time of falling farm prices. When my cousin and I first went there at the age of thirteen or fourteen the place had been abandoned. Nobody was about. We could do what we liked.

Behind the farm in a hollow lay a small field which had been used for games and picnics. Beyond it the hillside rose rocky and precipitous to Deerplay moor. We took other boys there, Jim Francis my school friend, and boys from the back street. My cousin Carlton came over the moor from

Bacup with his gang. We built fires and roasted potatoes and smoked Woodbines. We climbed the hillside and set off boulders which bounded past boys still climbing and smashed into the wall at the bottom. We crept with feeble torches down the abandoned drift mines cut into the flanks of the moor. A narrow-gauge railway, built to carry jinny wagons, ran down into an entrance which gave us the notion of riding all the way to the depth of the mine. We pushed out a wagon on to the top of the slope where they were parked and climbed aboard. It gathered speed. The mouth of the mine opened wide in front of us. We jumped. Much later came the echoing rumble of the wagon crashing into some obstacle deep in the mine.

Such activities could only have led to juvenile court, hospital or cemetery, but one day Harold Sutcliffe appeared in clattering clogs from among the abandoned buildings at Thieveley farm and enrolled Stanley and me for the peaceful pursuit of agriculture. 'Do you lads want a bit of haymaking?' he asked.

He was stockily bult, about forty, wearing braces over his union shirt. He had sandy hair and light eyebrows, so that from a distance his face was a blank. A cigarette hung from his lower lip, permanently we discovered. He spoke through swirls of smoke.

We followed him to the steep meadow. Most of the grass lay cut. A patient horse waited in the shafts of an iron mowing-machine. There was nobody else in the field.

'We mun get this in before t' weather changes,' Harold Sutcliffe said. 'These are my fields now. I own t' farm in t' bottom and I've bought Thieveley. It's all mine, this.'

He grinned in a proud, bashful way. It was indeed a magnificent place. The steep field overlooked the top of a wood and a long green valley where the river flowed towards Burnley.

Harold Sutcliffe led us down to an area where the grass had been cut some days earlier and scattered. 'Rake it into rows,' he said.

He had to show us what he meant by a row and how to hold the rake. He demonstrated, breathing hard through his cigarette smoke, his clogs clicking together as he moved. 'Canst thou do that?' he asked. 'There's nowt to it. I'll wap some more down.'

He left us and heaved himself into the iron saddle of the mowing-machine. The ratchet ticked as he backed the horse a little, then he shouted and snapped the reins. The horse with bent neck moved forward and the clattering blade lopped through the base of the standing grass. The meadow had not been manured for a year or two and was beginning to go back to moorland. The mowing-machine was frequently stopped by knots of coarse grass. Harold Sutcliffe backed off, leaning sideways, head over the wheel to watch the alignment of the blade. Then he shouted the horse to a fast start and the blade rattled again. It was a slow job. Our rows wavered across the field. The sun began to go down.

'That's all right,' Harold Sutcliffe said, 'but you mun try to keep 'em straighter. Shall you come back tomorn?'

We had never thought of spending the school holidays in the hayfield. Thieveley was a four-mile walk from home.

We had no bikes. 'Come on t' bus,' he said. 'I'll see you reight for a bit of bus fare.'

And so for our remaining years at school we spent part of the summer making hay. It could take weeks. The mower was the only piece of equipment that had not been available from shortly after the dawn of agriculture. The rougher areas still had to be scythed. The cut grass was dried by tossing and turning with pitchforks, several times if rain fell while the grass was lying. It was raked into rows and on steep farms like Thieveley, where carts might have overbalanced, it was loaded high on wooden sledges and led to the barn.

When we returned for the second year Harold Sutcliffe had prospered and there were more people in the hayfield. John Willy Sunter was a son of the family who had given up the place. He had gone to work as a labourer and through a turn of fate found himself employed by Harold Sutcliffe and back at Thieveley less than three years after his family had quit. He was a humorous dark little man with a passion for tidiness. When we led manure to the fields in the high-sided cart he scrupled to throw off heaps so evenly spaced that all across the meadow they marked the corners of perfect squares. The pattern would be undone a day or two later when we went with the shovel and skimmed the heaps across the grass but that was the correct way to do it and, if our spreading was equally consistent, it would ensure that every part of the field got exactly the same manuring.

Harry Frankland came as a tenant to the house, and cycled every weekday to his work in Burnley. He was a rueful socialist who always feared the worst and, as an insurance against the collapse of the mill where he was employed as a weaver, he worked part-time for Harold Sutcliffe and tried with no great success to revive the sweet-shop in the parlour. His jolly fat wife and their burbling baby lightened his despondency.

Alan Parker came up to the hayfield some days, a ruddy twinkling man in his mid-twenties whom Harold Sutcliffe in his rapid expansion had promoted from farm labourer. 'He's a foreman now,' Harold said. 'He worked in t' school holidays when he were a lad same as thee. Thou could do t' same. Thou might rise to any heights if thou stuck to it.'

Alan Parker winked at me. Everybody winked or grim-
aced behind Harold's back. He was considered a hard master
and had a reputation for tightness which deterred people
from the village from coming up to do a day in the hayfield.
Once when he had succeeded in recruiting a few he outraged
convention by providing, instead of the traditional beer
barrel at the gate, a crateful of bottles labelled 'Blood Orange
Drink'. It looked like water with tattered pieces of orange
peel floating about and tasted of nothing. When they had
gone Alan Parker tipped it into the wall bottom.

'How did thou like t' blood orange drink?' Harold Sutcliffe
asked later.

'Grand,' Alan said.

'It's only three ha'pence for one of them big bottles.'

'Go on.'

'Aye. We mun ha' some more o' that.'

Harold seldom worked at Thieveley himself but often
came up in the late afternoon or evening to inspect our work.
He usually arrived affable and exchanged a joke or two but,
whatever the task, when he saw what had been done his face
darkened. 'Is this all thou's achieved? What hast thou been
doing all day? Hast thou been sitting down?'

Neither John Willy nor Harry Frankland answered him or
offered excuses. 'Nay, nay,' they would say, shaking their
heads as though they too were perplexed to know what had
prevented more progress.

'Thou mun get thy back into it or I'll be givin' thee t'
sack.'

Back in the house Harry Frankland said, 'He's an objec-
tionable individual. He's a kulak.'

'What's that?' his wife asked.

'The Harold Sutcliffes of Russia,' Harry said. 'But they've
had their caper cut short there.'

'It's time he did these jobs on th' house.'

'He'll never do 'em.'

The house was humid with rising damp. There were
chinks in the wall through which the wind could blow with
such force that Harry and his wife had to hold on to the
bedclothes. The cesspool and the midden stank within fifteen
yards of the front door. Once Harry became a part-time

employee it was more difficult to press complaints. His wife tried.

'Aye, aye,' Harold Sutcliffe would say, moving off. 'Thou'll be reight.'

One day he became more specific. 'Thou can't expect a palace for what thou'rt paying. Thou'll be reight.'

One year he made John Willy try to mow the moorland grass which grew on the top side of a stony track across the meadow. 'We mun mow it year by year and before we all go to us reward it'll be yielding a good crop.'

John Willy looked doubtful. 'It's rough, mind.'

'Aye, thou'll need to get th' scythe to it in places. Wap it down. It looks bad from t' road.'

It was easier going when he worked with us. He would greet us in the normal way: 'Is this all thou'st done? Hast thou been sitting down?' Then in temper, his cigarette crackling bright with anger and exertion, he would work behind us, pushing us along fast.

But he tired. The pace slackened. He stepped out if he could and let us carry on, but we contrived to trap him in the middle of the line where he could not easily stop without us all stopping. He would toil on, puffing out cigarette smoke irregularly like the exhaust of a badly-tuned engine, then he would drop his rake or fork and flop down. 'We'll have five minutes.'

We all sat. Somebody went for the bottles we had left under coats at the wall side to keep cool.

Harold often graced our breather with an unexpected line of conversation. He spoke of institutions which he revered, the monarchy, the Church of England, totalisators at race tracks and the National Farmers' Union. On one occasion he generously included Burnley grammar school. He asked my cousin whether the German he had learned was sufficient to understand Hitler on the wireless. Stanley didn't know because he didn't have a wireless. Harold nevertheless expressed unqualified respect for the school. 'It's the best thing out is education. Thou can't ha' too much on it. And t' grammar school's t' best shop to impart it.'

On another sit-down he had come back impressed from a visit to a woollen mill the other side of Todmorden. He glanced up the valley in the general direction. 'It's nobbut a lile place,' he said. 'But,' he added in a voice low and quavering with reverence, 'it's t' biggest blanket-making firm in t' world.'

He would go about seven, leaving us with jobs which, if we had done them, would have kept us till dawn. 'Just bowl this lot in and rake up t' tails,' he would say, surveying a field of hay, 'then thou can go 'ome.'

One evening he decided he wanted his flock down from Deerplay moor. 'Just get yon sheep down,' he said, 'then thou can go 'ome.'

He was a born trader, always buying and selling things, and he changed his sheep so often that they never got hefted to the moor, so that if disturbed they would go in any direction rather than gather on their own ground. Moreover he had no rapport with dogs; he could neither train one nor keep a bought one under command. The evening we all climbed the rocky path to the moor he had no dog at all. We all galloped about in the gathering darkness, forming widespread cordons which the sheep easily and repeatedly streamed through. About midnight we reached the outskirts of Bacup. 'We mun't be defeated,' Harold said. 'We mun come again tomorn when we're fresh.'

The main farm in the valley bottom was given over to a poultry battery, row upon row of huts like an army camp in which thousands of hens were kept in multi-tiered lines of cages. It was a new idea. Up to then eggs were produced by hens that ran free round farmyards or in the henpens that surrounded industrial towns. Letters in the papers protested about the new batteries which were compared to prisons. The electric light burned day and night to keep the hens laying. After a few months the worn-out birds were cremated on a fire in the yard. They were too tough to eat.

I got the job after haytime of feeding and mucking out the hens. As soon as the door was opened they raised a hullabaloo. They squawked and rose on beating imprisoned wings, throwing up clouds of dried droppings. They calmed down, but individual hens would go wild again if one had to reach into their cage to retrieve an egg. The eggs should have rolled down to a channel at the front but some stuck in the mesh. Often these were the ones that had no hard shell because the hen had not picked up enough of the grit that we mixed into the buckets of mash. Harold Sutcliffe told me to get my fingers into the troughs and turn up the grit in the bottom. 'Grub it up for 'em,' he said. 'They mun ha' their calcium. We don't want no soft-shelled 'uns.'

Soft-shelled eggs were sold cheap to bakeries. The rest we graded, along with those Harold's lorry collected in the Yorkshire dales, and sold to wholesalers and multiple shops. It was a new sort of enterprise and visitors came from the farms to see the grading machine in a hut in the yard.

Bill the grader worked with a box of eggs in front of him. He held up each egg to a light to judge by the air space at its end whether it was fresh and let it roll down a chute into one of the small shallow trays which revolved on a spindle. Around this was a circular deck divided into segments. The trays tipped the biggest eggs into the first segment. Then mechanical weights were progressively added as the trays turned, so that first the medium and then the small and then the tiny eggs were tipped into their own segment.

My job was to pack the eggs and to carry new crates in for Bill. He was a man whose expertise was recognised, a trained technician, three shillings a week better off than a farm labourer. He wore shoes instead of boots and parted his hair in the middle. He had been on holiday to a distant part of the country and there, as he recounted, witnessed a happening which remained in his mind for months. He would switch off the machine to tell the story to any visitor who seemed a likely listener. He had gone to a wrestling match in which one of the pugilists outrageously violated the rules. He was warned by the referee, booed by the crowd, and in the end was disqualified. Eyes wild with anger, he prowled round the ring, 'like a caged tiger', as Bill said, menacing everybody. Shaking off his seconds, he made to climb over the ropes to get at individuals in the crowd. Finally he rounded on the referee.

'There were an enamel dish in his corner,' Bill said, 'and he up wi' th' enamel dish and brought it down wi' a clang on t' ref's bald head.'

'Nay,' the visitor would say.

'Aye. Laid him out cold on t' canvas.'

'Nay.'

They would both stand there silent, the visitor perhaps shaking his head, then Bill would switch the machine on again and the eggs would rotate and roll down the table.

The other workers thought that Bill's job, poised over his eggs every day, was an unhealthy one, highly paid though it might be. One day when rain was threatening he was impressed for the hayfield. Everybody told him he would benefit from the fresh air. He had never worked on the hay before. It was a humid day. By late afternoon he was wilting. By ten at night he could hardly walk down to the farm, let alone mount his bicycle to ride home. He slept on Harold Sutcliffe's couch. Ever after he stuck to his eggs and renounced every other branch of agriculture. He said if he was going to suffer like that he might as well be a wrestler and make some money.

In time I was promoted to travel in the egg-collecting lorry two days a week as loader for Alan Parker. He picked me up at six o'clock while Burnley was still asleep. We drove through Nelson, where the traffic lights blinked on empty streets, and up the steep hill at Blacko into the forest of Pendle, which is not woodland but a spread of fields and moors rising to Pendle hill. 'Witch country,' Alan Parker said. He would ask whether I believed in witchcraft but we never got far with the discussion because at the top of the hill the limestone peak of Ingleborough came into sight and he began to sing.

The Yorkshire dales lie north of the industrial belt, miles of undulating open country, divided by white stone walls and rising from broad river valleys to limestone outcrops. The northern valleys are steeper and the streams tumble faster. Some farmers left their egg boxes on milk stands by the road, but at most places we drove right up to the farm. We lurched slowly along green lanes, splashing through fords and passing beneath crags where sheep would appear suddenly like Indian ponies in a Western film. Old trees in the farmyards hummed with a million insects.

When we dropped down to Rathmell village Alan stopped outside the church. 'I'm going to say my prayers,' he said. 'Wilt thou come?'

I followed into the darkness of the church.

'Come on then,' he said. 'Get down on thy knees. Get supplicating.'

I demurred. He tried again. He pointed to a forward pew. 'That's where I get down to it,' he said, 'but I want to see thee properly installed first.'

I refused, embarrassed, and he gave up in a shout of laughter. 'Thou'rt too suspicious,' he said. 'I'll let thee off this time. Pick yon box up.'

A couple of egg boxes stood in the darkness by the door, left there, Alan explained, by the parson who was a poultry keeper. 'But it's a good gag, isn't it, reckoning I'm coming in to say my prayers? I've had one or two down on th' hassocks before today.'

In the late afternoon we were given tea at a farmhouse in the hills above Ribblesdale. Alan Parker penetrated the darkness of the kitchen and loudly greeted men eating at the table.

'Who's the lad?' one asked.

'Harold's taken him on for t' school holidays,' Alan said. 'He wain't say his prayers.'

'That's bad,' the man said. 'Sit down and reach up.'

The table was heavily laden with jam and bread and cheese and pies and cakes. A stout woman came in with a huge two-handled teapot. The men reached across with strong arms and talked with their mouths full. There would be a run of conversation, then a sharp comment I seldom caught and everybody roared with laughter.

In the darkness of the corner a very old man was sitting under a grandfather clock listening, if he still heard it, to the pendulum beating away the seconds of his last days. Kittens scratched at his boots and he prodded them off with his stick. Two small children came to play, his great-grandchildren perhaps, and he prodded them off too, without affection and without annoyance. A clown's face was painted on the clock dial above him, peering over the words of a scroll: '*Sic est vita hominis.*'

We ate and laughed. Somebody told a story about a man who had been taken to the infirmary and had the wrong leg cut off in error, and that led to a stream of anecdotes about medical misfortunes. The woman leaned against the door post and shouted the men down over points of detail. Then somebody said something brief that I didn't catch and we all got up in a bellow of crumbs and laughter, leaving the table strewn with the remains of the food and the old man sitting unheeded by the grandfather clock.

An old man of less advanced years used to signal us to stop as though we were a bus at Ribblehead near the viaduct of the Settle–Carlisle railway. He would climb up on to the egg boxes and rap with his stick on the back of the cab when he was settled.

'I'll teach the old devil to scrounge rides with me,' Alan Parker said.

He let in the clutch and accelerated fast down the switchback road. We could hear the egg boxes and the old man bouncing about behind us. When we stopped at Horton-in-Ribblesdale, tyres smouldering and windscreen caked with dead flies, all was silent for a moment, then the old man rapped with his stick by way of acknowledgment and climbed down. He grunted, which in those parts is an effusive expression of thanks, and walked off in the burst of our exhaust.

'Thou mustn't mention to Harold how we came down yon road,' Alan Parker said. 'He'll be riled if th' eggs are broken.'

The limestone country is honeycombed with caves, most of which can only be explored by potholers, but there is a show cave fitted with duck boards and electric lights for unequipped and unadventurous visitors. Alan Parker's brother-in-law, who came with us on one trip, paid for us to go through in return for his cramped ride.

We saw waterfalls and smooth shoulders of rock which films of water crossed in surges. We saw stalactites and stalagmites, and the guide explained how they were formed: dripping water left behind the minutest grains of calcium which had taken millions of years to grow into the formations we saw. We were not to be misled by the small stalactites forming above the light bulbs. The heat of the bulbs evaporated water and speeded the process on a scale inconceivable in nature. The natural formations had started at the beginning of time.

We looked impressed and, seeing that we had assimilated fact so readily, the guide proposed an exercise in fancy. Could we see in this formation the likeness of a bear?

Alan Parker innocently asked which way up. The guide replied sharply, 'The way up you're standing.'

Alan, in apology, divined its eye and its snout and its ears, and he agreed that the ribs of limestone could well be thought to resemble a bear's fur. He perceived other animals that were pointed out to us, an elephant and a monkey, and he went on to recognise further members of the menagerie unaware that we had finished with animals and were now required to perceive different kinds of things, such as churches, towers and castles.

'It's not a dinosaur,' the guide huffed. 'It's a wishing-well. We haven't come through here to act the goat.'

Alan apologised and asked, by way of placation, what we were looking at now.

'Snow White and the seven dwarfs,' the guide said. But he snapped off the light inside the rock grotto and stumped onwards to the platform that marked the end of the part of the cave open to the public. A rapid river disappeared into the darkness beyond the lights. The guide stood silent in a huff, then the offence wore off and he said the cave ran another mile or more under the mountain. The passage narrowed to eighteen inches, and the confined stream would then run almost the height of a man's head. Beyond that you reached a waterfall thirty feet high and, when you'd climbed that, a long crawl led to a wider passage which opened up into a lake you'd need a boat to cross. On the far shore was an underground chamber like a cathedral.

Outside the sun was blinding. Half the population of the villages was in the hayfields, including children and old people. In the dales the hay was raked into cops and the cops gathered into pikes six or seven feet tall and shaped like a conical tent, which would shed the rain and stand out for months. It looked like a child's painting, the many people,

the horses pulling mowing machines or hay carts, the yellow
pikes, the green meadows and white walls, the farm buildings low at the foot of the fells and the cumulus clouds
changing shape above the summits.

In the village children kicked up the white dust of the lane
as they came home from school. A shy girl in a rag dress
watched us at work on the lorry from an arch in a farm
building. An old parson with a shining face and a gold watch
chain trudged towards the churchyard carrying flowers. We
bought some crates of hens and sold them again further
along the route. We bought rabbits, which were snared by
the thousand and hung up in stables.

Driving back, Alan Parker considered how you'd get a
boat down to cross those big black lakes in the caves. He
supposed you'd have to take it down in pieces and nail it
together on the underground shore. He wondered if there
would be any fish. If so, they'd be numerous because there
were no anglers. Perhaps the fish, undisturbed for millions
of years, had grown to enormous size. That didn't happen
with animals because there was a limit to the weight that
legs might bear, but it could happen with fish. A cavern
chamber like a cathedral. What the guide meant was space.
We understood that, but the picture was of a building, nave
and transept, stained glass windows, altar and choirstalls,
evensong, on the far shore of the black lake.

Coming home one evening when we had loaded our boxes
at a farm near the foot of Pendle hill, Alan asked if I would
like to go and see an old woman who knew the witches.
She lived at the end of a stony track in a small cottage set
in a garden which weeds were taking over. She had once
supplied eggs, he said, but looking after hens became too
much for her.

She let us in and lit a paraffin lamp and hung it from a
beam. Alan gave her news about people she knew along our
route, then said, 'This lad is interested in t' witches.'

She glanced at me but kept on for a time with the conversation. She was bent and wrinkled but quick to understand
and ready in her brief responses. 'Did you show him the
barn,' she said, 'where they met?'

Alan said he hadn't.

She drew a curtain aside at a small window. 'There,' she said, 'on the top of the hill, if you can see in this light.'

'That's where they pranced round, is it?' Alan asked.

'Not in that building, that's more recent, but on that site, or so it's supposed.'

She reached down a small wooden chest and unlocked it on the table top. Inside were records of some sort. A black cat came and sat on the table. The old woman closed the lid of the box.

Witches, she said, sold their soul to the devil in return for the power to do harm. He might appear to them as a man but more often took the form of an animal, dog, cat, foal, hare or bear. The devil sucked the blood of a witch and left a mark by which she was to be recognised. He conferred on her powers to ride a broomstick, take on the form of animals, raise storms and kill people and animals by casting the evil eye upon them or by making a clay image and sticking in pins with muttered incantations. One witch made spells from skulls and teeth which she dug up from the graveyard we would pass just down the road. People who offended witches were stricken or killed. Their animals died. The milk turned sour.

'Fairies,' she said, looking at Alan, 'were often evil.'

He nodded.

After baptism, she said, they had no power over babies but until then small children were guarded day and night lest fairies snatched them from the cradle and left one of their own. Children who grew up physically or mentally detective often proved to be changelings. One small infant was imbued with the power of speech and informed its parent that it was three score and ten years old.

We risked a slight laugh. The old woman opened the box again and turned over some of the papers. 'These are records,' she said, 'gathered by my grandfather. He was ninety-six when he died.'

'So he'd know some of 'em,' Alan Parker said.

'No, they were dead before his time.'

The first covens, she said, were arrested in 1612 and tried for murder by witchcraft at Lancaster assizes. The most notorious witch, Old Demdike, who was eighty, confessed that she had sold her soul to a devil called Tibb who appeared as a brown dog, and through his power she killed by clay images a young girl and a gentleman.

Her daughter, Elizabeth Davies, 'a malicious, wicked and dangerous witch for fifty years', whose familiar also appeared as a brown dog, admitted killing two brothers and helping to kill a man who had refused her a penny.

Two grandchildren were also on trial, James and Alison Davies. James himself was under some sort of spell. He reached the court, as the old woman quoted from the record, 'so insensible, weak and unable in all things, as he could neither speak, hear or stand, but was holden up'. He had killed a woman who accused him of stealing turfs and a man who refused to give him an old shirt. Alison had lamed a pedlar who died.

All the accused gave evidence against each other. The principal witness against them all was Jenet, the nine-year-old sister of James and Alison.

Old Demdike died in prison. Her daughter and two grandchildren were hanged. So were four others. Only two were acquitted and one, who was accused of bewitching but not killing a woman and a horse, was sentenced to the pillory.

'Did witches have those powers then?' Alan Parker asked.

'Nay,' the old woman said, 'or where are they nowadays?'

They were poverty-stricken, ignorant people, she said, so terrified under questioning that they would confess to anything and make any accusation suggested to them. But what was the mental state, she asked, of magistrates and judges, educated men, who knew that the allegations were absurd and must have known how the confessions had been extracted?

She pulled out one of the papers. 'You'll have heard of Edmund Robinson,' she said. Alan Parker said we hadn't.

He was a boy of ten from Wheatley Lane, she said, whose accepted power to pick out witches put the whole district in fear. He first got among them, he told magistrates in 1633, when a greyhound he had put on a lead turned into a witch and another into a horse which carried him away to a witches' meeting. He watched their rites. He knew them. He claimed he could pick out witches he had not met before. The magistrates set him on. His father took him round churches where he denounced members of the congregation as witches. Nineteen he pointed out were arrested and sent to Lancaster for trial, including Jenet Davies, whose evidence twenty years earlier had helped to condemn her grandmother, mother, sister and brother.

Seventeen were found guilty but sentence was postponed until they could be examined by the Bishop of Chester. Four of them he found especially interesting and ordered them to be sent to London to be examined by the King's physicians and by the King himself.

'They were cruel superstitious times,' the old woman said, closing the box, 'and the highest in the land were afflicted no less than the lowest.'

We drove back through the lighted streets of Nelson and Burnley, past cotton mills and chapels and chip shops, work-a-day urban streets remote from the dark rural superstitions that had passed with bygone times. It was hard to imagine that people could ever have been so ignorant and vicious. But even then, though we did not know it, trials were being conducted in Moscow more grotesque than those held at Lancaster, and in Germany a malign power was gathering which would surpass the wickedness of witchcraft.

Nineteen thirty-eight was a year of deepening fear. War, which at the beginning had been unthinkable, had by the end become inevitable. One man was at the root of our fear, Adolf Hitler.

Up to then he had given less trouble than Mussolini, the Fascist dictator of Italy. But nobody was frightened of Italy, and Mussolini had always been something of a buffoon to us, a newsreel comedian with his pillbox hat and baggy breeches and the excited funny-foreigner gestures he made with his hands in delivering speeches from high balconies. His army, although it had proved capable of chasing primitively-armed Abyssinians, was, as the newspaper cartoons made clear, something out of comic opera, composed of ice-cream men and organ-grinders indistinguishable from their monkeys.

We took no such comfort in regard to Hitler, though he was unmenacing in appearance. He had a little moustache and a lock of hair which fell slantwise across his forehead. His eyes held the permanent sorrow of one who has been deeply wounded in childhood. His voice, as we heard it occasionally on the radio or the newsreels, was husky and rather old.

He began his speeches with a long silence, standing still for a minute or more until the huge audiences fell completely quiet. He would then rather hesitantly offer them quiet sentences build round simple emotive words: home, children, work, duty, fatherland. He might make a joke or two. Then, sensing their rising to him, he would speak louder and faster, throwing out a succession of themes to which the audience responded with increasing emotion – Jewry, international finance, Bolshevism, Versailles, living space – a well-rehearsed variety of grievances, threats and promises that whipped up the audience to hysteria and culminated in a great roar of 'Sieg Heil'. This was the part the newsreels showed us. Nobody had ever seen anything like the Nazi mass demonstrations with their uniformed phalanxes, torch-light and flags. It was mesmerising and frightening, not least because of the half-suppressed suspicion that if you had been there you too might have been carried away to join in.

The cautious passivity of the democracies contributed to the aura of Hitler's power. He threatened or acted. They reacted. He always had the initiative. Everybody hung on his words. When he had falsely claimed in 1935 that his Luftwaffe had grown to equal the strength of the Royal Air Force he was readily and fearfully believed.

That was the paramount fear, the dread of the bomber which, it was believed, woud bring death to the civilian population in devastating numbers. There would be no defence against it. 'The bomber will always get through,' Mr Baldwin, had warned. Pacifists and air marshals for their different reasons concurred. Exterminating raids on a scale only reached in reality at Hiroshima and Nagasaki were expected from the outbreak of war. The official British esti mate was 1.8 million casualties in the first two months. The authorities secretly prepared measures to deal with mass panic.

A further strong element in fear was a foreboding of defeat, which was not without cause. We knew how costly and close-run a thing the Great War had been and nobody had too much confidence in the result of a return fixture. The vigour of the German economic recovery contrasted with years of near stagnation in the democratic countries. Full employment had been achieved. The papers and the newsreels brought pictures of air formations, of healthy vig-orous leisure, of Europe's first motorways stretching through farmland and forest, and of the new car, the Volks-wagen, to be bought by instalments every family could afford (though in the event delivered entirely to the army).

Morale in Britain was low. In France, which had suffered grievous losses in the Great War and finished with its army mutinous, the mood was shaky and surly. Everywhere democracy was in retreat. In most countries of the continent, large and small, reaction prevailed. In the Left, which set the tone and agenda of public debate, a deep defeatism had developed. They had no confidence in themselves and, however they might try to bodge up popular fronts against fascism, at bottom they believed that the capitalist democracies were doomed.

There was certainly evidence for that. In old industrial areas like ours, despite a slight recent upturn, decline was still everywhere to be seen. Mills closed, woodwork rotted, people wore old clothes, homes were cold. We felt no match for a resurgent Germany. We waited with foreboding to see what Hitler would do next.

What he did in March 1938 was to incorporate Austria into the Reich. The democracies acquiesced. Then in September he demanded the return of the Sudeten territory where three million Germans lived in Czechoslovakia. Britain and France resisted and suddenly we were on the verge of war. It was difficult to follow quite what was happening. It was, as the Prime Minister Mr Chamberlain would say, 'a quarrel in a far-away country between people of whom we know nothing'. What part he was playing in this by his flying visits to Germany we did not properly understand, but his chances of preserving peace seemed slim. War was expected within days.

In London trenches were dug in the parks as shelter against bombs and forty-four old guns, representing the whole of Britain's anti-aircraft defence, were trundled out.

We had visions, derived from science fiction, of great armadas of silver bombers passing over as though in a pageant, devasting town after town. They were expected also to drop gas, a weapon of special horror. Thirty-eight million gas masks were distributed from schools and public buildings. The rubber masks fitted close against the face and had a snout which housed a filter. Children found they could make razzing noises and ran about playing porkers.

Stanley Stuttard, a classmate, offered a superior gas mask. His father was fire chief and Stanley promised that if we would enrol in the auxiliary fire brigade as boy messengers we would be issued a regulation army gas mask with a chest box and connecting tube instead of a snout. We would also get a tin hat, a lapel badge and a bike to ride when on duty. We joined. The Burnley brigade must have numbered more messengers than firemen.

The headmaster, out of humanity and possibly a prudent desire to preserve his post, sought an arrangement to avoid losing his school and his scholars at one blow. He negotiated as a place of refuge an area of Queen's park half a mile away. No trenches had been dug but we could hide in the foliage and cower behind the bandstand.

When the practice alarm sounded several hundred of us came jogging through the school gate. It was uphill to the park. Fat boys and fat masters sat panting on wall tops and at the edge of the pavement. The girls of the high school came to the railings and jeered as we passed. They had no place of refuge. Running *en masse* through the streets would have been thought unsuitable. When the silver bombers came they would all be goners.

Then just as suddenly as the crisis had come, it ended. Chamberlain had met Hitler again, this time in a four-power conference at Munich, the city whose name became the symbol of the policy of appeasement. He had been sped on his way by a House of Commons fervent for his success. When he returned, having in effect surrendered Czecho-slovakia to Hitler, he was met with mass acclamation. To the delighted throng in Downing Street he called from an upstairs window the words for which, poor man, he would always be remembered: 'I believe it is peace for our time.'

The settlement was welcomed almost unanimously in the press and overwhelmingly, according to contemporary observation, in the country. In my own small world it was greeted with profound relief and some shame.

Nobody had much faith in Munich for long. But it served a purpose. It was an inoculation against fear. The quaking of the Munich days was never repeated. The approach of war through 1939 was met by older people with resignation and by the young rather as though a holiday was on the horizon.

My cousin Stanley and I were then fifteen and our mothers had discovered that we could sit next year for the civil service examination at clerical grade which, if passed, would yield up a starting stipend of £1 13s a week with increments through life and a pension at the end. We did not argue. The civil service seemed all right. Stanley was reminded that he had an uncle who as a civil servant in Customs and Excise enjoyed an exciting life on the trail of smugglers. But whatever duties the examination might lead to, whether it would be intercepting kegs of grog or paying out the dole, we knew it was not going to come off. War was coming. It was pointless to try to follow little personal paths into the future, which now was wide open and unpredictable. Whatever will be will be. It was a heady year.

Stanley's family had moved into a large dark house on the top side of town commodious enough to take in lodgers as a means of eking out uncle Ben's wage. He had been doing badly and was reduced to smoking Erinmore Flake, a rank tobacco.

They were always shifting furniture from room to room. My cousin was called to assist, a big strong boy, bright at school but lacking in common sense. Lifting things with him, uncle Ben took his life in his hands. One day he nearly lost it. They had humped the base of a bed up two flights of stairs, Stanley backing at the upper end, uncle Ben hands above his head pushing below.

'Lower your end,' he commanded.

'Lower it?'

Uncle Ben was suffering under the weight. 'Come on, son. Drop it.'

'Drop it?'

'Yes, drop it.'

Stanley let go. The bed tobogganed down the two flights of stairs carrying uncle Ben caught in the midriff. He finished underneath it against the front door.

He rose slowly and felt his bruised limbs for breakages. Stanley apologised. Uncle Ben, a man of saintly patience,

merely said, 'That was downright foolish, son.' He inciner-
ated a pipeful of Erinmore Flake and sat on the bottom step
in a noxious cloud restoring his soul.

The first lodgers were two young probationary policemen.
They ate a lot, came and went at funny hours, but were
guaranteed to be of good behaviour. An officer had come in
advance and approved the lodgings. He would be back from
time to time to check on the lodgers' behaviour.

Leslie, a burly lad from Bolton, we saw little of. When
he wasn't on duty he was attending court, which policemen
had to do in their own time. He was a keen officer and
brought an incredible number of cases. It was as though he
sailed out of the police station and arrested everyone in sight.
We became chary of him. Everybody said he would soon
be a sergeant.

Joe Newton was a more spiritual and communicative
character. He came from Manchester, where he had acquired
a sophisticated style. He had a silver cigarette case and a
camel overcoat with a casually tied belt. He also had down
in Manchester a car and a dazzlingly beautiful girlfriend. He
lost both in a single day. She sacked him and he, lost in
misery, drove into a wall. He was anxious that this misfortune should not reach the ears of the Burnley police, who
were considering his application to join the road traffic
branch.

Joe never arrested anybody but trained hard for the day
when he might. He learned holds and throws in the police
gymnasium and came home and tried them out on us. He
would attempt to storm the attic steps with us at the top
thrusting chairs down at him in the role of villains resisting
arrest. We heaved and shoved and tried to twist each others'
limbs. He struggled to bring his handcuffs into play. When
he lost he claimed that in a serious tussle he could have
prevailed by felling us with his truncheon. He rewarded us
with a cigarette from his silver case and sat on the steps
keeping guard against auntie Abbie while we cooled down
and smoked.

One night uncle Ben came up to see what the noise was
about and sportingly demonstrated some holds. He was a
wiry little man with arms and wrists and fingers strength-

ened by years of woodwork. Once he had put on his grip
none of us could move. His success emboldened him to
demonstrate a spectacular throw. He hoisted Stanley into the
air, faltered and collapsed under his weight. A leg stuck out
at an ungainly angle.

We carried uncle Ben down the flights of stairs and laid
him out on the settee. Auntie Abbie and the two girls gathered round in tears. They skipped off and brought tea and
hot-water bottles. Joe Newton retrieved uncle Ben's pipe
from where it had fallen and charged it with Erinmore Flake.
Wincing at every move, uncle Ben sat up and took it between
his teeth. Joe applied a match and a rank cloud of smoke
rose.

The pipe, as always, healed uncle Ben's spirit. He exoner-
ated all present as we stood round and coughed. He described
the throw he had been attempting and specified in what
particular it had gone wrong. He had a week off work and
limped for several months. Auntie Abbie proscribed fighting
in the attic.

Just before Easter we bought a couple of old bicycles for a
pound each and rode far afield. There seemed to be few wet
Saturdays that summer. We set out at dawn while mist still
lay in the river valleys and returned at sunset. We rode in
the Yorkshire dales and out to the coast, to Morecambe and
to Blackpool, where we raced the streamlined trams up and
down the promenade. Two songs filled the summer,
'Bumps-a-Daisy' and 'The Lambeth Walk'. People danced
to them everywhere, on piers, at Sunday school field days,
on village greens. Hikers tramped about with floppy ruck-
sacks and baggy shorts. Little cars crammed with families
puttered about the hills. It seems, looking back, an especially
happy summer. People were carefree and nice to each other
as though they were all at a long garden party.

One evening we laid down our bikes and picked wild
flowers from the verge of a country lane near Settle. It ran
to a junction with a signpost and then rose between limestone
walls to the wooded horizon. Nobody came. A tethered
goat grazed at the crossroads and a horse looked over the
wall. The sky was streaked with collapsed cloud. We could

hear frogs. Gnats rose and fell. The flowers we picked were beginning to close.

Everybody knew that the summer was a passing season and that the time would not come again.

In July I sat for the School Certificate examination, to which our learning had been directed. Now it lost all its import. The future it might have guaranteed was not going to happen. The result would hardly matter.

I had studied in the spring evenings and gone towards dusk for a bike ride. The period of study became shorter and the ride longer. Some nights I knocked off and went to the park for a game of tennis. My mother became anxious. My grandmother responded in a positive way by sending in Horniman's tea coupons for a fountain pen with an enormous barrel which held such a volume of ink that you could write a whole day of exam papers without stopping to refuel. The gain was not only in time. The pen's broad nib and fast flow made for a bold hand on the page which must have carried some conviction with exam markers jaded at marking thousands of papers at a penny a time. We all passed at some level but the results, when they were published at the end of August, seemed of little significance even to our families.

A couple of days previously, early in the morning, I had called for my cousin to go for a cycle ride. Uncle Ben was reading the paper, which announced in big headlines the signature of the astounding pact between Stalin and Hitler. Uncle Ben had no doubt what it portended. 'Don't go sailing out into the countryside,' he cautioned. 'By this afternoon the sky'll be full of parachute troops. Bombs'll be falling everywhere, and crashed aircraft going off with thumping great explosions.'

He was always given to exaggeration. We rode off laughing. And indeed out on the fells the day passed as peacefully as any of the summer. But what he foresaw with his unrestrained imagination happened a week later in Poland and set the pattern for what would happen in many parts of the world in the next six years.

On Friday night the street lights were switched off. We walked through the dark town openly smoking. It was a warm night and people coming out of the cinemas lingered in the streets as though it were evening in a Mediterranean country. In one row several house doors were open and Territorial Army soldiers were getting their kit together on the table. It felt more like a holiday than the outbreak of war. Even now we did not really believe war would engulf us, although fighting had been going on in Poland all day. Some arrangement would be bodged up again.

'Up to the last,' Mr Chamberlain said, speaking on the wireless on Sunday morning, 'it would have been quite possible to have arranged a peaceful and honourable settlement, but Hitler would not have it.' We were therefore at war. My grandparents' friend, the redoubtable Mrs Corbett who was staying with us, rose and in a quavering voice led us in an embarrassed singing of the national anthem. That, it seemed, was her custom whenever a war broke out, now being practised for the third time.

I found uncle Ben and Stanley completing their air-raid precautions. They had placed a couple of boxes full of soil

outside the slit window of the cellar. Auntie Abbie and the
girls came out to see. 'That'll stand four direct hits,' uncle
Ben said. They went back inside.

'I was only saying that to reassure the ladies,' uncle Ben
confided to us. 'I don't want to exaggerate. If anything drops
within two miles we're all goners.'

The next night Arthur Askey in the radio programme
*Bandwagon* made his contribution to fanning the war along.
He sang the current hit, 'Run Rabbit', and in a reprise found
fresh words:

> Run Adolf, run Adolf, run, run, run,

We were astonished. The little man went on:

> We're going to knock the stuffing out of you,
> Old fatty Goering and Goebbels too.

The audience in the studio sat stunned, then a shock of
laughter ran through them and they applauded. We at home
had never heard anybody in authority mocked in public,
certainly not national leaders and certainly not by the BBC.
It brought home the reality of the war more powerfully than
the black-out or the Prime Minister's declaration or the news
of dive-bombers over Warsaw.

After that the war fizzled out for the winter. The greatest
number of British casualties it claimed were pedestrians
knocked down in the black-out by motorists who were for
bidden to use unmasked headlights.

Passing the School Certificate examination transformed us
from schoolboys to students. We wore sports coats instead
of blazers and lashed our books in a strap instead of carrying
slung satchels. We ceased to play football through the streets
on the way to school and instead waited on corners to walk
with girls going to the high school. Up to then they had all
looked like somebody's sister; now they blossomed into
young women, all different. Among our fellows also variety
broke out. Diverse personalities appeared. We began to
appreciate the virtues of quiet bespectacled boys who were

no good at games. We searched for style. We adopted and
changed mannerisms. We read the *Manchester Guardian* editorials and spoke like verbose parsons. We read John Gun-
ther, the popular staccato American reporter, and spoke like
machine guns. We made friends with older people, including
our teachers.

Our form master, the scholarly Walter Bennett, a small
grizzled man, saw the course of history as running through
centuries of fraud and farce towards the agreeable comedy
of liberal democracy. From arriving at the school as a young
man to take up the office of history master, he had devoted
himself year by year to the task of unearthing local history,
a life of patient scholarship which culminated in the publication on his retirement just after the war of his comprehen-
sive *History of Burnley*. It includes one of the most vivid and
detailed accounts of daily life in the Middle Ages. I suppose
that he alone could put a person and a life to the names of
the school founders that the bishop read out from the pulpit
at Founders' Day service. He saw woods and primitive ham-
lets where mill chimneys rose and canals and railways ran.

We read Shakespeare with Joe Chaplow, once the school
Victor Ludorum, a dear deaf man who was in charge of
school football teams. As referee he awarded no penalty kicks
to either side and never blew for fouls by our opponents. But
we won nearly all our home matches. We played up on
Walshaw moor, where visitors unaccustomed to the altitude
gasped for oxygen and stiffened in the cold. We also had the
strategy, taught by Mr Chaplow through the years, of playing the ball out to the top wing on a pitch which sloped
steeply from side to side. The sodden leather ball, lofted
back from on high into the goalmouth, came down like a
cannon ball and knocked unconscious anybody who
attempted to head it clear. Mr Chaplow in his gentle way
trained us to follow up like a pack of hounds.

Mr Key, the other English master, big and handsome
enough to be a Bengal Lancer, was in fact the squire of lands
in the Midlands which were said to be a severe drain on his
resources. He lived abstemiously in lodgings under the care
of a landlady who was reputed to regulate his comings and
goings and deny him the use of a wireless set. Literature

gave him great joy. He bounced and bubbled in his readings to the point of incoherence, head back, eyes closed, crooked finger in the air, enraptured. He threw himself into every part and assumed all the accents. He did a particularly powerful rendition of Joseph, the ancient yokel in *Wuthering Heights*. Mr Key was fired by a general distaste for peasants, having encountered some particularly boorish ones on his summer holiday in Poland, and he abominated the sanctimonious Joseph. He toiled to bring out all that was despicable in him. 'Master, master, he's stealin' t' lantern,' Mr Key would quaver, trying to disguise his own rich voice, to convey querulous old age, and to transform his county speech into old broad Yorkshire. It was a doomed performance that always drew a full house.

There was in those months a feeling of liberty and privilege. In the sixth form we should in any case have had periods during the day free from classes, but now because of the headmaster's continued determination to avoid presenting the assembled school as a target for bombers we had whole half days when we didn't have to turn up at all. We went up into the hills and froze with Mr Bennett, digging up the tiny stone implements of ancient man. We went up on Walshaw moor and re-dug the touchlines of our football pitches where the grass was too coarse for limewash. But these official outings soon fizzled out and we were left to our own devices. The athletes played ping-pong. The idle stayed in bed. The rich repaired to the pea booth, a cabin café that served nothing but peas and pop. We all went for bike rides. We were wholly free of the normal anxieties of sixth-formers about the future.

Part of our school time was idled away in discussion. Discussions were being fanned up everywhere. They became, along with knitting and making cigarette lighters in ordnance factories, a widespread wartime hobby. They cost nothing and were felt to be socially edifying. Indeed, staging discussions became a major industry within the army where intellectual agitators, operating under the cover of the Army Bureau of Current Affairs, circulated subversive pamphlets and had platoons wheeled into huts and ordered to discuss them intelligently on pain of being put on a charge.

At one time holding discussions threatened to become the army's principal activity.

In the winter of 1939, before the war had properly begun, we in school were led somewhat prematurely to cast our minds forward to the post-war settlement. We did not doubt that it would be dictated by Britain and France, nor that it would be liberal and socialistic. It would avoid repeating the injustices that had been done to Germany at Versailles. A democratic Germany, like Weimar but without night clubs and inflation, would be given its rightful place. And the Soviet Union, for so long excluded, would be invited into the concert of Europe.

On 30 November the Soviet Union took an unexpected step towards this end by invading Finland. We were shocked. Russia was the one inherently peaceful country on earth. It had no use for conquest. It was opposed to all aggression. Imperialism had no part in a socialist economy. True, the pact with Hitler had actually precipitated the war and the Soviets had occupied eastern Poland and three Baltic republics. But these could be seen as regrettable but necessary defensive measures taken when all attempts to make an alliance with the West had failed. The invasion of Finland should perhaps be seen in the same light. The frontier was dangerously close to Leningrad. The Finnish commander, Field Marshal Mannerheim, it was hinted, was really a fascist dictator. In any case it would all be over in a couple of weeks.

My cousin and I were now back in the same class for the first time since we left infants' school. We had enjoyed deep accord from early childhood. Now we spent most of the days and most of the evenings in each other's company, and we found a new pursuit, going for long country walks in the black-out. The landscape under frost and starlight assumed different contours as though it were an unfamiliar country. Our ideas bounded. We laughed at nothing. The odd person, coming upon us the other way, crept by in alarm.

The Finns held out. Our own war remained inert. Snow fell and lay long that winter.

Christmas was different from our usual family gathering.

Outsiders came, refugees from the silent war. A woman and her small daughter from London had stayed on next door with Annie Roberts when through the autumn other evacuees had drifted back home. They were welcome guests for Mrs Roberts. Her husband had gone off to serve in the balloon barrage and her father, a chapel caretaker, was often out in the evening. They all came round. The woman and her daughter wore their everyday clothes, which surprised us. We thought everybody had Sunday best to wear at Christmas.

But when the other guests arrived it was we who looked dowdy. They were rich German Jews, successors to the policemen as auntie Abbie's lodgers, a handsome ageing couple and their daughter who was approaching thirty. They were dressed as though they were going to the opera. They did a great deal of greeting and handshaking and rather overfaced my father and uncle Walter, who were shy men.

I never knew the family's name. Uncle Ben couldn't get his mouth round it, so for simplicity he called them by the only German name he knew, Hackenschmits, which was the name of a famous wrestler, actually Polish. On the head of the family, who was now handing round big cigars, he conferred the forenames Joe Bill. The daughter was shy, having suffered, as we learned later, the humiliation of being divorced by her German husband for racial reasons.

Uncle Walter and I went out to the fields to try a model aeroplane he had built for us. When we got outside he mentioned that he had been accepted by the RAF for pilot training. It was a great achievement. Their training establishment was very small at that stage and they accepted practically nobody. He lacked the required educational qualifications, having left school at fourteen to become a decorator, and he was twenty-six years old, an advanced age for entry. But he was already an apprentice aviator. He was in a club that flew, crashed and repaired home-made gliders, and he built on the kitchen table wireless sets that would pull in America. He was swotting up mathematics. The selection board was flexible enough to recognise a good candidate.

The model whose elastic we now wound was of a Flying Flea. It was a French aircraft, an early attempt at a Microlight, powered by a small car engine. It had a high mainplane and a low, very large tailplane with so short a fuselage that it looked like a staggered biplane. Uncle Walter and his gliding friends had made inquiries for components to build a full-size Flying Flea. They were fortunate to be baulked. The virtue of the plane was that it could be flown nearly as cheaply as running a motor bike, but it had the unfortunate drawback, it later transpired, of killing its pilots. Uncle Walter had painstakingly made the model accurate in every detail. It reared up and stalled and crashed.

On the way back in the gathering dark he told me about the training courses he would go on, how long they lasted and what he would learn at each stage. Up to then flying had seemed something one could dream of but never do, like bronco busting or sailing up the Amazon. His description of the courses brought it within reach. It would be the familiar process of classes and tests that everybody had done at school but with the added attraction of riding about the sky. I decided to apply as soon as I was old enough.

Over the Christmas high tea Joe Bill Hackenschmits told funny stories of life in the trenches. He had been an officer in the Kaiser's army. He compared dates and place names with my father and came convivially to the conclusion that there had been several occasions when they might have shot each other. He was a big bald expansive man. The lady from London said afterwards he looked more like a Prussian officer than a Jew. We could not comment; we had not previously seen either. Joe Bill certainly had a lingering pride in the Wehrmacht. He spoke with some admiration of the blitzkrieg against Poland, though he made it quite clear that his approval must be understood only in a technical sense. He generously concluded that it would be a different tale when the Germans came up against the English and the French.

He quite dominated the evening. Uncle Walter and my father never had much to say. Uncle Ben was outshone. My grandfather had made himself groggy with his Christmas cigar.

At one point auntie Abbie asked the guests if they would be offended by our singing carols. They said not in the least, but might they sing in German as they didn't know the English words? So we sang in two languages until, as we came to less familiar later verses, one by one we fell silent. Only Joe Bill knew all the words. He continued solo. He moved on from one carol to another. We listened and at the end applauded his performance. He stood and bowed.

The lady from London must have gone away with a curious impression of a northern Christmas.

Early in June 1940 the headmaster sent for me. He recalled that after a lecture on careers a year previously I had taken away a pamphlet about journalism. Was I still interested?

I mentioned an interview between us a few months back in which I had said my only interest was to join the air force.

He nodded. 'If you do want to do journalism there's now an opportunity. They're quite rare. They want a junior at the *Burnley Express*.'

I said nothing. The headmaster watched me, smiling in a friendly way, and without changing his expression delivered an ultimatum.

'As I see it, there are two courses open to you. You can stay here and work seriously for university entrance as and when that might be taken up, or you can go to the *Burnley Express* and lay the foundations for a career in journalism. What you can't do is to remain at school and continue to freewheel along until such time as you feel moved to fulfil your destiny in the air.'

Put that way, the *Burnley Express* seemed the best option.

'Be at the editor's office at six.'

The *Express* office was on a side street near the town centre. It looked poky and in need of paint. It was silent at the hour of Friday when everybody had gone home for tea before returning for the evening work of setting and printing. The only counter clerk on duty led me to the editor's office up a small carpeted staircase overlooked by photographs of generations of stern whiskery editors. I braced myself to encounter their successor.

Ted Parkinson, a young thirty-five, rose in welcome. His desk was covered with papers and proofs which had been banked up to make a space for his typewriter. He unrolled my school certificate and glanced at it. He carefully put aside school magazines containing articles of mine, as though to read them later. He asked me some questions which I responded to easily. It was like talking to somebody I had known for years.

The job, he explained, had once been an indentured post, of which the holder would receive training by legal agreement, but all that remained of that was the nominal salary of 11s 9d a week. The incumbent might expect to do some reporting but his job, at least initially, was really office work. He took down the black-out blinds in the morning and put them up at night, answered the telephone, returned photographs to lenders, filed blocks and cuttings in the fireproof records room and typed the editor's letters, to which end he would need to join the typing class at night school.

We both permitted ourselves a smile at the meniality of the job and the implied descent from the cultivated leisure of the sixth form. Knowing only the slow procedures of the educational establishment, I supposed other candidates would be interviewed over several weeks and the outcome communicated in a few months' time. I decided I would anticipate that by writing a pleasant letter withdrawing my application.

'Well, that's it,' he said. 'Do you want the job?'

'Yes.'

'Come in at nine o'clock on Monday.'

He handed me back my school certificate and the magazines unread. I hesitated on the way out to say I might not stay there long.

'In this profession,' he said, 'nobody knows how long he'll stay anywhere.'

As I went back down the carpeted stairs the electric motors started up and the linotype machines on the top floor began to bang and rumble.

My parents were very good about the 11s 9d, which was a poor contribution after five years at the grammar school, only a third of what was paid by the job my mother had picked out for me in the civil service. My father said that if that was what I wanted to do, the money didn't matter.

I could not bring myself to confess that I had accepted the job against common sense and better judgment simply because on brief acquaintance I took to the editor. Instinct served me well. Ted Parkinson was the best guide and teacher I ever had. The job led to an interesting life.

The reporters' desks, half a dozen of them, were ranged along a wall and overlooked by three big windows. Ted's small office was at the end of the room through a partition in which was set a hatch where the reporters dropped their copy into a wire basket. Ted opened a small door on his side and drew the copy through, sub-edited it and sent it up to the composing-room in a small hoist at the side of the hatch. The hatch and hoist served the purpose of an internal telephone system. Conversations, being shouted, tended to be briefer and franker than they might have been over a wire. Tom Bracewell, the printer, up aloft in the composing-room, made known his displeasure by unaddressed chunnering which grumbled through the system. He was a mild man, a church organist on Sundays, with spectacles and a strand brilliantined across his pate. He excused any excess of language by adding 'to use vulgar parlance' as though he had merely been quoting somebody else.

The most friendly of the reporters was Edgar Hartley, a bit of a performer who welcomed a new audience. He was athletic and in his early thirties, a man about town. He had a gold tooth, a gold ring and suede shoes and wore dark shirts with light jackets in a style seldom seen except aboard liners in screen romances. At a time of shortage he obtained a steady supply of cigarettes from under the counter. He was quick with winks and sharp cracks spoken quietly out of the side of his mouth and usually aimed at the management or at the local establishment of which the paper was a pillar. As sports editor he ran a semi-independent enterprise, came and went in his own time and was largely exempted from routine reporting duties. His page was less impersonal than the rest of the paper and he was allowed to sign himself Sportsman, which was the nearest anybody came to a by-line.

The loathed office of Uncle Tim, conductor of the Children's Corner, was passed round the room, and everybody was supposed to contribute to Over the Teacups, a ladies' column signed Elizabeth Ann. Clifford Harman, the chief reporter, scowling through his cigarette smoke, rewrote most of the paragraphs in what was respected as a light, gossipy and feminine style. It was to be several years yet before they thought of hiring an actual woman, but Edgar Hartley's wife got around in social circles, and he always weighed in with a few Elizabeth Ann paragraphs. He also excelled himself, again outside his own sporting sphere, by obtaining early intelligence of changes in the meat ration from his brother, who was president of the butchers' association. It was the only scoop we enjoyed.

We were in fact not in the scoops business. We were, like all local newspapers then, a paper of record, and of that kind of record that nobody would ever be likely to consult. Court cases of every sort we reported at length, inquests, meetings, committees, and once a month the council, covered by a shock group of several reporters including Edgar in his dark blue shirt.

It was made clear that I would not be permitted to join this mainstream of activity until I could write verbatim shorthand and also until I acquired the habit of accuracy. In taking down messages on the telephone I misspelled some names and got some details wrong – not enough, I thought, to worry about. But it worried Clifford Harman, a shy taciturn man in his mid-thirties. He approached holding the offending message. His dark eyes were full of concern and he stammered at the gravity of it. Evidently I was not sufficiently abashed. He reported the offence to Ted Parkinson, who appeared at the hatch and called me into his room.

'Accuracy is essential.'

'Yes.'

'Spell names back. Don't guess. How many ways are there of spelling Smith?'

'Several.'

'Those men through there have made fewer mistakes in their life than you've made in a week.'

He patted the file of *Burnley Express*es. 'We should be able to go through every issue there and every one in the records room going back into the last century without finding a single error.'

He allowed time for it to sink in. 'A newspaper in which the facts are wrong is no good. No other virtue compensates for inaccuracy.'

It was my bike that got me started. One Monday morning to keep me occupied Clifford Harman gave me a list of church calls to try. Before the war, when they had a big paper and a large staff, several reporters spent Monday morning doing the round of vicarages and manses to pick up paragraphs on the weekend's events. Clifford told me to see what I could do on the telephone. I got nothing. There was only one telephone in the room, housed in a glass kiosk that stank of cigarette ends, and I had to give way to other reporters. Most of the parsons were not on the telephone anyway. The rest were too surprised at the call out of the blue to respond.

I already knew the telephone was a poor way of making inquiries. It was my duty in the early morning to telephone police, fire and ambulance. I seldom got anything, although often there had been happenings which officers remembered when reporters called personally at the station during the day. I asked Clifford if I could try cycling round the parsons. He looked unhappy. My duties in the ofice, he said, were 'paramount'. But he let me take a couple of hours and from this start, with petrol rationed and bus services infrequent, my mounted sorties became established as the only arm of the *Burnley Express* capable of reaching outlying parts at short notice.

From the moment of appointment I had given much thought to the question of image. I fancied a trilby hat like reporters on the screen who snarled into the telephone: 'Hold the front page. Getta load o' this.' But my head was the wrong shape; hats blew off. Then I thought of getting a man-about-town ensemble like Edgar's with suede shoes and a light jacket. But clothes were rationed and I couldn't very well confront him in the office looking like a clone. The bike, a racing model, offered a quite different sort of image:

speed, thrust, panache, the up-to-the-minute virtues we
reluctantly admired in the Panzers.

I rattled through the cobbled streets, banged on doors,
asked rapid questions and sped away. At one manse I rapped
with such éclat that the old parson was moved to reproach.
'Surely,' he protested, looking round at the smouldering
knocker, 'Surely.'

The next week he tried to anticipate me, moving out of
his study into the hall the moment he caught sight of me
leaping from the saddle. He did not quite make it. He had
just reached the door and suffered the full volume of the
hammering. He wrote in complaint to the editor. 'Cultivate
a more circumspect approach,' Ted Parkinson counselled.

But my mechanised operation had come to stay. Most of
the news tips I rode out to investigate yielded little – I would
be shown a corpse and given a tearful biography – but I did
let on a few good stories, and when Harold Hutchinson was
called up for the army Clifford gave me charge of the district
of Padiham which he had covered. It did not warrant a full-

time reporter. I attended the police court every fortnight, the council once a month and the Whit Monday processions once a year, but my main job was to compile the column of Padiham paragraphs, for which I cycled down on each of the two press days, Tuesday and Friday. It was my ambition, which I never quite realised, to fill a whole column from top to bottom. In the composing-room, where late copy had to be taken up to Ted Parkinson who was making up the pages, I became a marked man for my voluminous trivia. 'What the hell is it now?' Tom Bracewell the printer would ask. 'Another chip-pan fire? Somebody else slipped off t' flag edge?'

Padiham was an easy beat for the *Burnley Express*. Half the work was done for the reporter by Major Hargreaves, Labour councillor, magistrate, secretary of the Weavers' Union, but not actually a major; that was not his rank but his Christian name. He was approaching seventy, only slightly more than five feet high and nearly as broad, with a round head like a cannon ball, steel spectacles and prickly white hair and moustache. He moved slowly, smoked a short pipe and spat into a brass spittoon. His desk was a big table in the meeting-room of the Weavers' Institute. Everybody came to see him at some time, not only weavers, but anybody at all who wanted advice or something signed. They waited on the bench seats round the room while he carried on with his observations and anecdotes. He was not to be rushed. He was quite free of anxiety. I never saw him stumped.

Major Hargreaves knew of everything that happened in Padiham. The biography of the whole town was in his memory or his wooden filing cabinet. He usually had half a dozen news items but he brought them out in his own good time. I waited with the supplicants and listened to his slow orations, delivered in a broad accent, full of jokes from the mills and quotations from classic works of political philosophy, Greek and Latin, English, German and American. He was an erudite man.

I soon saw how much better the news items he provided were than those I collected directly. There was always some colour. Even if it were only the obituary of an ordinary working life he would think of some incident that made it warmer and more interesting. I saw that in haring round and going for volume I was missing facts that would have given some life to my stories.

The only other person I lingered with was Annie Burney, the secretary in the Conservative office, a slight dark woman approaching thirty who, now that party politics were suspended, had little to do. The agent, who was based in Clitheroe, and the MP hardly ever came. Annie was shy and lame like my predecessor on the territory, Harold Hutchinson. It had been a bond between them. She made tea and they smoked one of her scented cigarettes together and exchanged supportive conversation. I inherited this graceful social occasion along with the news beat.

But now, determined to give myself more time on stories, I went through the list of regular calls and struck off everybody, apart from Annie, who had not come up with anything worth while. Among the casualties was a headmaster who compiled the total of national savings invested in Padiham for each week a fortnight in arrears. Ted Parkinson asked what had happened to the item. I said I had dropped it; I didn't think it interesting.

'It may not be interesting,' he said, 'but it's our patriotic duty to publish it.'

One night at some sort of church event I was introduced to a merchant seaman who had been torpedoed, spent twenty-six days in an open boat, been picked up and then torpedoed again. It was misfortune, as he said himself, on the Laurel and Hardy scale. It made the back page lead. Ted Parkinson was pleased. It occurred to me that everybody on leave must have some sort of story to tell. I made an effort to dig out a few, then, once we got going, readers came down to the office or wrote in to offer stories.

I learned how to interview people. I always had to overcome some slight inner resistance to pick up a telephone or knock on a door (and still do) but for an interview at length this shyness was an asset. People do not blossom in response to a series of questions. This is of course the method for a broadcast interview where the performance has to be kept going like a ping-pong match, but what emerges seldom has much surprise and variety because the agenda is being imposed by the regular interviewer. Listening rather than questioning is what makes people talk. They will stop and then, unprompted, go on again to fill a silence. Often they say unpredictable things and go off in unexpected directions quite outside the scope of any question an interviewer might have thought of.

I stumbled on the method, if it can be called that, by accident, partly because of diffidence but also because I could not write fast enough in my mixture of longhand and short-hand to keep pace. I would nod and scribble away. Almost invariably the person would start up again. I got through many interviews almost without asking questions. Through the years I have discovered a further bonus to this method. The people to whom one mutely listens don't, as might be supposed, think one dumb but, on the contrary, perceptive and understanding. It is a rare pleasure to be permitted to talk about oneself at length without interruption. Most people respond volubly.

On Wednesday and Saturday mornings when the paper was published I was alone in the office, tidying up and returning borrowed photographs, until the reporters came in towards noon. Ted Parkinson would arrive at his office in mid-morning and go through the paper alone sitting at his desk. Everybody worked hard but Ted was probably the only person in the building who deeply cared about the paper. It had been locally owned but now belonged to a chain, Provincial Newspapers, based in London. Nobody ever came down and I doubt if they would have known Ted's name without consulting a list. What he could do was severely limited by finance and established practice. Nevertheless he thought of it as his paper.

He would call me in and again turn through the pages, putting into words his thoughts about the stories and make-up. He sometimes praised members of staff but never anything he had done himself. His editorials made him wince. 'On the one hand and on the other hand,' he would comment, and indeed that was what they amounted to.

A local paper has to watch its step in making comments.

It is chary of antagonising people who are indispensable sources of information, and there was a wartime political truce which further restrained comment. I think only the weight of tradition prevented Ted from abolishing the column. Leader-writing even without the restraints was really not his forte. Essentially he was a news man, better at telling it as it is than at proposing how it ought to be. He went on to make a distinguished career in BBC news.

That was in the future. Now on publication mornings he turned his talents to assessing the remuneration due to correspondents in the surrounding villages who contributed news paragraphs to a section of district news led by my Padiham column. Correspondents tended to hand the job on to their pals and heirs. Nobody knew on what basis any of them had been appointed. Their copy arrived by post on all sorts of paper. Some wrote with a poker on the back of pieces of wallpaper, others on scented pages with scalloped edges in the tiny precise script of wife-poisoners.

Ted battled with all of them. They were paid by the column inch. Their aim was to blow out the items, Ted's to chop them down. He had no time to rewrite but he was adept with his thick pencil at subbing down a prolix work to sharp masculine sentences, cryptic, almost cablese, in their brevity.

On publication mornings he got out his ruler and assessed the result of the battle, measuring up all the contributions and marking on the paper in black crayon what was to be paid. The amounts were niggardly. Many correspondents were rewarded with sixpence or ninepence, barely enough to cover the stamp and the wallpaper. They retaliated by adding to reports of events long lists of participants, which put Ted in a bit of a quandary. We liked names. Every name in the paper, even of people charged with burglary, guaranteed half a dozen copies sold. But lists of names spoiled the look of the page, there was not really space for them, and Ted suspected some of the correspondents of swelling the number by including people who were removed, dead or entirely fictitious.

Our conversations in the leisure of Wednesday and Saturday mornings often turned into brief tutorials. Ted was a

good teacher because, like the best journalists and broad-
casters, he remained a student all his career. He was ready
to question anything. It was easy to discuss with him errors
and uncertainties one might have concealed from another
boss. He encouraged me in other ways, not least by finding
space for my special efforts in his slim paper (four pages on
Wednesdays, six on Saturdays). He ran for a few weeks a
comic column I wrote, which distressed Clifford Harman
and my father; he ran a series I wrote of Major Hargreaves'
memories of his Victorian childhood; and he usually managed to squeeze in something of the stories of variable quality
I hunted out in my own time.

We all put in a long working week, five and a half days,
plus two press nights, and there were some engagements on
other evenings and at weekends. As a concession to my
youth I was released at nine o'clock on press nights. Clifford
tried to keep me clear on the other week nights to go to
night school and on Saturday afternoons to play football.
Any evening event had to be written up that night, however
late. I had to be in the office at nine o'clock in the morning
and everybody else at nine-thirty all ready to go.

I enjoyed press nights. I was allowed to hang about in the
composing-room, an exciting, urgent place, hot from the
lead that simmered in the tanks of linotype machines and
noisy with the clank and rattle of their mechanical parts. The
copy came banging up the hoist and was fired across the
room on overhead wires. The linotype operators, sitting
erect, stroked the keyboard like tranquil organists. Everybody else looked tense. Ted and Clifford crouched over
the pages of type at the opposite side of the stone to the
compositors. Damp page proofs were pulled, acrid with the
smell of printers' ink. People smiled in a feeling of mounting
achievement. The room had a wonder quite beyond the scale
of our modest prosaic production.

On other nights in winter I went to shorthand and typing
classes. There were only two other boys for shorthand and
I was the only one for typing, which meant that I had the
pleasure of walking home under the stars in an ever-changing
variety of company without needing to go too far out of my
way. On some nights the sky to the south glowed red from

the incendiary bombs dropped on Manchester, and spent shrapnel rattled on the slates.

Frank Brierley protested against our long hours. Approaching seventy, he did not enjoy the boons of being let off to play football and to type with the girls, and he tried to insist upon union hours. He had been for many years a courts reporter in London for the Press Association and came back from retirement when Edgar Hartley joined the air force a few months after my arrival. Frank was bald and ashen, suffering from a stomach ulcer which caused him to sit doubled over at his desk writing his copy. He was a socialist. He claimed to have been a friend of Shaw and Wells and to have got a piece of Philip Snowden blown into his eye at the scattering of the Labour leader's ashes. He had been a long-time campaigner for the National Union of Journalists. When Clifford gave him a Sunday assignment he demanded a half-day off in compensation, which was his right under union agreement. Clifford was reduced to looking unhappy and stuttering, as he was by any problem, but behind this shaky front he was unshiftable. He was moreover father of the union chapel, which under his influence had established a firm tradition of never meeting. Frank did get one grudging half-day off but that was the end of it. He told me that at eleven and ninepence I was being exploited.

No doubt that was true and if I had been of a later generation, reared in rights and resentment, I might have taken it to heart. But it was only a temporary job, a stop-gap, and it was enjoyable. In the event, being let loose on all sorts of engagements because of lack of trained staff, I gained quite a lot of experience in a short time. When several years later I left the air force I had no trouble in getting a job in journalism.

I learned things of wider application. One day there was a discussion in the office about how journalism ought to be regarded. Clifford thought it was a profession. Frank said it was a trade and the sooner journalists recognised themselves as ordinary workers the sooner they'd win tolerable conditions. Billy Bury, another old reporter, liked the term craft, though he agreed it smacked of wrought-iron work and basketry. I thought, though I didn't say, that essentially it was a game. We produced the paper twice a week. Some were good editions and some bad. We won some and we lost some. Whether we had shining faces or mud in our eye, next morning was a fresh start. We kicked off again. I have regarded every job I have done since in the same way, as a game. You play your hardest, then as soon as the edition has been printed or the programme transmitted you forget it. What was once said of the Hapsburg empire applies to journalism and broadcasting: things are desperate but not serious. Games players last longer.

I also learned that the essence of professional production is speed and volume. There is a constant battle against time and mounting costs, and on most projects one must call it a day when they could still be improved by more work. Perfectionism leads to diminishing returns. It is the right spirit in which to set out, but the point comes to give it the chop. Somebody said that a poem is never finished but only abandoned. That is true of lowlier forms of endeavour.

I learned that success is not necessarily related to effort. Some trivia which one has knocked off can go down well, while a big work on which one has toiled passes unnoticed. Things done quickly may be rough but often gain energy and sparkle from the speed of their generation.

I gained some measure of the extent and limits of my own abilities. I also learned that different competent judges may make quite different assessments of one. Ted thought quite well of me; Clifford didn't.

If anybody was exploited it was Clifford. Ted was also overworked but he had the compensation of the editor's status. The social events he had to attend and the war-support committes he had to sit on, though crowding his diary, gave him a break from the office.

Clifford had no such status. When they went to Rotary together Ted joined the members, Clifford sat below the salt with his notebook and pencil. He came into the office through the works entrance. He did not even have a tele-phone on his desk.

His job as chief reporter encompassed three functions. He did the main weight of the reporting, he worked as news

editor organising the coverage, and on press nights he acted
as a sub-editor in making up the pages, all this with a staff
shrunken in size and composed largely of dilutees. Several
of his young trained reporters had gone off early into the
abounding number of information jobs the war created, then
within a few months of my arrival Clifford lost his two
remaining regular staff, Edgar Hartley and Harold Hutchinson. Harold was a quiet, humorous pessimist who brightened the office with lugubrious jokes. At twenty-four he
had just completed his training. His call-up to the Army Pay
Corps was an unexpected blow because it had been assumed
that his lifelong lameness would exempt him from service.

Clifford was left with me, old Frank Brierley and Gerry
Bradley, a likeable open-faced man around thirty, whose
withered hand kept him out of the army. He was a photogra-
pher and filled in as a general reporter and sports editor now
the picture pages had gone. Frank was too ill to do much
except report the courts.

The only other reporter, the tubby and ageing Billy Bury,
was permanently detached to cover the area of Nelson and
Colne and lived out on his territory. He had survived a
shaky start. As a boy in the days when the *Burnley Express*
reported some world events he had received over the office
telephone news of the relief of Mafeking in South Africa
and, forgetting his duty, had danced out into the street and
told the town. He was lifted shoulder high and plied with
beer. The town centre filled with cheering crowds. The news,
hounds of the *Burnley Express*, standing by for the tidings
and holding up printing until late at night, were the last to
hear.

Billy was given the opportunity to redeem himself by
monitoring the last moments of a bigwig who was expiring
in his mansion some way out in the country. The editor was
determined that if the gentleman was gleaned on a press day
the *Burnley Express* should be the first with the news. The
pages containing the death notice, obituary and appreciations
were held ready until 3 a.m. while Billy Bury trudged out
to the mansion. Few private houses had a telephone in those
Edwardian days.

The old man hung on. Twice a week through the winter

weather Billy made his nocturnal expedition. On better nights he rode a horse. A footman received him at the trades- man's entrance, and their exchange followed a decorous for- mula. Billy would inquire about the master's health. The footman would reply that it still gave cause for concern. Bill then returned to the office and reported, 'He still hasn't snuffed it.' The paper went to press without the prepared pages.

Eventually the old man died only five minutes after Billy had left. When Billy reported, 'He still hasn't snuffed it,' he had. He was cooling at the very moment when the pages announcing his death were again put aside. The *Burnley Express*, not printing again for three days, was beaten to the news by the two local evening papers and all the nationals. It was not Billy's fault, but the memory of Mafeking was still fresh and one of that gallery of whiskery editors whose photographs overhung the front stairs kept him under a disapproving eye. He only redeemed himself by rising in the Great War to be a sergeant-major in charge of a huge office employing a hundred military clerks.

Now he had a lifetime's experience as a reporter but enough on his plate with his own area. Clifford at head office had only one trained reporter to call on and that was himself. He was permanently worried about how to cover everything and ever anxious about the errors which our inexperience let through. He took more and more of the reporting upon himself. He had hardly any time off and came to regard holidays, especially his own, as a worrying nuisance.

There were many like Clifford who kept civilian indus- tries, large and small, running through the war. Most were middle-aged and some, like him, not in perfect health; he had been turned down for medical reasons by the army. They lived on rationed food and wore shabby clothes, their pay remained at 1930s levels, the shops were empty. They slogged on long after they were weary, doing their own job and running around to make good the mistakes of half- trained staffs. Few got the recognition they deserved.

Clifford in fact was rewarded. He was promoted editor when Ted left for the BBC. Sad to say, he did not have a long life.

\* \* \*

Gerard Mulholland was imported direct from Ireland as an answer to Clifford's trained manpower problem. His reputation came before him. He was a widely experienced journalist, about forty years old and currently a sub-editor on the *Irish Independent* in Dublin. He came our way only by the good fortune that his wife haled from Lancashire and wished to return. Ted at first meeting found him charming and cultured.

Indeed he was. The tone of the office improved from the moment of his arrival. He was tall with steel spectacles, hairy ears and wavy hair and, though he spoke in a snuffling brogue as though he had a permanent cold, he made good jokes and laughed generously at other people's. He sat at the desk in front of Clifford's, his long legs out sideways. Both of them were chain smokers. At times they were scarcely visible through the haze.

Gerry did not type but wrote beautiful pages with a fountain-pen. From time to time he would raise unseeing eyes, searching for phrases which he tried out under his breath. But for the main part he wrote fast and fluently. He covered sheet after sheet. But there was a problem for the paper. What he wrote was less of a factual report as we understood it and more of a literary essay.

There was also another problem. He filled the office with priests. Gerry Bradley was our resident Roman Catholic, the accredited correspondent of the *Universe* and the *Catholic Herald*. But Gerry Mulholland somehow eased him out of the territory and, instead of the brief paragraphs usually given to church events, we got rolling essays a third of a column long full of Catholic phrases. Ted indulgently let the essays pass, and thus at an early stage lost the battle to curb Gerry's prolixity. Clifford said with his unhappy smile that he was very devout.

Gerry's zeal did not stop at church reports. He was an excellent talker, full of anecdotes, but quite suddenly, provoked by some phrase in the conversation, his face would fall solemn and he would set about proselytisation. He had me marked. We came from cultural extremes far wider apart in the narrow world of the 'thirties than any could be now. I had been reared in the aridity of industrial Nonconformity,

Gerry in the fancy and superstition of bog-Irish Catholicism. He regarded me as a ripe case. One day he spotted a book on Marx on my desk.

'What have we here?' he snuffled. 'Oh dear, oh dear, Donald. That's terrible stuff, terrible. Won't hold water at all.'

I asked him if he had read Marx.

'Oh no, God forbid. Not a word of truth in it. Not authenticated at all. Oh dear, oh dear.'

He was fond of Catholic anthologies and would read out extracts to me in the office and sometimes as we walked home together – passages from Belloc, Baring and Chesterton. He read with the book held high in an excited, chuckling, adenoidal voice. He was vibrant with pleasure and quite oblivious of people on the pavement dodging out of his way. 'Oh, good things,' he would say. 'Pearls of wisdom.' He would pass on in a lowered confidential voice to contemporary miracles, ('Now that is a fact, authenticated by the *Irish Independent* and boards of scholars'), and thence naturally and without a change of gear to incivilities committed by the Black and Tans.

He trained the priests to come into the office through the works door. Nobody else did that except employees. When people came to see us we would talk to them across the counter of the general office downstairs. Father Veale made a small drama of his entrance, standing framed in the open door until Gerry looked up and bounded over, all solicitude.

'Father, Father. Come in, Father. You know Clifford Harman?'

Clifford put on his happier smile.

'Course I know Clifford. How's Clifford now?'

Father Veale was Irish, around fifty, fat and with cold grey eyes that were at odds with the warmth of his manner. He wore a Holy Joe hat and told coarse tales.

' "I'm a member of the board," says he. "Paul," says I, "the only board you're fit to sit on is one with a hole in it." '

'Ho ho ho, Father, Father, Father. Ho, Father. One with a hole. Ho ho ho. Father, Father, Father.'

Father Veale spotted me. 'And is this a good lad, now?'

'Good lad, Father. Oh a good lad, Father, Father.'

'And teetotal?'

'Ho ho, teetotal, Father. Never touches a drop. Father, Father.'

'Did you hear Lenihan had gone?'

'Lenihan, is it, Father? What age was he?'

'No great age at all.'

They would sit, two big men huddled at Gerry's desk, mumbling smoke, proposing phrases for a eulogy.

Gerry had been an occasional drama critic for the *Irish Independent*. There was no corresponding post at the *Burnley Express*, nor had there ever been, but, just as unasked he had increased the area and imposed an esoteric style for Catholic church reporting, so he now established a bridgehead for drama criticism. He attended in his own time amateur dramatic performances, starting with those at Catholic churches, then broadening to take in any local drama. His first brief notices became longer, half a column, a whole column, two columns of fluent prose, rolling and sparkling like the tide, full of quotations and rhetorical questions, mesmerising in its attack, unlike anything ever seen in the *Burnley Express* before and, alas, all but incomprehensible.

That was no defect in the eyes of the players. The benevolence and warmth and length of it flattered them. They were, if anything, charmed by being described in erudite passages they could not quite understand. They bought many copies of the paper. Gerry started to sign his articles with the initials G.J., which Ted must have let pass, then boldly broke cover with the full pseudonym, Gabriel Joseph, the name, he informed us, of a nun who taught him, adopted when he first set out on his career as a drama critic.

It was only too apparent that Gerry was not and would never be the work-a-day news reporter Clifford so badly needed and briefly hoped he had got. And there was worse to come. The Old Vic and Sadlers Wells came and holed up in Burnley for the duration of the war. Gerry threatened to fill the whole paper with their doings. He spent hours at the theatre and they began at his invitation to invade our office, artistes of one sort and another mingling with the priests and filling the place with excited conversation, smoke and laughter. This happened after my time. I believe that Edgar Hartley on leave came upon the salon in full voice and fled across the street to take refuge in the bar of the Bull.

Early one Wednesday morning when I was alone in the office a knock came to the inner door. A small man with a bony face and penetrating grey eyes stood there.

'Mr Preston from the Co-op. Come to put the clock on the beat.'

He smiled a pleasant smile, exposing big teeth. His hat brim was turned up all the way round. He carried an old attaché case.

I moved a chair so he could climb up to the clock on the end wall.

'Am I obliged to remove my hat?' he asked.

I said not.

'Can I continue to smoke my pipe?'

I said he could.

He climbed up and tinkered with the clock, shifting its angle on the wall by small degrees and listening intently. I stopped what I was doing to be quiet. He stepped down, stood back and listened with eyes closed.

'It's on the beat,' he said.

I thanked him.

'Accurate,' he added, 'within the limited measuring capacity of the instrument.'

I nodded.

'Time,' he said, 'will do away with all things, good, bad and indifferent.'

He spoke slowly, relishing the thought.

'Nothing endures. Empires perish, cities crumble, the ice and the desert return. Wealth moulders to dust, the mighty of the earth sink into oblivion, intelligence passes, that brief flicker of matter made conscious, all returns to the void.'

He glowed with pleasure. I offered him a chair. He chose to remain standing under the clock. The present war, he said, might well be part of the last throes of capitalism but we should not underestimate how long the system might endure. It might still remain for our lifetime or indeed for a thousand years – 'a mere moment in historic time'.

Time informed all his thoughts. He apologised for having
taken up mine. I said I had enjoyed listening to his discourse.
He said he had enjoyed delivering it. 'We might resume if
you're agreeable,' he suggested, 'if our paths should cross
again.'

As we worked only round the corner from each other our
paths did cross and he did resume. After the first few meetings he dispensed with any greeting but, turning sideways
to the flow of pedestrians, plunged straight into his address,
always beginning by placing his ideas in time. 'I had a good
thought last Wednesday at ten past two in the afternoon,'
he would say and launch himself happily into the cosmos
and with pity and contempt into the affairs of men and the
puny senseless war which would shrug a few more million
of them into eternity. He made no distinction between the
combatants. Churchill he sneered at rather more than Hitler.
All wars in this phase of history were imperialist wars, whatever their additional accidental characteristics.

'Time is always of the essence,' he said. 'If I could find
the time I'd like to have a proper crack at undermining the
war effort.'

He regretted that he wasn't better placed to exert a wider
influence. The Co-op clock shop only employed half a dozen
people. 'If I was in a big factory, somewhere like Metro-
Vickers down at Trafford Park, I might well be able to seize
the opportunity to address thousands in their dinner break.
I think if I got into my stride I could work up a mob.'

My cousin and I encountered him out walking on Crown
Point moors. He was on particularly good form, enjoying
the doubled audience and an easy dummy to knock about in
the form of a National Day of Prayer just announced. 'The
jackboots beneath the surplice,' he sneered. 'The flame-
thrower behind the cross.' He had even more contempt for
God than for Churchill, 'the feeble ghost that man creates
to protect his doomed universe from the oblivion of Time.'

One Saturday morning Clifford marked me down in the
diary to cover a meeting next day of the People's Convention.

'We don't want much. Quarter of a column at the outside.'
If it had been a meeting of which he wanted a proper

report, two columns with verbatim quotations such as might
be warranted by the respectable political parties, he wouldn't
be sending me. The only reason he was doing anything at
all on the People's Convention was the implicit obligation
to give some news coverage to any organisation which took
advertising space in the paper.

The People's Convention was a front organisation of the
Communist party created to unite pacifists and pinkos in
opposition to the war (later disbanded when Russia was
attacked). It attracted the usual retinue of eccentric actors,
rogue clergymen and disaffected academics but also a large
number of consistently-minded people who had supported
the peace movements through the 'thirties and still saw no
gain in war. Most of them were getting on in years.

The convention, however, aimed to reach out beyond
them to much larger numbers who would not be asked to
oppose the war, and still less to embrace communism, but
to give their support on a single issue about which they were
already agitated. It was the usual tactic for rallying a 'broad
cross-section'. The chosen issue, the inadequacy of air-raid
shelters, was a good one. The government could not divert
any further weight of resources from the war effort to civil
defence, and even if it did they would never be enough. The
fact that continuing casualties would have to be accepted
could not be publicly argued without danger of misrepresen-
tation. Deaths from the air almost every night kept the
campaign fresh and rolling.

People came by bus and train to the meeting and the Co-
op hall was full. The afternoon began in a lively knockabout
manner with a blowsy woman on the platform jibing at an
elegant detective who had sidled in with his notebook at the
back. The main speaker was a professor of some sort in
ginger tweeds, a big bald man with a squeaky voice. He
piped on about air-raid shelters. The audience sat bored.
Only one bomb had been dropped in the vicinity of Burnley,
on a dummy airfield up on the moors. Nobody had spent
even half an hour in an air-raid shelter. The professor may
well have raised storms of indignation in London. All he got
for his pains in Burnley was polite applause.

What most of the audience really craved for was the good

old anti-war story, munition barons, scheming imperialists, stupid generals, 60,000 dead on the first day. But that had far too narrow an appeal for the convention, quite apart from the danger of sailing near to a breach of the Defence Regulations for which the elegant detective had come to watch. Air-raid shelters was the line. That was the line in London and, since the party had only one line, it was the line everywhere else as well. But similar sources of dissatisfaction could be touched upon. A 'war worker' was produced to carp about the canteen and the washrooms.

Questions were invited. People planted in the audience asked something suitable. Old men rose and launched into quavering speeches. They were stopped by the chairman. The persistent were beaten into silence by his bell. He tried to close the meeting. But a man at the back had been trying to speak and those round him set up a call for him to be heard. The chairman relcutantly agreed. Mr Preston removed his pipe and commenced his dissertation.

I had not at first recognised him, seeing him for the first time without his hat, but there was no mistaking the slow tones, the scorn and the smiling reason. He brought balm to the souls of old campaigners parched by the aridities of the afternoon. He sailed by way of overture through the decay of capitalism, the futility of imperialist war, the fraudulent pretension of monarchy, and the hypocrisy of religion. The old-timers applauded. The chairman banged the bell and instructed him not to make a speech but to put a question.

'I am putting a question,' Mr Preston replied, 'but I must place it in its relevant historic context.'

'People are dying in rotten air-raid shelters,' somebody on the platform said. 'We're concerned with action, not historical theory.'

Part of the audience shouted agreement.

'But what action and to what end?' Mr Preston asked. 'We learn from Marx that capitalism will perish from its inner contradictions through time and irrespective of the wishes and actions of men, which would seem to put all action under a cloud of being redundant if not heretical.

However, there is a yearning to mould his own environment deeply implanted in the soul of man –'

The chairman banged on the bell. Others on the platform called, 'A question, not a speech.' They had rented the hall to hear about flooded air-raid shelters and blocked factory lavatories, not to consider our mortal lot *sub specie aeternitatis*. Some of the audience stood up and shouted at him.

'Reason,' Mr Preston chided. 'Reason. A fallible light, true enough, but the only one we possess. Its desertion is the bane of revolutions. Its loss perverts their course and leads to the establishment of tyrannies more malign than those they deposed, as we saw in France and see today in Russia, the graveyard of all our hopes.'

A cry of horror escaped many in the audience. Those on the platform were convulsed into angular shapes as though an electric current had been passed through them. The chairman pounded the bell. People rose and shouted, 'Fascist!' Two bruisers stepped out, raising heavy faces in query towards the chairman. He waved them back but went on pummelling his bell. It jammed and stopped.

In the moment of silence Mr Preston said gently by way of reconciliation that none of the differences that passionately divided us today would have any meaning in a hundred years. All our strivings were footling seen in the span of cosmic time. Millennial societies would arrive but in their turn would pass, whether they were the thousand-year Reich or the socialist society of our aspirations.

Dissension broke out again but only sporadically up and down the hall. Mr Preston came smilingly to his conclusion.

'We see now that Marx was wrong in believing human society would reach a final state. The only unchanging factor in the universe is change, which is of course the visible aspect of time. Nothing else endures and in the end time will sweep away all things, good, bad and indifferent.'

Mr Preston sat. Booing and counter cheers broke out all over the hall. The chairman flapped his hands downwards in quietening gestures. Somebody else shouted, 'We don't want trouble. Clear the hall.' The bruisers moved between agitated groups.

Out on the pavement Mr Preston was surrounded by an

admiring circle of people, several of them asymmetric and most in strange clothes. He had enjoyed his turn and now he listened agreeably to the opinions they squeaked at him. His hat with its upturned brim was back on his head, his pipe aglow. He recognised me.

'Do you think mine was a good question?'

I said I did.

'And well put?'

Everybody joined in agreement that it had been very well put.

'You know,' he said, 'these socialist meetings have the same defect as the capitalist meetings. Too much thumping on the bloody bell.'

I decided to concentrate my report not on the main speeches, which had been a bore, but on the altercation. It made considerably more than the quarter column Clifford had asked for. I left the copy in his basket on Monday morning and watched for his reaction rather in the hope that he might be moved to congratulation. But as he read it his face darkened with deepening emotions, surprise, perplexity, disbelief, consternation. He returned it to his basket until he was feeling stronger. When I got back from my church calls he summoned me to his desk.

'We can't have this kind of thing, Donald,' he stuttered.

The *Burnley Express*, he pointed out, was not a students' rag-day sheet. It was a respectable newspaper, responsible to its readers for furnishing objective, impartial and accurate reports at a length the subject warranted. A mirthful and probably libellous essay on an uproar at a subversive meeting did not fall within the ambit.

'Don't get carried away,' he said. 'There is such a thing as the Defence of the Realm Act. This sort of stuff could land Ted in Strangeways.'

I think that was the day on which Clifford decided that my industry no longer compensated for the nuisance I caused. When some time later I told him I would be leaving he expressed polite regret but hummed to himself half the morning.

Thinking back on the people of those years, what strikes me is how confident so many of them seemed. There were reasons, not least that most people still lived within the certainties of tradition. It was still basically the Christian tradition learned in childhood with an emphasis on social responsibility developed through a century of hard and close urban living.

They knew the difference between right and wrong without ever thinking how they knew, and everybody took much the same view. In almost any of the fairly limited situations that might occur they knew what was expected of them and how to behave. The existentialism of the late 'forties, in which moral choices were made without criteria and in anguish, would have been incomprehensible, as indeed would the moral relativism of the last thirty years.

Individually they had a strong sense of their own being. They knew who they were. Everybody was somebody. We exist in the reflection of each other's eyes, and people then were longer under regard. Families sat round together most evenings, if only for lack of anything else to do. Everybody got a turn at being listened to. Many people now grow lonely for lack of everyday attention in homes where those who might have listened to them are for much of the time out or half-occupied with television or cocooned in the sound of a Walkman.

Outside the home also people had more to do with each other. They were less rushed. They spent their time as though they had a bank full of it. They stopped and talked in the street. Shopmen offered a patter of conversation from opening until the blinds were lowered at night. Club collectors, even in the rush of Friday nights, would always linger for the exchange of a few civilities. On our egg round it would have been thought very odd if we had loaded the boxes and driven away without, if need be, seeking somebody out for a word of conversation. You did not have the impression then of everybody being on the starting blocks. The pace was slower.

Farming, with little machinery, was in its nature a plodding job, and even in much of industry the pace was not relentless. The cotton strike of 1932 was brought on by an employers' proposal to increase the number of looms per weaver from four to six, and one of the reasons for opposing it was that it would destroy the social enjoyment of work, the lip-language conversations across the mill floor, which an easier pace permitted. One price of higher productivity is greater personal isolation at work. A hill farmer I know,

proud of his achievement on his bleak place, was nevertheless aware of the cost to the quality of his life.

'I've worked my stock up to a hundred and fifteen cows and two hundred ewes and the only time I can take off is a couple of hours in the pub after market once a fortnight. All my grandfather had here in the 'thirties was a garden, four or five cows and a few hens. He was a poor old man. But he was a sidesman at the church, he was known at the pub, he held an office in the farmers' union. He had some time at his disposal. He was somebody. Who am I? I don't even have time to say "Good morning" to people.'

The sense of being somebody was supported by other people's attention, and it was enhanced by willingness to recognise each other's bit of authority, not only in such pillars of the establishment as the policeman, the parson and the schoolteacher but within his small circle of competence in anybody holding any office or job. Nearly everybody got a turn, the sales assistant in the shop, the conductor on the bus, the gas collector around his meters. Their jobs, all jobs, commanded respect. Most were in them for life. The job became part, often the greater part, of their identity. They took pride in their own function and in the organisation they served. The gas collector in the homes he visited was not so much an employee of the company as its representative. He offered advice. He took complaints personally, bore them back to the office and could be relied upon to follow them up. The installation of electricity by any of his clients darkened his day. He was the Gas Chap and it meant something to him, and also to us.

In the home old people especially enjoyed a bit of authority. Grandmothers were consulted about all sorts of matters of experience, especially children's health. We were reassured by my grandmother's pronouncements, and the exercise of her judgment left her pleased. My grandfather took a similar pride in his unopposed opinions on politics and society at large. Both of them deferred, except in their specialised areas, to my father as head of the household and to my mother as the manager of the home. For all of them their measure of authority, granted by others without thought, helped their self-regard. As children we felt secure because of it.

The sense of identity, of being something more than the victim of bad times, helped people to get by. They were also helped by their patience and passivity, old characteristics of the poor, which rather lingered on in the cotton industry, partly because of the predominance of women in the labour force. They accepted their bad luck. They bent with the wind. They did not kick rocks and then complain that the universe was hostile.

The Catechism, with which most had been reared, taught them 'to honour and obey the King and all that are put in authority under him . . . to order myself lowly and reverently to all my betters . . . and to do my duty in that state of life unto which it shall please God to call me'.

The words would have caused smiles, but the sentiments prevailed. People spared themselves the conflict of contesting authority and the distress of yearning for what they could not have. There was no protest industry to goad them and no television commercials to mock their indigence. They lived fairly content in a society which shared a sparse equality. Loyalty to whatever one happened to belong to – family, church, trade union, football club, town, country – was taken for granted. To denigrate one's own was thought unnatural.

People in whom tradition abides are less the product of their own time than of much longer earlier periods. The character of people who were adult in my boyhood was influenced by the depression but by no means created by it. The manners, attitudes and habits of better times persisted People were light-hearted, at least in public. Cheerfulness was a social requirement. Grumbling was scoffed at. One comedian sustained a long career with a single line, mournfully delivered, 'It's being so cheerful that keeps me going.' It never failed to raise a laugh. Mournfulness, like drunkenness, was comic on stage but reprehensible in life.

Nearly everybody seemed ready to offer opinions on all sorts of topics. In politics most were untouched by the totalitarianism of the time, and indeed for a long time found it hard to credit the atrocity stories reported from Germany and even longer those from Russia. Except at elections, party views were seldom expressed with much force. Most people combined in their own thought the main strands of the democratic tradition. They were conservative by temperament, liberal in their tolerance, and socialist in looking for collectivist rather than individual solutions.

I think there was a greater variety of opinion then and less caution about expressing it. Discussion of sex was inhibited and certain subjects – religion, the monarchy, democracy – were usually treated deferentially even by critics. But there were no censored areas, as there are now, ruled by illiberal insistence on compliance with 'liberal' views, OK sentiments expressed in the approved vocabulary. Beliefs were eclectic; they did not come in ideological packages from which, knowing one opinion, you might guess the lot. Nor could you deduce people's views by their appearance, speech and background nearly so well as you might now. They were unpredictable. They said what they thought and expected others to think differently.

The time was easy-going, tolerant and not very stressful, the society more caring and compassionate than the one that later popularised the words. They were certainly more peaceful years. Crime was at an all-time low. Small children played out in the streets and fields. Old people went about after dark. House doors were left unlocked. A few old men with the authority of a peaked cap kept order in parks and on recreation grounds.

The war when it came was of a kind for which their life experience had prepared people of the 'thirties, a dour struggle waged with little panache but long perserverance. 'Victory at all costs,' Churchill proclaimed. 'Victory however long and hard the road may be.' They were the right people for it. Steady slogging was what they did best.

# 17 · LEAVING

I travelled by stopping train to my first RAF medical examination at Blackburn. A boy who had been at school with me got in, bound for the same destination. He also wanted to fly and turned out to know a lot about it, about the training stages and operations and aircraft types and performances. We had the feeling as the train puffed along of heading for a great free life.

It was a rudimentary physical examination with the usual soundings, tappings, eye-sight tests and bottle fillings. The medical officers grunted and shoved us along to the next cubicle, but in the end one, an older and more senior officer struck up a conversation while one was laid out on a leather couch.

'Can you guess,' he asked, 'what most of the people we get here suffer from?' He spoke in a quiet confidential way. I feared it might be something unmentionable.

'No, I can't guess.'

'Black feet,' he said.

'Black feet?'

'Black feet.'

I looked down at mine. They did not seem too black.

'They don't wash 'em,' he said. 'They have the effrontery to come here with black feet.'

He stood back and looked at me.

'That's not very good,' I toadied.

'It isn't,' he said. 'It's bad.'

He picked up his fountain pen and on my documents wrote the big single word, 'Intelligent.' I was on my way.

But I ran into trouble at the parting interview with the recruiting officer, a little man with fine straight hair and spectacles, whom I recognised as the person from whom I obtained figures for the paper when he came recruiting to Burnley town hall. I did not know whether it would be proper to acknowledge this acquaintance. He had no such qualms. 'Come in, Donald,' he said. 'Take a pew.'

He turned over my documents. 'So it's goodbye to the headlines and the thundering presses, eh?'

He made a little aimiable conversation, then said we must proceed to formalities. He put on his cap and gloves. This was the stage, he said, at which if I chose to do so I might formally volunteer for flying duties.

I said I wished to do that.

'Do you understand that that means flying and fighting in the face of the enemy?'

I said I did.

'Do you know what that means?'

'No,' I confessed. 'I don't.'

He stopped, looked puzzled and sat back. 'Flying and fighting,' he said.

'Yes,' I said.

'It means what it says, doesn't it?'

'Yes.'

He sat and thought. 'Are you making the point that while you volunteer to fly and fight you do not know what that might mean in terms of subjective personal experience?'

'I can't,' I said, 'I've never tried it.'

'We're not here to discuss our inner experiences or lack of it,' he said crossly. 'Britain is at war.'

I apologised. He gave himself time to regain his composure.

'When I asked if you were volunteering to fly and fight and further asked if you knew what that meant I was making doubly sure that you well understood the duties for which you were volunteering. It was a reiteration or reinforcement of the question, not a second and supplementary one opening a different field of inquiry.'

'Yes,' I said.

'Everybody's understood that until this morning.'

I apologised for having spoiled a good run. He sulked for a moment, then said we would proceed to attestation. I cannot remember what was involved in the ceremony, whether I read from a card or repeated words after him or whether or at what stage a Bible was brought into play. I was preoccupied by the thought of having made a bad start. Whatever he would write would certainly detract from the doctor's assessment. I was obviously better at discussing black feet than at discussing flying and fighting, and that could not abode well for a career in aviation.

He wrote something brief I could not see and wished me luck in a tone that suggested I would need a lot of it.

But I was through that stage. I walked back to the station elated. The boy I had come with on the train who knew so much about flying was waiting on the platform, sitting in gloom on a porter's trolley. He was C3, unfit for any combatant duties and most military trades. He had always imagined himself to be in excellent health. At the age of seventeen or eighteen it was a shattering blow. It not only ended any prospect of flying, on which he has set his heart, but cast a shadow over his future life and the way he thought of himself. We said almost nothing on the way back.

Another of my school contemporaries made out well from rejection at his medical. They diagnosed a chronically weak heart. He was advised to walk home slowly from the train and henceforth to avoid any exertion in what regrettably would be a short life. A series of specialists, to whom his father sent him, reversed the verdict. The boy had intended to challenge the medical board but, as the months passed with daily bulletins of RAF losses, the appeal of flying and fighting diminished. He prudently decided to remain a civilian. He spent most of the war years at university, played football until he was thirty-five and died in his sixties from excessive smoking.

The general medical examination was only the first stage in enlisting for flying. There was then an aircrew selection board with a more searching medical, written tests and an interview, lasting in all three days. Only a small proportion of candidates got through. All sorts of minor blemishes that would not have come to light in a normal lifetime were disqualifications. Some men were rejected for being too tall to fit into a cockpit and others for being too small to reach the switches.

The board I attended was at the big hutted camp built on a bog at Padgate near Warrington. Its main purpose was the initial training of groundstaff. The roads were swept and the ropes round the headquarter's building blancoed. It was a spruce, clean place, whose sharp outlines were blurred only by the permanent mist. Flights of recruits marched up and down flinging their fists to shoulder height, herded by corporals who barked round them like cattle dogs. They were pink-faced and wore smart new uniforms, transformed from pale shabby civilians in a matter of weeks.

I had not before slept in blankets without sheets, nor been awakened by a bugle sounded over tinny loudspeakers. My father smoked in the early morning but that was only one cigarette. Here everybody in the hut lit up, some groping under the bed before their eyes were properly opened for the half-smoked fag they had docked the night before. It was like waking up in a gas chamber. I have always been a bad starter. This was the worst to date. There was then a huge breakfast eaten from tables covered with oilcloth in a concrete hall full of clatter and bustle. Birds swooped about the iron rafters. Big tanks of boiling water used for washing the eating irons gave off a smell of chlorine.

It was still dark when we were lined up in a cold hangar with the doors wide open. NCOs with script boards and torches went up and down checking names. We were kept waiting a long time. Men stamped and blew puffs of breath into their cupped hands. One bold soul said he wasn't in the air force yet and lit a cigarette. Matches flared across the dark hangar. In our threadbare wartime clothes we looked more like an assembly of tramps than potential aviators. I could well have gone back and told my recruiting officer, no doubt still abed, that I had indeed not known what was involved in flying and fighting. At that low ebb I felt I had no chance whatever of passing the board in competition with these cheerful hobos who drew on their fags and stamped their feet before the break of day.

The throng grew less as the sun came up and the day wore

on. After each medical test we were sent to sit outside a different room to await another. Candidates who failed any test were finished. They were sent instead to an officer who condoled with them and invited them to state a preference for a ground trade. By night the hut where we slept was less than half full. We were elated still to be in the running. The examinations had become a game and we had gone some squares along the board. Progressing from room to room was like throwing sixes and missing the heads of snakes. Some of the tests were quite painful, though. In one a quack with a reflector on his forehead prodded the nostrils with steel probes. In another you had to blow up a column of mercury and hold it for some ridiculous time. That was the most notorious test. Most candidates knew about it in advance and made themselves dizzy for weeks by going about practising holding their breath.

The second day was better. There were more medical examinations, written papers and aptitude tests. Later, psychologists infiltrated the organisation and aptitude-testing for flying became a large industry. The most complicated piece of apparatus at my time was a sort of fun-fair contraption, a cockpit modelled on a child's pedal car. It was fitted with a control stick, by which a wandering spot of light had to be kept centred on a screen, and levers which had to be snapped back or forward when coloured lights showed. A Waaf who assessed the score on a script board was gracious enough to look agreeably surprised at everybody's earnest effort.

At night, reduced now to a small band, we sat in the Naafi, listening to the tales of a couple of policemen from Liverpool. They were about twenty-five, much older than the rest of us. One with hair *en brosse* was in the mounted branch. The other, a foot-patrol constable, did not look like a policeman at all. He had a slim dark moustache which, because of his sallow skin and his ensemble, made him look not, as perhaps he hoped, like Clark Gable but rather like a film dago. He wore a dark overcoat and a white silk scarf with tassels. His homburg hat sat on the table. They made everybody laugh with their stories of maintaining the King's

peace in Liverpool by running in or riding down the citi-
zenry.

Somebody said they would miss the life when the air force
got them. The dark one said he would miss his new wife.
The other said he would miss his old horse. Everybody
laughed. The dark one, who was the more serious, said
volunteering was a gamble but a reasonable military record
might serve better in a police career than staying on the beat.
As police they were in a reserved occupation from which
they could obtain release to the armed services only by volunteering for aircrew or submarines. They had seen enough
of submarines when the *Thetis* went down in Liverpool Bay.

By that stage we were all through the medical tests and
fairly sure of being accepted for flying. In what category
would depend on the result of the written tests and, crucially,
on the interview. Nearly everybody wanted the pilot–observer category (later redefined to pilot – navigator – bomb
aimer) and boys from grammar schools usually got it. It was
clear to me that I must repeat the success of the blackfeet interview and, while presenting an appearance of eager
truthfulness, avoid the excessive pedantry that had unhinged
the recruiting officer. I knew they looked for participation
in group activities as evidence of team spirit, and I figured
that my own evenings – hanging about for newspaper stories, typing with the girls and going for walks in the dark
with my cousin – would not score highly. I decided to make
the best of my footballing and my bit of cycle road-racing.
I thought up and mentally rehearsed some answers, clear-
cut, modest and understated. As soon as I sat down in front
of the board my mind went blank.

The chairman was an ageing group captain with a grey
moustache, one of the generation of aviators who had
stepped down from the cockpit beating the snow off their
chests. He was flanked by a lame flight lieutenant with an
observer's brevet who asked most of the questions, and an
administrative officer who said little and seemed to be in
charge of the papers. I heard their questions and with some
surprise I heard my own answers. Not bad, it struck me, as
though I was no part of the proceedings, quite perky. My
heart-beat slowed. I began to feel I was among friends. I

saw that the group captain who had looked quite severe
could have made a Father Christmas at a department store.
I risked a slight joke.

The observer smiled. He said I had just mentioned that I
had been keen on flying from boyhood.

Had I said that? I hastened to agree.

'Then why haven't you joined the Air Training Corps?'

There were reasons. The corps was part of the 'youth
movement' then rearing its chummy head and had a boy-
scout aspect which was off-putting. I didn't think that a
good point to make. I said the newspaper where I worked
was short-staffed and I couldn't join any organisation that
required regular attendance.

'So your career in journalism takes priority over learning
the rudiments of flying?' the observer observed.

Yes, I said, so long as I was employed by the newspaper
and not the air force.

The group captain nodded. The observer, now in the role
of prosecuting counsel, turned to the written tests and read
out one of the simple questions. I was, as they now say,
psyched up to the point where I immediately knew the error
I had made in the answer.

'Yes,' I said, 'I wrote the reciprocal.'

'That's careless,' the observer said.

'An error like that in the air,' the administrative officer
piped up, 'could kill yourself and people you were responsible for.'

'This could rule you out,' the observer said. 'We must
take a severe view.'

'Careless,' the group captain said, not in the least now like
Father Christmas. 'Do you know you're careless?'

'Yes, sir, I do,' I heard myself say. Boy Scout's honour,
no excuses, straight as a die, whatever the consequence.

The group captain and the observer exchanged a glance.
Everybody relaxed. The observer carped on a bit about other
written answers, but the group captain was already writing
his charitable endorsement at which I later sneaked a look.
'A good type. Alert and intelligent.'

I spotted the two Liverpool policemen sitting in the Naafi
and went over and joined them, not noticing at first in my

own elation that their jolly mood had passed. The mounted
one had been accepted for the pilot category but not the
other. He didn't know why. It occurred to me that perhaps
his moustache and his clothes hadn't helped. So he would
be an air-gunner. There would be no good war and quick
promotion in the police force on his return. The prospect
was a short training course and an early death.

I do not know whether anybody given a category he did
not want could at that early stage have withdrawn his offer
to fly. I never heard of anyone who did. The policeman, as
he had said, had taken a gamble and he accepted that he had
lost. He asked the other about the time of the train home
and said he wasn't looking forward to telling his wife.

From the selection board I was sent home for a few months
to await a training course and given a little silver badge to
wear. I went round telling everybody. Major Hargreaves
spat into the spittoon.

'Thou daft bugger,' he said. 'They'll kill thee.'

A long-faced hospital almoner was in the office. 'Thou
won't last six weeks, lad,' she said. 'Thou shouldn't let 'em
push thee into it.'

'I volunteered,' I said.

'Thou mun go back,' Major Hargreaves said, 'and volunteer to be a clerk.'

From Mr Preston I expected disapproval but he reacted
instead with his brightening smile. 'It's the right thing,' he
said, raising his pipe with the sticky end pointing towards
his ear. 'This imperialist war will inevitably turn into revolution, if not this year or decade then in the longer passage
of time. You've made a shrewd move.'

I enjoyed those last months. They were a long farewell. I
took work easier. I gave up the evening shorthand and typing
classes and instead dropped in on the Air Training Corps
which I was required to do, though as an out-patient, without wearing uniform. They taught me some elementary
navigation, signals and engines, and I wished I had gone
earlier. The corps was commanded on highly social lines by
Edgar Hartley's brother, a Great War aviator who, it may
be recalled, was now president of the Butchers' Association.

He kept the ATC canteen well supplied with meat-and-potato pies.

Most evenings I went out visiting. There was never a time when I had so many friends within walking or cycling range. I took girls to the pictures, usually with press passes. I played football on Saturday afternoons and in the evening dropped in on one or two dances, sitting it out with pleasantly aching legs in a circle of happy young people.

I felt a sense of high privilege and of confidence in myself and in my luck. It sprang, although I did not know it then, from the good fortune of growing up in a steadfast, generous and good-natured community, a few of whose people I have remembered in these pages.

My calling-up papers arrived, and one Monday morning I took the train to London. I never returned to live in Burnley again, but it is the place I still think of as home.